All Our
Yesterdays

Detroit-Windsor International Freedom Festival

All Our Yesterdays

A Brief History of Detroit

by
Frank B. Woodford
and
Arthur M. Woodford

A Savoyard Book

Detroit
Wayne State University Press
1969

Published simultaneously in Canada
by The Copp Clark Publishing Company
517 Wellington Street, West
Toronto 2B, Canada.

Standard Book Numbers 8143-1366-3 (cloth)
8143-1381-7 (paperback)

Library of Congress Catalog Card Number 68-27691

To Margaret

Contents

Maps

Acknowledgments

In the preparation of this book many persons have given freely of their time, advice, materials, and specialized knowledge. To all these we wish to express our heartiest thanks.

The major portion of the research for this book was done in the Detroit Public Library, particularly in the Burton Historical Collection. Therefore, a special word of thanks is due Mr. James M. Babcock, chief, and his associates Mrs. Bernice Sprenger, Mrs. Alice Dalligan, Miss Irene Dudley, and Miss Madeleine Shapiro. More than once they found the answer to a seemingly unanswerable question.

Mr. James Bradley, chief of the Automotive History Collection, and his assistant Mr. George Risley were always prompt in answering a hurried telephone request. Also, a special thanks to Mr. Joseph Marconi of the Sociology and Economics Department for his assistance in locating material dealing with the labor movement.

Others, the value of whose help must not be measured by the brevity of this expression of thanks, include Mr. Henry Brown, Detroit Historical Museum, Mr. Robert E. Lee, Dossin Great Lakes Museum, Mrs. Barbara Marconi, Language and Literature Department of the Public

Library, and Mrs. Patricia McHugh, Technology and Science Department of the Public Library. We are especially indebted to our friend Mr. Hazen E. Kunz for his counsel and encouragement, always given at the moment they were most sorely needed.

For the selection of the illustrations we were fortunate in having the assistance of Mr. Arthur Greenway, Department Report and Information Committee, City of Detroit, and Dr. Philip P. Mason, archivist, Wayne State University.

F.B.W.
A.M.W.

1

As It Was in the Beginning

The Lay of the Land

Detroit is the largest city in Michigan and the fifth largest in the United States with a population of about 1,650,000. The city is in the southeastern corner of the lower peninsula of Michigan on the west bank of the Detroit River. Its latitude is 42 degrees, 19 minutes, 51 seconds north, and its longitude is 83 degrees, 2 minutes and 54.6 seconds west of Greenwich. This places it on almost the exact latitudinal line as Alma-Ata, Kazakstan, U.S.S.R., and the same longitudinal line as Havana. This is something that is seldom a topic of drawing room conversation in Detroit or as far as is known in Alma-Ata or Havana either.

One of Detroit's most unusual geographical features is that it is the only major United States city north of Canada. This is due to the sharp turn to the west which the Detroit River takes soon after its waters leave Lake St. Clair on their way to Lake Erie. This bend continues past the downtown center of the city. After a short distance it twists back to its proper direction which is south. But for a matter of a mile or so anyone standing on the Detroit shore looking at Canada looks almost due south.

At this point at the foot of the Detroit Civic Center the river is its narrowest, being little more than half a mile wide, and it flows past with a current of about two miles an hour. The connecting link between Lake St. Clair and Lake Erie, its total length is twenty-eight miles, its average depth (due to channel dredging) is now thirty-five feet, and its course is studded with about fifteen islands, some of them on the Canadian side of the international boundary line. The larger of the islands are Belle Isle which has been a public park since 1879, and Grosse Ile which is big enough to sustain a city-size population. Both are United States possessions.

The river accounts for Detroit's existence; it has determined nearly every phase of the city's destiny. The history of Detroit is inseparable from the ages-old story of the river. That story, if the geologists are correct, began billions of years ago when the sun threw off a fiery spark which spun through the firmament for countless ages. Eventually the spark's outer surface cooled, but its insides continued to boil, giving off burps and hiccups which resulted in the formation of mountains and other topographical features. For a long time, measured in millions of years, much of the earth's surface including the present Detroit area was covered by salt seas. When these receded they left behind layers of sandstone and limestone which the early settlers quarried to build their walls and chimneys and their successors find necessary for the manufacture of steel. They also left behind thick layers of salt. Today that salt is mined from huge caverns under the city, caverns whose chambers are more vast and lofty than the greatest cathedrals.

The process of making the land did not end when the seas subsided. There followed ages in which glaciers covered the surface of much of the earth. These glaciers moved slowly back and forth, ebbing and flowing like an icy tide. The last one is believed to have receded from the Detroit area about 18,000 years ago. The great weight of those mighty ice fields gouged great scars in the land which their melting waters filled to form the Great Lakes. They were also responsible for the soil composition, the lakes and marshes, and the many small streams found in this part of Michigan. Like a giant bulldozer, the last glacier left a wide plain, fairly level and split down the middle by the Detroit River whose course has not appreciably changed for thousands of years.

This plain is almost flat. One has to go back almost fifteen miles from the river to find anything left by the glaciers that has even the appearance of a hill. The elevation at Detroit is about six hundred feet above sea level. From the river the rise is so gradual as to be almost imperceptible. This flatland was drained by numerous small streams or creeks. The most important is the River Rouge on the southern and western border of the city, a stream which drains a large close-in area. It has been made navigable and today is an important channel of commerce, serving primarily the fleet of giant freighters carrying cargoes of coal, iron ore, and limestone directly to the furnaces of the industrial complex of the Ford Motor Company. There were many lesser streams nearer the present center of Detroit, but these have mostly vanished, having long ago been converted into drainage ditches and then into enclosed sewers. One of them was the Savoyard River. It had its origin in some marshy land behind the present Wayne County building at Brush and Congress streets. It flowed westward through a meadow, cutting across what is now

15

the center of the city's business district, following closely
the line of Congress street. If one stands today at the corner of Fort street at Griswold and looks south, he will note
a fairly sharp dip in the street. That depression marks the
course of the Savoyard. Once wide and deep enough for
scows, the stream meandered on a few blocks, then turned
south near Fourth street and emptied into the Detroit River.
In the early 19th century some of the city's building material, stone and lumber, was floated up the Savoyard. Today
it is an underground sewer which passes beneath the Buhl
building.

Other important streams were Conner's Creek,
May's or Cabacier's Creek, and Parent's Creek. These were
named for early French families who settled near their
mouths. In the early years of Detroit these creeks served
useful purposes, furnishing access to the country back from
the river and waterpower for mills. Not too many years ago
there were venerable Detroiters who could recall when some
of these little streams provided swimming and fishing holes.
Today they have virtually disappeared, suffering the igno-
minious fate of being turned into parts of the metropolitan
sewerage system. Only a pond in the center of Elmwood
Cemetery remains as the last visible mark of Parent's Creek
which we will hear of later under the more intriguing name
of Bloody Run.

The Detroit River has been a well-behaved stream.
There is no record that it ever overflowed its banks, at least
where it washes the shore at the center of the modern city.
It has never required levees to control its flood. From time
immemorial it has flowed swiftly and smoothly past the site
of the town, as predictable as tomorrow in its movement
toward the lower Great Lakes and on to the Atlantic Ocean.
Unlike its sisters, the St. Mary's and the Niagara, it contains
no rapids or falls; here and there it does have a sand bar

or mud bank, but even where these exist there are safe channels and navigation is not impeded. The river's only show of temperament has occurred on occasion in the winter. Prior to 1855 it used to freeze over regularly so that people and wagons could safely cross it. One entrepreneur used to set up a shack in the middle of the river where he sold liquor to those who could not wait to get to the other side. Railroad ferry operations and industrial waste now keep the river open most of the time, although in severe cold spells it will still freeze over for a day or two.

Long before the river's banks became populated its shoreline varied only slightly from today's contours. Originally its edges were scalloped in a series of shallow bays. These have long since been filled in and the shoreline has been straightened. Before this was done, however, the shore was bordered by a bluff about twenty feet high. At its foot was a narrow shingle which was barely wide enough to accommodate a cart track, but which provided a place where small craft could be pulled up out of the water. Today one may see where this bluff stood. Let the viewer stand on Jefferson avenue at the Civic Center; he will note that from Jefferson, which once marked the approximate edge of the bluff, the ground slopes sharply down towards the river. Grading and filling below Jefferson have provided two or three hundred additional feet of made land between what was once the bluff and the river's edge, and where the water line is now. As one stands at the spot suggested, he can look across the river to the Canadian side. There he will see the reddish-brown earth banks stretching along the water's edge, having almost the exact appearance of the American shore as it was before the people of Detroit began tampering with it beginning about 1827.

First Visitors

While the geologists dig into the earth's core to study what changes the ages have wrought, the archaeologists sift between the layers in hopes of finding out about the earliest inhabitants. So far they have not been too successful when it comes to explaining about prehistoric human inhabitants of the Detroit region. That they were Indians is about all that can be said with any certainty, and the best guess is that the first red men moved in about 6,000 B.C., probably coming from the central plains of the United States or Canada—an area sufficiently large to make any reasonable guess a safe one. Those first people found this a strange land. It is said that they hunted the bison, the mastodon, the giant beaver, and other huge beasts. Venison is believed to have been on their menu, as the white-tailed deer, still plentiful in Michigan, is about the only known mammal to have survived from those early times.

Later tenants of the area are a little better known. They were the so-called Copper People, so named because they worked the copper deposits on Isle Royale in Lake Superior. Archaeological studies indicate that they may have been around as early as 4,000 B.C. and continued to live and work in the Lake Superior region for nearly 3,000 years. Who they were, what they looked like, and where they came from remain mysteries. They attained a relatively high culture, attested by the copper weapons and utensils they made as well as the tools they devised to work the copper into form. Some investigators claim these copper products were widely traded and have been found in many distant parts of the United States. There is no evidence that the Copper People ever lived in or around Detroit, but it can be assumed that in carrying on a commerce with far distant aborigines either they or their customers passed through the Detroit River and that this region knew them at least as transients.

The Copper People were followed by the Mound Builders, another group whose place of origin and whose antecedents remain unknown. The Mound Builders occupied a large part of the present American Midwest. Compared to the Indians first known to the white man, these people were fairly sophisticated, as proved by their pottery, jewelry, and tools. Some of their mounds were huge, elaborately designed, and exhibited considerable engineering skill. It is not entirely certain whether the mounds were burial sites only, or whether they were also used for religious ceremonies. The more spectacular mounds are in Ohio, Indiana, and other states, but some smaller ones were built within what is now Detroit's city limits. One was near the River Rouge not far from the present Ford plant, another was within the Fort Wayne military reservation, and a third was in the city's northeast section, giving name to the present Mound road. Perhaps there were others which escaped the notice of the pioneers and long since have been graded or bulldozed into flat obscurity.

The Mound Builders, whoever they were, occupied the area from about 1,000 B.C. to A.D. 700 when they vanished or, as is more likely the case, were absorbed by the historic Indians who may have been their descendants and are known to have been in the Detroit area as early as A.D. 800. By 1600 they were well established although not too much is known about them prior to that time. These people, depending upon where they lived and their background, were hunters and fishermen; many were agriculturists and remnants of their gardens are still to be found. They moved about from locality to locality, depending for transportation on canoes or pirogues. Some of their hunting and traveling paths became Michigan's main highways and important Detroit streets, such as Woodward, Grand River, Gratiot, and Michigan, were originally Indian trails. They knew how to make maple sugar, one of their staple foods; they built huts of saplings, the ends of which were set into the ground and the tops were bent inward to form a conical type house covered with bark or skins. They were frequently at war with neighboring tribes and went joyously into battle. When captured they died stoically under the application of the most exquisite forms of torture. They wore their hair in roaches into which they fastened a feather or two. They painted their faces and bodies for war or ceremonial reasons, and plastered themselves with rancid bear grease to keep off the black flies and other stinging insects. White men who came in contact with them reported they smelled perfectly awful.

The Indians who lived around the borders of the Great Lakes were of two language groups: the Algonquin who generally lived north of the St. Lawrence River and along the rims of Lakes Huron and Superior, and the Iroquois who were more or less centered along the south shore of Lake Ontario and the north shore of Lake Erie. The Algonquin tribes included the Ottawa, Chippewa, Potawatomi, Sac and Fox, and Miami. The more prominent Iroquois tribes were those of the Five Nations in central and western New York, the Hurons around Georgian Bay, and the Neutrals who occupied the land along the north shore of Lake Erie and into southern Michigan, including Detroit. The Neutrals were closely allied to the Hurons, but they were caught between that tribe and the Five Nations, and suffered the fate common to him who is caught in the middle. They were less warlike and got their name because they acted as buffers and traded with both sides. They were nearly obliterated. Remnants have survived and some of their descendants can still be found in and around Detroit and on the Canadian side of the Detroit River.

Inter-tribal wars and the later inducement to establish themselves to the advantage of the white fur traders resulted in fluidity and migration. Consequently the early Detroit fort and trading post at various times had neighboring villages of representatives of most of the tribes— Hurons, Ottawa, Chippewa, Sac and Fox, Miami, Potawatomi and others. Other near neighbors at times in Detroit's history were Delawares and Shawnee. Descendants of many of these people reside today on Canadian reservations at Walpole Island in Lake St. Clair and near Chatham, Ontario. Both places are within an hour or two by automobile from Detroit.

The Indians had several names for the region on the river which became Detroit. Some called it *Yondotega*, meaning the great village. Others called it *Wa-we-a-tun-ong*, which refers to the bend in the river and has been translated as the crooked way. Another name was *Karontaen*, or coast of the straits, while the Iroquois referred to it in grunts that came out sounding like *Teuchsa Grondie*.

It is almost anybody's guess as to who was the first white man to see the Detroit area, but the best one is that he was a young French explorer named Adrien Jolliet who paddled down the lakes and through the Detroit River in the late summer of 1669. There may have been others before him. Claims have been made that in the mid-14th century, long before Columbus's first voyage to the New World, a party of Norsemen sailed into Hudson and James Bays

21

and made their way south into the Lake Superior country. The claim of Norse discovery has been challenged, but the possibility exists. If the Vikings reached the Great Lakes at all, is it not possible that they saw the site of Detroit? If they did, they left no record of their visit, so the theory cannot be taken seriously.

Most historians hedge by suggesting that French coureurs-de-bois or their water-borne counterparts the voyageurs may have paddled their canoes through the Detroit River before Jolliet passed by at a comparatively late date. The coureurs-de-bois were a hardy far-ranging breed who in many cases spent more time among the Indians than in civilized society. They had a tendency to go native, which accounts for the fact that so many French-Canadians today look like Indians and so many Indians look like French-Canadians. They traveled far distances in search of furs; their canoes poked into many corners of the Great Lakes. They may very well have camped on the shores of the Detroit River, but because they were illiterate and because to them one day's journey was much like another, they left no record of where they went and what they saw.

The king of the coureurs-de-bois was Etienne Brulé, a true adventurer in every sense of the word. A protégé of Samuel de Champlain, the father of New France, Brulé plunged into the wilderness a couple of years before the Pilgrims landed at Plymouth. Once in the woods, he seldom came out. On rare visits back to Quebec he gave oral reports of his travels, and on the basis of these it is believed he reached the vicinity of Duluth on western Lake Superior in 1618. There is supposition that he crossed the Ontario peninsula from Georgian Bay to Lake Erie in 1625 or 1626, and historians almost jump to the conclusion that anyone visiting Lake Erie must have visited Detroit. The supposition is reasonable because the explorer returning from Lake

Erie to the upper lakes and the Ottawa River route back to Quebec would very logically have gone north through the Detroit River on his way to Lake Huron. But it still remains supposition, just as it is that some English or Dutch explorer accompanying a raiding party of Iroquois might have been our first tourist.

Other claims for first visitors have also been advanced. The theory has been held that Champlain himself was in the area in 1610 or thereabouts; one historian maintains that Jesuit missionaries visited a camp of Indians on Parent's Creek about the same time, and one of the first known explorers, a Recollect friar named Louis Hennepin who saw Detroit in 1679, flatly declared that he had been preceded by Jesuits and coureurs-de-bois. None of these arrivals and departures can be substantiated, and after giving full consideration to all the claims and possibilities, and after sifting through all the speculation, the award for first-comer has to be given to Jolliet.

Adrien Jolliet was from Quebec and was the elder brother of Louis Jolliet who with Father Marquette was the discoverer of the upper Mississippi River. In the spring of 1669 French officials in Quebec sent Adrien along the shores of Lake Superior in search of a copper mine of which the Indians had spoken. He failed to find it and on his return stopped at Sault Ste. Marie. There he learned that the Iroquois were peaceful and that it was safe for a Frenchman to cross Lake Erie. At the Soo he met an Iroquois prisoner who, like so many confirmed New Yorkers, did not appreciate the Middle West and wanted to go home. The captive offered to guide Jolliet, so off they went paddling south through Lake Huron, the St. Clair River, Lake St. Clair, the Detroit River past the present-day Detroit site, and on across Lake Erie. There they abandoned their canoe and set out across country. This was in September

1669. They had not gone far across the Niagara peninsula, reaching the vicinity of present Hamilton, Ontario, when Jolliet met another party camped on the shore of Lake Ontario. The leader of this group was Robert Cavelier, Sieur de La Salle, out to claim a continent for God and King and turn a profit if the opportunity presented itself. La Salle was headed for the Ohio River to lay title to its basin for France.

Accompanying La Salle were two Sulpician adventurer-priests, François Dollier de Casson, who had given up a distinguished military career for the priesthood, and René Brehant de Galinée. Dollier was described as "a man of great courage, of a tall, commanding person and of uncommon bodily strength." He came out to New France in 1666 as chaplain of a regiment sent overseas to keep the Iroquois in check. Galinée was more of a theologian, full of missionary zeal.

Jolliet sketched out a map of his travels down the lakes for La Salle and the two priests, and he told the latter of seeing many Indians along the way who had not been exposed to missionaries and were ripe for conversion. He suggested they would find a fertile field for soul-saving if they retraced his steps. As they listened to him, the idea grew in appeal. They felt their brand of conversion was vastly superior to that of the Jesuits and were eager to move in first. Competition has always been fierce in Detroit.

So Dollier and Galinée separated from La Salle who went off to the Ohio River. The priests wintered at present Port Dover, Ontario, and in March 1670 entered the Detroit River. What was most notable about their trip is that they were the first to make a written report about their journey, although their narrative did not contain a detailed description of the Detroit region.

Actually, when they discussed the strait through

which they passed, Dollier and Galinée included all the waters between Lakes Erie and Huron. Somewhere along the way—and guesswork has put the spot near the mouth of the River Rouge—they came upon a strange object. This was a peculiar stone formation resembling a human figure. The Indians had made it an idol, painting and decorating it and placing before it thank offerings for safe passage across the tricky waters of Lake Erie. The sight of such a heathen abomination greatly offended the priests and their zeal demanded they do something about it. They proceeded to attack it with their hatchets and smashed to bits what would later have been a first-rate tourist attraction. They put the pieces they hacked off into their canoes, carried them out to deep water, and dumped them overboard. Legend says that unregenerate Indians fished the pieces out of the river and set them up on the lower end of Belle Isle. Having accomplished their labors for the Lord, Dollier and Galinée continued on to Sault Ste. Marie, and then to Montreal and Quebec. It was the last Detroit saw of them.

La Salle was back in the neighborhood a few years later. He spent 1678-79 near the site of Buffalo where he constructed a small armed merchant vessel, the *Griffon*. He proposed to sail to the head of the lakes and open a regular transport service, supplying a string of trading posts and bringing back cargoes of furs. The *Griffon* sailed through the Detroit River in August 1679, the first ship ever to traverse those waters. The *Griffon* was lost with all hands later in the year in Lake Michigan or Lake Huron and never completed the down passage. It was almost a hundred years, according to one historian, before the next vessel of any size was to pass Detroit.

Accompanying La Salle was Father Louis Hennepin, chaplain of the expedition. Hennepin had a tourist's eye. It is from him that we receive the first descriptive account of what the Detroit region looked like. He wrote:

> This strait is finer than that of Niagara, being thirty leagues
> long, and everywhere one league broad, except in the middle
> which is wider, forming the lake we have named Ste. Claire.
> The navigation is easy on both sides, the coast being low and
> even. It runs directly from north to south. The country be-
> tween these two lakes is very well situated and the soil is
> very fertile. The banks of the strait are vast meadows, and
> the prospect is terminated with some hills covered with vine-
> yards, trees bearing good fruit, groves and forests so well dis-
> posed that one would think Nature alone could not have
> made, without the help of Art, so charming a prospect. The
> country is stocked with stags, wild goats, and bears which are
> good for food, and not fierce as in other countries.
>
> Those who shall be so happy as to inhabit that noble coun-
> try cannot but remember with gratitude those who have dis-
> covered the way by venturing to sail upon an unknown lake
> for above 100 leagues.

In the years immediately following the expedition
of La Salle and Hennepin traffic increased considerably and
as long as the Iroquois behaved the lower lakes route to
Montreal and Quebec was easier than that by way of the
Ottawa River. French travelers came to know the region
well and they gave it a name. They called it simply the
Strait or in their own tongue *le Détroit*.

2

In the Shade of the Old Fleur-de-Lys

Beaver Empire

Someone once remarked that Detroit was founded so King Louis XIV of France could wear a beaver hat. That is a little farfetched, but like so many glib statements, there is a grain of truth in it. Detroit was founded as a French outpost to prevent the British from encroaching into what is now Michigan and the Old Northwest. The English were unwanted because the French wanted to control the rich fur trade in the area.

The fur trade, principally the greatly desired beaver, was just about the chief asset New France or Canada had to offer the mother country. In the cold unheated houses of Europe furs were not a luxury, they were a necessity to keep the chill and damp out of milord and milady's bones. For a long time Europe could meet the demand, but as time went on the harvest of peltries ran short. Poland, which had been a chief source of beaver for the French market, became trapped out.

After Columbus discovered America in 1492 and established Spanish claim to the Caribbean area, other European powers sent explorers across the Atlantic. England claimed what became the United States seaboard and France was left out in the cold—literally. She wound up with Canada. Each colonizing power demanded a profit on its investment. Spain acquired the gold and silver of Mexico and Peru; England prospered by shipping tobacco out of Virginia and codfish and naval stores out of New England. Canada produced neither gold nor silver or much tobacco, but it was rich in fur, and by 1544 cargoes of beaver skin were being shipped back. King Louis one day appeared in a high-crowned narrow-brimmed hat of beaver and a new fad was started. Parisian hatters threw out their satins, velvets, and velours, and began to use fur. This increased the demand; the fur trade prospered. The crown declared the gathering and importation of fur to be a royal monopoly.

France's claim to Canada was established in 1535 when Jacques Cartier discovered the St. Lawrence River and sailed up it to the site of Montreal. In 1608 Samuel de Champlain came out as governor and about that time the period of settlement began. Emigrants arrived, but many found the fur trade more enticing than prosaic farming, and they took to the woods. This spurred the fur trade even more and to control it, as well as to offer protection against the Iroquois, a string of outposts was established. Some of these were where the missionaries had already set up missions. Eventually, years before Detroit was founded, several of these forts or trading posts were flourishing in Michigan. They were at Sault Ste. Marie as early as 1668; Fort de Buade at St. Ignace in 1686; Fort St. Joseph, where Port Huron is now located, in 1686; and others at or near modern St. Joseph (1679) and Niles (1691).

Most of this expansion of trade was carried out under the vigorous administration of Louis de Buade, Comte de Frontenac, the governor of New France. But Frontenac discovered, as have so many others in like situation, that success breeds as much trouble as profit. Where there are profits, there follows the power play, and that in turn leads to political infighting. Endeavoring to keep tight control of the fur trade, Frontenac ran into trouble from small independent operators. The clergy, particularly the Jesuits, frowned upon the trading post system, regarding its establishments as dens of licentiousness and depravity, which in truth they frequently were. The Jesuits feared the souls of the Indians would be lost before they could be saved. Brandy was a chief trade item; the Indians lapped it up, and often all they had to show for a winter's trapping in the woods was a monstrous hangover. This pained the Jesuit fathers and led to dissension with Frontenac and the other fur tycoons who operated on the principle that the customer should be given what he demanded. An Indian with a cultivated taste for liquor was bound to be a repeat customer. The cross currents thus generated led to Frontenac's recall in 1682. Matters did not greatly improve, however, during his absence. He was a favorite at the court of Louis XIV and had great influence there. In 1689 he was sent back to New France where a new set of problems awaited him.

The infighting continued unabated between the Frontenac faction, which wanted the Indians to bring their furs to the trading posts, and that which found it advantageous for the individual traders to go directly to the Indian villages. The latter system, much preferred by the small operators, reduced the chances of exercising the governmental monopoly and for that reason upset the higher authority. Frontenac also discovered that attempts were being made to eliminate brandy as a trade item, and that caused the Indians to carry their furs to the British who had no scruples against the use of firewater. The West Indies, which the British controlled, supplied molasses which New Englanders made into rum, and this proved cheaper than French brandy. The Indians discovered they could get drunk quicker and stay that way longer on the liquor yield per beaver pelt from the British than from the French. This was a definite threat to French trade. The situation from the French standpoint became even more grave when the anti-liquor faction prevailed in 1696. The government decreed that all furs had to be delivered by the Indians at Montreal, and the forts strung around the Great Lakes were ordered closed and abandoned. Only the Jesuits henceforth were to be permitted to maintain mission settlements in Indian country.

Frontenac had a favorite lieutenant whom he had established as commandant at the key post of Fort de Buade at St. Ignace before it was closed down. He was Antoine Laumet de la Mothe Cadillac, a professional soldier who had the stars of empire in his eyes. La Mothe, or Cadillac as history knows him best, was most unhappy just sitting around Quebec waiting for something to turn up. Nobody in New France was better informed about conditions in the West than him. Nobody knew better than him that the policy of closing the West was tantamount to surrendering the Ohio, Mississippi, and Great Lakes basins to the British. In 1698 he sailed for France to present Louis and his ministers with a plan to remedy a deteriorating situation.

His plan was well thought out. It provided, in simplest terms, for colonizing the West on a permanent basis. Michilimackinac, he insisted, was not the place to start. The northern region was too cold and too barren. A better place could be found lower down the lakes, a place like *le Détroit* where the land was fertile, where the waters narrowed and a defense could be made against British intrusion. There he recommended a fortified town be built, a place at which the Indians could be induced to establish their villages, and where French soldiers and farmers would be encouraged to marry Indian maidens and everybody would live happily ever after. Everybody, that is, except the English and the Iroquois. If this model settlement should work out satisfactorily, others would be planted. Cadillac specifically had in mind a place at the mouth of the Mississippi, and another part way up that stream. He never did get around to building them, but his plan was followed by others, resulting in New Orleans and St. Louis. For the moment Cadillac was concentrating on the Detroit River.

His plan for financing this scheme was the most attractive feature of the whole proposition—at least from the standpoint of the king and his chief counselor, Count Pontchartrain, minister of marine. It boiled down to this: if Louis XIV would grant him a generous piece of land on the Detroit River with seignorial rights together with a trade monopoly, Cadillac would hire soldiers for the garrison and furnish civilians for farming and trading, all at his own expense. The farmers would make the post self-sustaining, the traders and Indians he expected to attract would make it financially stable, and the soldiers would maintain French sovereignty in the entire region. All the government was asked to contribute was 1,500 livres, the equivalent of $300, to pay for the construction of a fort.

When Cadillac laid out his grand scheme it looked like a bargain to Versailles and the reception was quite enthusiastic. As a matter of fact the adventuring Frenchman from overseas was quite popular at court and something of a favorite of Pontchartrain. He was a career officer, he had the attributes of a courtier, and most important, he was offering something for almost nothing. Pontchartrain, whose jurisdiction extended over the colonies, favored the plan and early in 1701 Cadillac returned to Canada with the king's orders in his pocket. Arriving at Quebec, he discovered his patron Frontenac had died during his absence and had been succeeded by a new governor who was unfriendly to both Cadillac and his plan. But the royal seal on the orders took precedence and there was nothing the new governor could do about it.

Thus Cadillac, as it turned out, became the first in a long list of promoters who have graced the Detroit scene. He differed from the modern breed in that there was no aroma of gasoline about him. He would be very much at home today among the gray flannel set at the Detroit Athletic Club or the Recess Club. He would probably even have an ulcer. He was hard-boiled, imaginative, ruthless, capable, and not overburdened by conscience. He was a blend of empire builder, idealist, and bravo. He was a soldier, explorer, possibly a pirate, politician, and able administrator. He was, in short, a man of parts and a successful one.

Cadillac was born March 5, 1658, in St. Nicholas de la Grave, a tiny village in the south of France, in that part known as Gascony. It was the land of the troubadours and crusaders, and it produced characters like D'Artagnan and Cyrano de Bergerac. Gascons are a proud, high-spirited and short-tempered breed, and Cadillac ran true to form. The sons of Gascony provided Louis XIV with his best swordsmen, and Cadillac was said to have been superb with the rapier. In fact, one of his biographers insists that he was the prototype for Cyrano, due to the fact that like Rostand's hero, Antoine had a prominent nose. This appendage earned him the nickname of the Hawk. He was the son of Jean Laumet, a small town lawyer. His mother was Jean Pechagut whose family connections consisted of upper middleclass landowners. The Laumets were not nobility, but they were gentry. Cadillac had a reasonably good education, which included a military school from which he graduated into the army, a career which took him to Canada in 1683 when he was twenty-five years old.

He located at Port Royal (now Annapolis), Nova Scotia, where his early activities are obscure. He seems to have formed some kind of connection with a merchant and trader named François Guyon. Guyon was a shipowner and there is evidence that Cadillac made coastal trading voyages in his vessels. He may even have commanded one, because Cadillac won the reputation of being a first-class navigator. It has been hinted that Guyon was also a privateer. At any rate Cadillac became familiar with the coastal waters and lands from the New England colonies northward. Like many another enterprising young man, he improved his fortunes by marrying his boss's niece Marie Therese Guyon who lived in Quebec. The Guyons were a prominent family; Cadillac's marriage to the seventeen-year-old Therese gained him admittance to the best society of Quebec and New France.

About this time there was another change in Cadillac's status. The whole story is somewhat obscure, but up to the approximate time of his arrival in Canada he had been just plain Antoine Laumet, the name by which he had been baptized. But that name obviously was not grand enough for a young man on the rise because he was soon flaunting the more impressive one of Antoine de la Mothe, Sieur de Cadillac. It was as such, rather than as plain Laumet, that he was henceforth best known. Where he acquired these titles that have the ring of nobility is not entirely clear. It has been suggested they were derived from family estates which, if the truth were known, were somewhat unpretentious farms or manors in the neighborhood of his birthplace. However, for a young man intent upon building a reputation and establishing court connections, the new name was vastly more impressive.

Along with fancy titles, Cadillac also became a substantial landowner. He was granted a huge domain of about 187,000 acres on each side of the Donaquec (now Taunton) River in what is now the state of Maine. Today this grant includes Bar Harbor and Mount Desert. The land remained in his possession and was passed on to his heirs. After the American Revolution the state of Massachusetts, of which Maine was then a part, confirmed title to the tract to the granddaughter of Cadillac who was designated "Lord of Donaquex and Mount Desert" in the original deed.

Because of his familiarity with the Atlantic coastline, Cadillac was called back to Paris in 1689 to advise the court regarding plans for a sea attack against New England. Apparently he made a favorable impression at Versailles and returned to Quebec with the confidence of Louis and Pontchartrain. He already stood high with Frontenac who regarded him as one of his most able and trusted lieutenants. At any rate, he was rewarded by assignment to the post at Michilimackinac, Fort de Buade on the site of St. Ignace. The command at Fort de Buade, which he assumed in 1694, gave him supervision over all posts and governmental interests in the entire West. The experience was useful. At Michilimackinac he acquired a knowledge of conditions relating to trade, the Indians, and British encroachment that shaped his thoughts of empire, and resulted in his securing orders to establish a new post on the Detroit River.

Cadillac's Village

Cadillac organized his expedition at Montreal. With him were fifty uniformed soldiers and fifty Canadians who handled the twenty-five large canoes. These Canadians were engaged to become settlers, and among them were traders, farmers, and artisans whose special skills were necessary for community life. Also with him were Captain Alfonse de Tonty, the second in command, and two junior officers, Lieutenants Chacornacle and Dugne. The first sergeant was Jacob Marsac, a bull of a man from whom at least several score of present-day Detroiters are descended. Two priests, one a Recollect whose name is unknown and a Jesuit, Father François Valliant de Gueslis, and two interpreters, the brothers Jean and François Fafard de Lorme, completed the party. Cadillac took along his ten-year-old son Antoine, but the rest of his family was left behind at Quebec. There were no women in the original expedition.

The flotilla of canoes pushed off from the vicinity of La Chine on June 5, 1701. Because the obstreperous Iroquois were being induced to sign a peace treaty, it was thought best not to provoke them by taking the easy route up the St. Lawrence and through Lakes Ontario and Erie. Instead, the way chosen was the old wilderness road of the voyageurs up the Ottawa River, through Lake Nipissing, and down the French River to Georgian Bay. This entailed some back breaking portages, but it was safer and for the moment more diplomatic. Once in Georgian Bay and out into Lake Huron, the eastern shore was followed south until July 23, 1701, when the Detroit River was entered. The present site of Detroit was passed, and that night the party camped on Grosse Ile which was seriously considered for the location of the settlement. But because of the width of the river there, close to the head of Lake Erie, Cadillac had second thoughts. The following day, July 24, Cadillac went back up the river where it was at its narrowest and where the high banks made it most defensible. This was the site he chose and there his canoes were drawn up on the narrow beach. The landing point, as far as can be determined, was at the foot of present-day Shelby street a few feet below Jefferson avenue. If one were to seek the spot today, he would find it where the Veterans' Memorial building stands. It has been said that a temporary settlement had been established at this site eighteen years prior to Cadillac's landing. It was probably no more than an encampment of traders. The historian Silas Farmer states that upon his arrival Cadillac was greeted by two coureurs-de-bois. Cadillac at once paced off the limits of his planned village between the Detroit River and the small Savoyard River to the rear, marked the corners of his stockade, and within two hours his ax-men were in the nearby woods felling timber for construction.

There is a cherished tradition that the first building erected was the church located at what was to be the eastern end of the village. The exact spot, close to modern Griswold street and Jefferson avenue, is in all probability today covered by the pavement of Jefferson just before it dips down to become the John C. Lodge expressway. It has been said that the little church was completed in two days and that the first Mass was sung on the feast of Ste. Anne in whose honor it was dedicated and for whom it was named. Regardless of where it was placed and when it was ready for use,

36

it gained the distinction of becoming the second oldest continuous parish in the United States, first honors going to a
parish in St. Augustine, Florida.

But before anything else was done Cadillac gave
his town a name. Remembering with gratitude the support
of his patron the French minister of marine, he called it in
his honor *Fort Pontchartrain du Détroit*. The Pontchartrain
part has since been appropriated by a couple of hotels and
other commercial enterprises. The Detroit part stuck.

The next few weeks were devoted to putting down
the municipal roots. The stockade or palisade was erected,
a wall of twenty-foot logs, about four feet of which were em-
bedded in the earth. A bastion or blockhouse was set at
each corner of the enclosure to permit enfilading fire. A
moat was dug outside. At least two gates provided access,
one on the river side, wide enough to permit large loads to
be brought in, and another in the east wall near the church.
There was really only one street—Ste. Anne's—which par-
alleled the river along the top of the bluff. It was twenty-two
feet wide. Another shorter street above Ste. Anne's and two
north-south streets, more properly alleys or lanes, completed the highway layout. Lots were marked out, the ordinary house lots being no larger than twenty-five feet square.
But Cadillac knew what he was doing. The more lots he
could squeeze into his village, the more rents he would be
able to collect. Some houses were built almost immediately.
These were made of small oak logs or posts set perpendicu-
larly into the ground like the stockade, chinked with grass
or mud, and roofed with bark slabs. Something a trifle more
elegant was put up for Cadillac, and before much of anything else was erected, a large warehouse was built for storage of public property and furs, and for use as a trade store.
Business has always come first in Detroit. The whole village
—stockade, streets, and buildings—occupied an area which

today consists of about one city block. It can be bounded roughly by Griswold, Jefferson, Shelby, and Larned. In time the stockade was extended to about Washington boulevard. It was never extended that much eastward.

Having gotten the place put together, the new Detroiters were ready for their first big social event of the season. That was the arrival in September 1701 of Mmes. Cadillac and Tonty, the first white women to set foot in the new city. Not until the following year did a few other women come to join their husbands or to find spouses. It was probably a dull winter of 1701-02 for the men who had to confine their admiration to the Indian ladies of the neighborhood. However, they were reasonably busy and their minds were kept on other things. For instance, in October 1701 ground was broken adjacent to the fort and about fifteen acres of winter wheat were sown. There was a crop the following July, although it was said to have been rather poor. Nevertheless, it was demonstrated that the land could be cultivated and that the village could be made reasonably self-sufficient. From the standpoint of trade, matters went well from the beginning. A band of Hurons set up a village near the foot of present-day Third street; the Ottawas settled across the river near the foot of Belle Isle; and the Potawatomis and Miamis set up housekeeping a short distance downriver. Before long Cadillac would report 2,000 Indians in the neighborhood, and in the spring distant tribes from as far away as Lake Superior and the Illinois country came in to trade. All this pleased Cadillac greatly. In a report back to Quebec he broke out in prose that was almost lyrical:

> The banks of the river are so many vast meadows where the freshness of these beautiful streams keeps the grass always green. These same meadows are fringed with long and broad avenues of fruit trees which have never felt the careful hand

of the watchful gardener; and fruit trees, young and old, droop under the weight and multitude of their fruit, and bend their branches toward the fertile soil which has produced them. . . . On both sides of this strait lie fine, open plains where the deer roam in graceful herds, where bears, by no means fierce and exceedingly good to eat, are to be found, as are also the savory wild duck and other varieties of game. The islands are covered with trees; chestnuts, walnuts, apples and plums abound; and in season the wild vines are heavy with grapes of which the forest rangers say they have made a wine that, considering its newness, was not at all bad.

The climate of the neighborhood, he declared, was temperate—"Winter, according to what the savages say, lasts only six weeks at most." (Oh, those lying Indians!)

There was, however, a little crabgrass in these Elysian Fields. With so many Indians around, members of different tribes whose hereditary jealousies were inflamed by strong potions, there was bound to be an occasional outburst of trouble. In 1706 Cadillac made one of his periodic trips to Montreal and Quebec, and during his absence Lieutenant Etienne Venyard, Sieur de Bourgmont, was given temporary command. De Bourgmont must have been a prime ass; at least he lacked Cadillac's ability to control the savages. One June day an Ottawa brave, nosing around the commandant's quarters, was bitten by de Bourgmont's dog. The Ottawa gave the animal a kick that rattled its ribs and brought de Bourgmont storming out. He beat the Indian senseless, an act that upset the Ottawas no end. Probably they got drunk, certainly they got quarrelsome and started to take out their anger on a group of Miamis camped just outside the stockade. To prevent the slaughter of the Miamis, de Bourgmont called out the troops and ordered them to fire on the Ottawas. Several were killed. The remainder withdrew and as they moved away from the stockade they met the village priest Father Constantin

Delhalle and promptly murdered him. He died on June 6. Detroit had its first martyr and its first victim of violence.

Even more serious trouble broke out a few years later in 1712, threatening the continued existence of the settlement. This occurrence, too, can be attributed primarily to intertribal animosities. A band of one thousand Foxes with some Mascoutin allies came to town and began to throw their weight around. They were mean, arrogant and looking for trouble, and were thoroughly disliked by the Ottawas and Hurons. The latter tribes were absent, away in the West on a war raid. The commandant at the time—Cadillac had been replaced before 1712—was Charles Regnault, Sieur Dubuisson. He had only thirty men in his garrison and was less than enthusiastic about having troublesome Indians around. He ordered the Foxes to leave the vicinity; they replied that they intended to burn the fort and the war started. Dubuisson had the church and one or two other buildings torn down to prevent the Indians from setting them on fire. The Indians, whose camp was where the Penobscot building now stands, began a siege and lobbed fire arrows into the village but without causing much damage. After a few days the absent Ottawas and Hurons returned and reinforced the French. Now it was the turn of the Foxes to be besieged in their village. For nineteen days the struggle continued. Finally the Foxes withdrew, seeking escape along the river toward Lake St. Clair. The French, Hurons, and Ottawas pursued and overtook them near Windmill Point at the head of the Detroit River. A pitched battle followed and the Foxes were virtually annihilated; it is said that a thousand were slaughtered. Other Indian trouble beset Detroit from time to time, but most of it was among the Indians themselves. The French suffered only to the extent that the peacemaker and innocent bystander always does.

When Cadillac returned from Quebec in 1706 he

brought several families of settlers with him and for the next few years his little settlement prospered. He amassed a considerable fortune and his success, together with a somewhat high-handed system of running things, created jealousy and rivalry. The result was that in 1710 he was removed and appointed governor of Louisiana Territory. In 1711 he left Detroit never to return. After a brief visit to France he came back to America to his new post with headquarters at Mobile. In 1720 he returned to France for good and was given the governorship of Castelsarrasin, a small town near his birthplace. He filled that position until his death on October 15, 1730.

Much to his disappointment, Cadillac never was given a seigneury at Detroit. However, he did possess certain feudal rights and apparently appropriated more. Among them was the granting of land to the settlers. At first these grants consisted of house lots inside the stockade; the farmers worked the public domain outside the palisade walls. Beginning about 1707, however, he awarded farms to the deserving on both sides of the river. These farm grants, known as the private claims in today's land abstracts, consisted of river frontages of from one to four or five arpents (an arpent was about 200 linear feet), and extended back two or three miles in some cases. The rear line of most of the original grants that are now within the city of Detroit is somewhere in the vicinity of Holden and Harper avenues. They became known as ribbon farms because of their long narrow shape, and their boundaries are marked in modern Detroit by streets which bear the names of the original grantees, such as Beaubien, Riopelle, St. Aubin, Chene, Campau, and Livernois.

The first of the farm grants, and a fairly typical one, was made by Cadillac to one of his interpreters François Fafard de Lorme. In his right of tenure Fafard was permitted to trade, hunt, and fish on his property, but he could not kill hares, rabbits, partridge or pheasant. He paid an annual rent of five livres and an additional fee of ten livres for trade privileges. He was required to have his grain ground at Cadillac's mill for a small fee or share, and each year he agreed to help plant a Maypole in front of Cadillac's home. He could not engage in any occupation such as that of blacksmith, such business belonging exclusively to Cadillac's own artisans.

Before the passage of many years the ribbon farms lined both sides of the Detroit River from Ecorse up to Lake St. Clair. Some lands were retained as commons, such as Belle Isle, where the settlers kept their pigs safe from marauding wolves. For many years, until the mid-nineteenth century, it was known as *Ile aux Cochons* or Hog Island.

Cattle were imported early, and milch cows as well as oxen were among the possessions of most of the farmers and many of the townspeople. Small, hardy, shaggy horses of a special breed—ponies, really—were brought in from the St. Lawrence country. They thrived at Detroit to the extent that herds ran wild in the woods behind the farms. The settlers developed or derived from Canada a light high-wheeled caleche and a high-wheeled farm cart. The latter continued in use for more than a century, being the most efficient vehicle for the navigation of roads that were nothing more than knee-deep quagmires in wet weather. Each farmer had his canoe or pirogue, and the river with its canoes in summer and sleighs in winter provided the principal means of transportation.

After Cadillac's removal and departure other governors and commandants were sent out from Quebec, but for the most part they failed to distinguish themselves and left no mark on the community. They are no longer remem-

bered in Detroit, not even to the extent of having automobiles named for them. For several years after 1712 the
village declined. Few new settlers arrived; some who had
come with Cadillac departed. Trade dropped off, partly due
to a glut of furs on the European market. The stockade
fell into disrepair, so much so that one resident reported that
a stag entered the village through a hole in the wall. For
about a decade it seemed hardly likely that the settlement
would survive. However, about 1725 or 1730 things began
to look up again. French wars with Great Britain persuaded
the authorities in Paris and Quebec that the outpost would
have to be strengthened if it was to be held against English
encroachment. The British conquest of Acadia displaced
many of the French in Nova Scotia, some of whom, thrown
out of Evangeline's country, found new homes in Detroit;
among them were families that have been prominent in the
business and social life of the city ever since. Many of the
newcomers established themselves in the town but owned
and worked ribbon farms on either side of the river. Among
them were quality folk like Robert Navarre, descended from
the old kings of France, who came out as the settlement's
intendant or business manager, and remained under later
British and American rule as the town's notary or legal
counselor. Also about that time the first alien note was in-
jected by the appearance of Michael Yax and his family.
They were Germans who had been captured in Kentucky
by the Indians. Taken to Detroit and ransomed by sympathetic townspeople, they were permitted to remain and were
given land out near Grosse Pointe. The descendants of Michael Yax were still listed in the Detroit telephone directory
in 1967. Some of the newcomers were silversmiths who
found employment making medals and trinkets for the Indians as well as utensils for their white neighbors. Today
examples of their work are considered collectors' items and

fine pieces are preserved in the Detroit Institute of Arts.

For fifty-nine years after Cadillac's founding of Detroit it was a completely French town, socially as well as governmentally. In more than half a century under the fleur-de-lys it had its ups and downs, but except for an occasional Indian alarm, life went on quietly and peacefully. The French settlers were not a particularly progressive people. Conservative by habit, they were content to live in a semi-feudal society, existing off the fur trade and their small farms. There were no economic innovations, no attempts at or interest in developing even the most primitive industrial enterprise. They lived as their ancestors along the St. Lawrence had lived for a century, and as their peasant forebears had lived for hundreds of years before that in France.

Yet early Detroit's society was not a sterile one. The people were warm-hearted, gay, hospitable and friendly. The winters were long and cold and the spring crop of children was large. A dozen or more offspring per family was not at all uncommon. From about 1730 on, more people lived on farms than in the village itself, but it was all Detroit—on both sides of the river. For the most part the farms produced wheat, oats, and some corn. Most of what they raised was consumed by the family. The surplus was sold or given for the support of the town, the garrison, and the church. Most farms had cattle, pigs, and chickens. The nearby forest supplied the family table with venison, birds and muskrat, and the river at the front door was a never-failing source of sturgeon, muskellunge, and that jewel of fishdom the whitefish. Each farm had its orchard of apple, peach, and pear trees. Detroit was especially famous for the pear trees the habitants planted and some, old and gnarled, still stood along Jefferson avenue until well into the twentieth century. The apple crop made a superior cider, the peaches produced an excellent brandy, and there were both wild and cultivated grapes and berries aplenty, so that the wine crocks were always full.

The houses of the habitants became a little more livable as time went on, although they were never pretentious. The early rough pole structures eventually were clapboarded over; lofts or second floors, lighted by dormer windows, became common. The houses were whitewashed and the Dutch doors were frequently painted apple-green. The yards, enclosed by picket fences to keep the live stock in and the Indians out, contained the usual outdoor bake ovens and wells with long sweeps. Similar houses can still be seen along the St. Lawrence. Travelers entering the Detroit River from Lake Erie, and approaching the town, frequently commented on the neat comfortable farms. The proximity of the buildings gave the impression of a continuous village street stretching for miles along the shore. Many of the more prosperous farmers had a slave or two. These were Indians, some with a mixture of Negro blood. For the most part they were captives taken by the Hurons and Ottawas in raids against western tribes. Some were Pawnees and as a result the common name for slave in Detroit was *pani*. These people were adaptable and, it is said, could be trained into excellent house servants.

Paris fashions did not reach the remote outposts. The people dressed simply in homespun, much as the peasants in France dressed. The women wore full skirts with many petticoats, although for farm work and on market day they usually appeared with the outer skirt worn short or kilted up. The fabrics were hand woven, most of the thread and yarn being imported. Very little wool was raised in Detroit, but some farms had small fields of flax and a little linen was produced. The men working in the fields wore smocks; winter coats were made of brightly colored blanket material, belted by brilliantly dyed wool sashes, such as are still seen on festive occasions at Quebec. Pants, jackets, and leggings were of soft doeskin. From the Indians moccasins and shoepacs were adopted, although for both men and women working in the fields wooden shoes or sabots were not uncommon.

Social life centered around the home and the church. Dancing was a popular pastime and in nearly every home there was a fiddle and someone who could scratch out a tune. Weddings and baptisms were events at which everybody turned out to sing, dance, and tip the cider and brandy jugs. In the winter horse racing on the frozen streams was the most common sport. There were no schools except those in which the children were taught their catechism. As a result, hardly anyone except the priest, the notary, and a few officers could write. Newspapers were unheard of and unneeded. When there was news or an official announcement to be made, it was done in a fog horn voice by the beadle from the porch of Ste. Anne's after Sunday morning Mass. The church festival days were observed, particularly Christmas and the Feast of Corpus Christi, the latter being an occasion when everybody, civilian and military, turned out and formed a procession through the streets of the town. New Year's Day was the big holiday and was observed by everybody's holding open house and racing sleighs up and down the river to make calls on friends and relatives, which included just about the entire population. If anyone got sick there was the garrison surgeon to physic or bleed him. About 1720 Dr. Jean Chapoton arrived at Detroit as garrison surgeon. In 1734 he left the army and settled permanently in town. Doctors by the name of Chapoton dispensed pills to sick Detroiters for some five or six generations after that first one.

French sovereignty vanished from Detroit more

than two hundred years ago, but French influence never has. It exists today in place names and the names of old streets. But more important, it persists in the people. In and around Detroit there are thousands descended from the settlers who came with Cadillac or followed close after him. For many years after the last French governor had withdrawn, the French language and culture continued to be dominant. Neither has yet entirely died out. In the early years of this century, within the memory of persons still living, aristocratic old ladies in lace caps and elegant shawls poured tea in their Jefferson avenue mansions and gossiped in the language of their forefathers. Up to the 1950s some of the old-timers living around Ecorse held their annual muskrat dinners and muskrat was sold in many Detroit butcher shops. For many years, not far from modern times, sermons were delivered in French in some of the older churches.

If one cares to seek it out, he may still find lingering traces of the old French way of life thriving within a few minutes' drive of downtown Detroit. He need only cross to the Canadian side of the river and drive west and then south along the shore road (route 18). He will pass Sandwich and see a monument that marks the site of the old Huron mission and village. Continuing half a dozens miles farther, he will come to the little village of La Salle, once called and still known as *La Petite Côte*. Along the road just beyond it the farmhouses stand close together, a reminder of the old ribbon farms. Look at the names on the mail boxes. There will be Reaume and Druillard, Renaud, Bondy and Laframboise. And if the passerby stops at one of the farmhouses and knocks at the kitchen door, he will be cheerfully admitted. But he had better know his French, because that is what he will hear spoken. The younger people are bilingual, of course, but the oldsters, the *grandpère* and the *grandmère,* have in many cases forgotten their English and French is the language of the household. The old tongue is a dialect, to be sure, and a modern visiting Frenchman would find it as hard to understand as the English speaker. But there are those who insist that this patois, once the only language of old Detroit, is the pure French of the sixteenth and seventeenth centuries, and Louis XIV and Cardinal Richelieu would understand it easily.

Distance is short but history is long. Stand with those French-Canadian farmers on their doorsteps along the Petite Cote. From where you stand you can clearly see the lofty towers of downtown Detroit—fifteen miles away as the wild goose flies, but two hundred and fifty years away in the annals of mankind.

3

The Lion's Tale

The French Depart

In 1760, after fifty-nine years of French rule, Detroit
became a British possession. When the English took over
this rich territorial asset, they found they had acquired a
fair share of trouble. For thirty-six years Detroit managed
to tie knots in the lion's tail. The British had trouble with the
French inhabitants, with the Indians, and finally with the
American colonists. It cost them more to maintain garrisons
and to subsidize the Indians than they bargained for. The
profits from the fur trade, while substantial, were in large
part skimmed off by Scotch and Scotch-Irish traders, some
of whom had been run out of the mother country as unde-
sirable. There must have been times when the British would
gladly have given Detroit and the western country back to
the Indians. And in the end they lost it all anyway to a
rabble of rebellious colonists.

Detroit changed from a French to a British possession as spoils of the French and Indian War. That conflict

was one of a series of wars which began in 1689 and involved almost all of Europe for the better of a hundred years. They represented a power struggle between the English, French, Austrians, Prussians, and Spanish. Eventually they spilled over into North America where the stakes were the colonial empires of France and Britain.

The French and Indian War, while an offshoot of the long European power struggle, was almost entirely a home product. It is simplifying things to the extreme to say that it grew out of the covetousness of the English seaboard colonies for the vast rich Ohio River and Great Lakes basins which were French property. Yet, over-simplification or not, that is the basic fact. The English colonials felt hedged in by the Allegheny Mountains, beyond whose ridges lay fertile lands and profitable trade opportunities. Adventurous American traders penetrated the Ohio and Kentucky regions and found the Indians willing to sell them furs. The French attempted to stifle this competition by building a chain of forts from Lake Erie down to the forks of the Ohio. A Virginia military expedition, led by a young tidewater aristocrat, Colonel George Washington, moved against them in 1754, the year that marked the beginning of the French and Indian War. Washington was repulsed, but in 1755 a strong force of British regulars led by General Braddock and supported by colonials commanded by Washington crossed the mountains to attack Fort Duquesne (Pittsburgh). This army was bushwacked and badly defeated by Indians, and French soldiers, and coureurs-de-bois, most of whom came from Detroit.

But the British tried again and profited from the lesson of Braddock's defeat. They sent out competent generals who did not blunder through the woods as though they were on parade in London. They used regular troops, supplemented by locally raised bands of rangers who knew how to fight the Indian on his own terms. They took Pittsburgh on October 28, 1758, and Fort Niagara in July 1759, forcing the French to abandon all their strongholds east of Detroit and concentrate all their strength at that place. At times as many as two thousand uniformed infantrymen, French-Canadian rangers, and Indians, along with fairly strong batteries of artillery, were crowded into Detroit. The place was so congested that soldiers and inhabitants faced serious food shortages. The ribbon farms simply could not meet the demands.

The governor of Canada had sought to strengthen the town by sending out new settlers. For each family that agreed to go to Detroit, he offered free land, a plow, livestock, and other inducements. Few accepted the invitation. Most of those who did ate the livestock, shot off the free gunpowder, and promptly returned to Quebec where the living was easier. But additional troops were also sent out, the stockaded area was substantially enlarged, and as the citadel of French power in the West, Detroit became a pawn in the game of world politics.

One of New France's most capable officers, François Picoté, Sieur de Belèstre, was placed in command and took immediate steps to enlarge and strengthen the fort. The palisaded limits were pushed out until the western end reached what is now Washington boulevard. The northern limits, restricted by the Savoyard River, remained much as before, although the walls were repaired and put in better shape for defense.

The Iroquois, never real friends of the French, allied themselves with the British, as did some of the Hurons. Someone devised a scheme to use the latter to capture Detroit and massacre the inhabitants. The Hurons were instructed to sleep inside the fort—which they frequently were permitted to do—and in the farmhouses adjoining the stockade. At a specified time each Huron was to kill the inmates of the house in which he was lodged. But a squaw heard some of the braves discussing the plan. She warned the authorities and Belèstre took measures to thwart the plot. In spite of safeguards, however, atrocities were committed from time to time, and a number of the French settlers were killed and scalped within sight of the fort.

Detroit never came under direct attack from the British. The issue was settled elsewhere, on the Plains of Abraham just outside Quebec. On September 13, 1759, General James Wolfe scaled the high bluff that appeared to make the city impregnable and decisively defeated the defenders. Only Montreal was left and it was surrendered to General Jeffrey Amherst on September 8, 1760. Detroit and all the remaining French possessions were included in the capitulation.

While the French empire along the St. Lawrence and in the Great Lakes basin was crumbling, life continued much as usual in Detroit. Far removed from Montreal and Quebec, and temporarily quite out of touch, neither Belèstre nor the citizens knew what was happening. They were soon to find out, however. Four days after the Montreal capitulation, General Amherst sent off an expedition under Major Robert Rogers to take over the remote western posts. This Rogers was quite a fellow; his exploits have been recounted in Kenneth Roberts' fine historical novel *Northwest Passage*. A native of New Hampshire, Rogers organized a company of rangers consisting of experienced woodsmen and dedicated Indian haters. This body of half-wild men fought the savages on their own terms and in their own fashion. They were a miserable lot to meet in the woods, as both the Indians and the French discovered. Rogers' Rangers, or the Royal American Rangers as they were officially called, could wield a war hatchet and scalping knife with as much artistry as the best Indian warrior.

With two hundred of his roughnecks packed in fifteen bateaux and whaleboats, Rogers moved up the lakes with a stop at Erie, Pennsylvania, where he was reinforced by Captain Donald Campbell and a detachment of thirty-six men of the Royal American Regiment from Pittsburgh. The Royal Americans henceforth were to be closely identified with Detroit. The regiment was composed of troops recruited exclusively in the British seaboard colonies, mostly Pennsylvania, and were officered in large part by German or Swiss Protestants, including such well-known men as General Frederic Haldiman and Henry Bouquet. Unlike their counterparts in other regular British regiments, the Royal Americans or 60th Foot were distinguished by the green uniforms they wore.

Rogers and the Royal Americans proceeded from Erie to the site of present-day Cleveland where an imposing-looking group of about thirty Ottawas stepped out of the bushes and brought the British to a halt. Why, they demanded, were the English moving through their precincts? Rogers explained that he and his gentlemen-adventurers were prompted only by the purest motives. They were on their way to Detroit to take over that post from the French. They had no intention of trespassing on Indian land. They were there only to bring comforting protection to the benighted, and better and cheaper trade goods. The Ottawas allowed Rogers to continue his journey without interference. But playing it safe, they sped off their fastest runners to warn Belèstre.

That was the first inkling Belèstre had that something had gone wrong. He found it impossible to believe his government was in serious trouble, let alone that it had ceased to exist at all. To show his confidence to the Indians, he tacked a large poster on the gate of the fort with a cartoon depicting a crow perched on a human head, pecking out the brains. He explained that he was the crow and if the British came around, he would pick them clean. Meanwhile, Rogers was approaching. He reached a spot about where the Ambassador Bridge now has its Detroit terminus and sent two officers to Belèstre demanding Detroit's surrender. Belèstre was still skeptical, but when he saw a copy of the capitulation and written orders from his superiors in Canada, he realized the jig was up. On November 29, 1760, with drums pounding, the soldiers of France marched out of the stockade for the last time and Detroit was surrendered with the honors of war. Rogers and his crew marched in and raised the Union Jack. The French garrison of three officers and thirty-five enlisted men soon started on their way to Philadelphia and from there shipped home to France. It was a particularly happy occasion for seventeen Englishmen the French had been holding as prisoners of war. Rogers remained in Detroit for about a month and then, with everything under control, departed for Pittsburgh. Captain Campbell was left in command with his Royal Americans.

Now began the transition to an English colony. It was not easy. The Indians, always opportunists, cheered loudly for the new landlords, but the cheering probably emanated more from the rum jug than from conviction. The French did not cheer at all. They felt a vast distaste for their hereditary enemy. The best that can be said is that they gave a Gallic shrug of their shoulders and went about their business, convinced that eventually right would triumph and John Bull would be thrown out on his royal American. Captain Campbell, who had to live with this situation, proved to be amiable and tolerant, and did everything in his power to make friends with the inhabitants of Detroit. He kept his troops in check so they would not create any sticky incidents, and before long the girls were batting their eyes at the young soldiers. Campbell kept Navarre in office as notary and made no radical changes in the way public affairs were conducted. He even gave a series of balls and card parties to which he invited the leading French families and soon the thaw set in. The French never were enthusiastic about the British, but at least for the time being, they gave no trouble. Presents were given to the Indians and treaties were made, and for the moment the whole atmosphere was calm.

When Rogers and Campbell moved in, Detroit was still more of an area than a village. The entire population up and down the river on both sides was about two thousand, exclusive of the garrison. Perhaps five hundred people lived in the village or adjacent to it. There were about three hundred buildings in the stockade and the adjoining fields. The fort itself was considerably larger than the one Cadillac built; its dimensions were about one hundred yards north and south by two hundred yards east and west. There were bastions or blockhouses at the corners and over the main gates. These towers were armed with cannon of varying size. The streets inside the stockade were much as they had always been, but some of them had been extended beyond the walls, so the village actually included more than just the fort. In fact, more people lived outside the walls than inside.

The Indians soon became disillusioned with the British and their cheers of greeting turned to unfriendly grunts. The good things of life the savages had anticipated were not forthcoming. The English were not friendly like the French; they did not integrate. The host of traders that swarmed into the West proved to be unscrupulous and hard bargainers. The officers at the fort, with the possible exception of Captain Campbell, were a cold-eyed, disdainful and suspi-

cious lot who treated the Indians with a frosty arrogance.
To top it all off, General Amherst issued orders limiting the
distribution of ammunition, causing the Indians to suspect
the British were planning to get rid of them by starving them
to death.

Pontiac's War

This state of affairs led to the most dramatic and
best known event in Detroit's long history, a bloody Indian uprising called Pontiac's Conspiracy or Rebellion.
The Pontiac who gave his name to the affair had met
Major Rogers at Cleveland. A cruel and wily warrior,
he was also something of a statesman. At least he was one
of the few Indian leaders who understood that only by united
action on the part of all tribes could sufficient strength be
mobilized to challenge successfully the white interlopers.
So Pontiac developed a plan of confederation and during
most of 1762 traveled long distances seeking the coopera-
tion of far distant tribes—the Chippewa, Shawnee, Delawares, Miami, Potawatomi, and Hurons. He proposed that
these people join with his own Ottawas, and that each select and be responsible for the capture of a single fort or
settlement. At an agreed upon time each tribe would rise
simultaneously and by surprise or treachery hit its prescribed
target. The attacks were to be simultaneous so the English
garrisons would be unable to go to the aid of each other. By
threat and coercion Pontiac enlisted many of the western
tribes, and by the spring of 1763 he was ready. He sum-

moned a big council which was held on the Ecorse River below Detroit in April and final instructions were given. Pontiac reserved for himself the principal fort—Detroit. His first step was to move his village from the Canadian shore at Walkerville, across from the lower end of Belle Isle, to the American side. He set up his encampment on the farm of Baptiste Meloche on the east side of Parent's Creek. The location today is approximately at Lieb and Wight streets a short distance west of the Belle Isle bridge. Some of the ground may now be occupied by the huge Parke, Davis & Company plant.

Pontiac had a worthy foe to contend with, the British Commandant Major Henry Gladwin of the 80th Light Armed Foot who had been sent to Detroit with a troop detachment. He had arrived September 3, 1761, superseding Campbell who remained as second in command. Gladwin was a professional soldier to the core, stolid and unimaginative, but completely reliable. He was of the stiff-upper-lip carry-on-old-chap type that built the British Empire and permitted no nonsense from the lesser breeds within the imperial borders. Rudyard Kipling would have loved Henry Gladwin. Pontiac definitely did not.

On May 7, 1763, soon after the Ecorse council, Pontiac was ready to make his move. He had concocted an elaborate plot which almost worked. He requested a parley with Gladwin at which he proposed a group of his chiefs should be present. About noon the delegation of sixty tribal leaders appeared at the east gate—the location, marked today by a plaque at Griswold and Jefferson, was known thereafter as the Pontiac Gate. The group was admitted to the Council House which stood just inside the gate near the southeastern corner of the stockade. Pontiac planned to deliver a flowery speech and at its conclusion present Gladwin a belt of wampum, green on one side, white on the other. If in Pontiac's opinion conditions were favorable, he would hand over the wampum green side up. That would be the signal for his chiefs and warriors to draw the sawed-off muskets concealed under their blankets and mow down the garrison. If conditions did not look right, he would deliver the wampun white side up and the ruckus would be postponed.

Unluckily for Pontiac, Gladwin knew all about his plan. For a couple of centuries Detroiters have cherished the romantic legend that he found out from a beautiful Indian maiden who did the laundry and other things for him. Actually, the secret was wide open. For some time, the local blacksmiths reported, there had been an unusually active business in saws and files, and several people reported seeing the Indians cutting down their long gun barrels. Many of the French knew of the plot; Pontiac tried to enlist their help. It is generally believed, and there is evidence to support it, that a daughter of the Beaubien family warned her fiance James Sterling, a local trader, and he in turn told Gladwin.

At any rate, Gladwin was ready. When the Indian delegates stalked into the fort the garrison was drawn up under arms, and troops lined the streets and walls. Inside the Council House, Gladwin was surrounded by his officers, all wearing their side arms. Pontiac blandly inquired as to the reason for this military display. With equal blandness Gladwin replied that by occasionally exercising his troops they remained alert and ready for business. It was evident to Pontiac, of course, that his scheme was discovered and that Gladwin was ready for him. He became even more certain when Gladwin stepped over to one of the Indians, drew his blanket aside, and revealed his hidden gun. Gladwin then gave Pontiac a tongue lashing consisting of a stern lecture on the dangers of perfidy, and then had him and his friends escorted out of the fort. The wampum was delivered white side up.

Two days later Pontiac returned to the fort but was denied admission. Enraged, his warriors immediately went on the warpath, and murder and atrocity became the order of the day. A widow and her two sons who lived on the common somewhere in the neighborhood of Grand Circus Park were scalped and killed. Another party visited Belle Isle and wiped out a family named Fisher. A surveying team headed by Sir Robert Davers was ambushed and murdered as it returned from Lake St. Clair. Captain Campbell volunteered to go to the house of Antoine Beaubien at the corner of Jefferson avenue and Beaubien street to try to talk some sense into Pontiac. He got nowhere and at the conclusion of the parley, instead of honoring his flag of truce and permitting him to return safely to the fort, he was held prisoner and taken to the Ottawa camp. A few days later that amiable officer, a true friend of the Indians, was brutally murdered and his body was frightfully mutilated.

Gladwin buttoned up the fort and settled down to the serious business of withstanding a siege. His garrison consisted of about one hundred and twenty-five regulars, and a few British and French civilians who served as militia. Several sorties were made to burn houses and barns near the fort in order to provide a clear field of fire and destroy cover the Indians were using. Supplies on hand were not large, but fortunately Gladwin had at his disposal two small armed schooners, the *Huron* and *Michigan*, which could bring food, ammunition, and reinforcements from Niagara. Some of the French farmers were friendly to the British and smuggled what food they could into the stockade. Their neighbors, at the same time, were feeding the Indians. While much has been said of the hardships suffered by the garrison during the siege, the stories have been exaggerated.

Actually, Gladwin's supply line was kept open and his people never were in serious danger of running out of food and ammunition.

What worried Gladwin more than the Indians was the attitude of the French. Gladwin neither liked nor trusted them. To a large extent he had reason to feel as he did. The French inhabitants up and down the river had no love for the British. They were confident that ultimately France would triumph and the English would be tossed out. They had no quarrel with the Indians and wanted none. As a result their attitudes varied. The majority was neutral; many, however, actively sided with Pontiac, even to the extent of joining the besiegers. A few remained faithful to the British and these included some of the more influential families such as the Navarres, Babys and Campaus.

Day after day the siege went on and Pontiac resorted to a form of psychological warfare. British traders caught in the woods were scalped and killed and their bodies were shown to the fort's defenders. Atrocities were of the most repulsive kind. The Indians had cast-iron digestive tracts and would eat anything, including a Britisher. Cannibalism was quite common in Pontiac's camp.

One by one the posts were taken—soon everything west of Niagara except Detroit was wiped out. Sandusky, St. Joseph, Fort Miamis, Ouiatenon (Lafayette, Indiana), and Mackinac were captured and their garrisons either massacred or held prisoner. Only a few escaped; one whose life was spared and who managed to make his way back to Detroit was the independent trader Chapman Abraham, the first known Jew in Detroit.

At least two relief expeditions were sent from Niagara. The first, commanded by Lieutenant Abraham Cuyler of the Queen's Rangers, set out on May 13, not knowing that Detroit was then under attack. His command con-

sisted of ninety-six men in ten bateaux which also carried
one hundred and thirty-nine barrels of provisions. A bateau
was a flat-bottomed vessel of French design with high sides
and pointed ends. Propelled by sweeps or a single small
sail, it was used for carrying heavy loads. Cuyler and his
cumbersome scows landed at Point Pelee about twenty-five
miles from the mouth of the Detroit River on the night of
May 28. Before a proper camp could be made the party
was jumped by a body of Indians. Some of the soldiers, including Cuyler, managed to escape in a couple of the boats,
but the rest, nearly fifty men and eight boats, were taken.
Two days later, on May 30 a flotilla coming up the river
was observed from the fort and the garrison naturally believed it was a rescue party. The troops and loyal townspeople lined the walls cheering, but their joy quickly evap-
orated when the boats continued past Detroit and it could
be observed they were manned by Indians. Four soldiers
in the leading boat suddenly turned on their captors and
tossed them overboard, and three managed to make their
way safely to shore, bringing seven barrels of provisions
with them. The fate of the others was sealed. They were
taken to Pontiac's camp. There they joined a group of eighteen soldiers or boatmen and a woman taken the day before
as they were downbound from Mackinac. A murderous
spree followed and the watchers on the ramparts of Detroit
were sickened in the days that followed as they saw logs
floating by to which the bodies of the Indians' victims were
bound.

The second effort to relieve Detroit was more successful, at least in its initial stages. On July 29 Captain
Dalzell (sometimes written like Dalyell) arrived safely with
two hundred and sixty men, consisting of a detachment of
the 60th Foot, and another of rangers commanded by Major
Rogers. The addition of these troops materially strengthened

the garrison, but it led to immediate trouble. Dalzell was a glory seeker and persuaded Gladwin that an offensive action would defeat and scatter the Indians. He proposed taking his men on a surprise march against Pontiac's camp. Gladwin had misgivings but gave his reluctant approval, and an hour before daybreak on July 30 Dalzell led two hundred and fifty regulars and rangers out of the fort along the river road, now East Jefferson avenue. A surprise attack was impossible. There were enough French informers ready to warn Pontiac, and his own warriors watched the expedition as it march off.

Nothing happened until Dalzell's column arrived at Parent's Creek, close to where the Players' clubhouse now stands. The creek ran at the bottom of a little ravine, spanned by a foot bridge which permitted only two men abreast to cross at a time. When the first files were across all hell broke loose. Indians hidden in the bushes poured in a murderous fire from all sides. Taken completely by surprise, the British became confused and the head of the column crowded back on those following. Attempting to rescue a wounded man, Dalzell was shot down. Rogers, who was in the rear, relied on his knowledge of Indian fighting. He rallied the men, then dispersed them in the farmhouse and outbuildings of Jacques Campau, and succeeded in holding off the enemy. Gladwin, apprised of the disaster, sent a couple of bateaux mounting swivel guns upstream and the survivors were evacuated. Only ninety men were saved. So many dead and dying soldiers fell into Parent's Creek that its waters ran red, and from that time on the stream was known as Bloody Run. Dalzell's body was taken to the camp of the Indians, whose losses numbered only twenty, where it was hacked into small pieces. A few days later these were collected by Campau and carried to the fort. Dalzell's remains, along with the other dead of his command, were buried in the military cemetery just outside the palisade. The site today is just below Jefferson at Griswold across the street from the new Michigan Consolidated Gas Company building. Unfortunately, all trace of this burying ground used for military and Protestant interments has long since disappeared.

The Dalzell disaster at least served the purpose of teaching the British to stay behind the walls of their fort and not go rambling around the countryside looking for trouble. As long as the defenders stayed put they were safe from bullets and tomahawks. Thanks to the schooners *Huron* and *Michigan*, they were reasonably well fed. Pontiac realized he could not starve out the garrison as long as the two vessels remained operative. He made unsuccessful attempts to destroy them. He floated blazing fire rafts down the river, but the schooners eluded them. On other occasions he sent canoe loads of warriors to attempt to board, but they were beaten off. Once, at the mouth of the Detroit River, a group of Indians did manage to get on board at night, but a leather-lunged officer bellowed an order to touch off the magazine. The savages understood the order and went over the side in a hurry. The schooner then proceeded safely upstream to the fort.

Thus, without anything decisive happening, the siege continued through August, September and October. The Indians wearied of it, and the Hurons and some of the other allied tribes hitched up their leather leggings and went home. As autumn approached only the Ottawas and a few others held on. Even the French could see that the uprising was not going to succeed, and they became more friendly toward the British. Finally a couple of local Frenchmen returned from a visit to St. Louis bearing a letter from the French commandant there to the effect that a peace treaty between France and Great Britain had been signed.

The official peace confirmed the transfer of French possessions in North America and indicated the Indians could expect no help from France. That was all that was needed. On October 31, 1763, Pontiac sent a message to Gladwin offering to make peace. Gladwin replied that he lacked authority to make an agreement but would forward the offer to General Amherst. Pontiac decided not to wait. He gathered his remaining followers and retired to his ancestral home on the Maumee River. The siege was at an end and of all the western posts, only Detroit had survived. Pontiac wandered away and Detroit never saw him again. In 1769 he was murdered at East St. Louis. As far as is known all that remains of him lies buried under the streets of downtown St. Louis, Missouri.

Frontier Citadel

After the war whoops ceased echoing through the forests, life in Detroit settled down to a peaceful and normal pattern which more or less continued for about a dozen years. Freed from the necessity of standing watch on the ramparts and dodging Indian bullets, the garrison turned to other pursuits of a more social nature. With time on their hands, the officers gave balls and organized a Masonic lodge. Known as Zion Lodge, they obtained a charter from the Grand Lodge of New York. Civilians were admitted to membership and several of the more prominent Frenchmen around town joined. The oldest Masonic organization west of the Alleghenies, it is still in existence and in 1964 celebrated its two hundredth anniversary. Business prospered and a number of merchants and traders established commercial enterprises in Detroit. Most of these entrepreneurs were Scots or Scotch-Irish, and from a social and economic standpoint they quickly became the dominant faction in the community.

But the peaceful days did not last. In the eastern colonies there was unrest and strong resistance to British colonial policy. To offset that as much as possible and to prevent its spread to Canada, which remained predominantly French-Catholic, the British took conciliatory measures. In 1774, following the Boston Tea Party, the Quebec Act was passed by Parliament. It provided that all the Indian country north of the Ohio and east of the Mississippi would be annexed to the Province of Quebec, with a lieutenant-governor assigned to each important post; that English criminal law would be continued, but that French civil law and customs would be reinstated; that an appointed legislative council instead of an elected one would be provided for Quebec; and that the Roman Catholic religion would be protected. This set of rules, added to others already in force, completely closed—or was supposed to close —the western country to settlement by the people of the seaboard colonies who claimed all the territory south of the Great Lakes. The Quebec Act was regarded by the predominantly Protestant Americans as a slap in the face and a serious threat to their religion, their system of self-government, their enterprise, and their safety from the Indians. Their resentment was in part responsible for the explosion of temper at Lexington and the Revolutionary War.

Detroit played a key, although not decisive role in the American Revolution. Chiefly it served as a base from which expeditions were sent to harass the American settlements in Kentucky and western Pennsylvania and New

York. These marauding parties caused great havoc on the frontier and were composed of Indians led by white partisan raiders. The names of the latter are written in infamy in records of American history. They include Walter Butler whose rangers, both white and red, carried death, terror, and desolation to the Mohawk, Cherry, and Wyoming valleys of New York and Pennsylvania. Billy Caldwell, Henry Bird, Matthew Elliott, Alexander McKee, and the notorious Simon Girty kept the Kentucky border in turmoil and brought home scores of scalps and prisoners. It has been estimated that more than two thousand men, women and children were killed and scalped by Detroit-based Indians under these leaders. One of those killed was a backwoods Kentucky farmer named Abraham Lincoln whose grandson and namesake would become president of the United States. In 1782, it is said, more than five hundred prisoners were held at Detroit, brought in by the Indians and held for ransom. When possible they were bought by the British inhabitants of Detroit. Those who were not were sometimes adopted by Indian families; some were disposed of in the most convenient manner. One distinguished Detroit guest was the noted frontiersman and "b'ar" killer Daniel Boone. He was captured in Kentucky in 1778 by a Shawnee war party and remained in Detroit for several months. British authorities tried to ransom him, but he was such a prestigious catch the Indians refused to give him up. They took him to a village near Chillicothe, Ohio, where he made his escape back to Kentucky.

Behind all this border fury was Henry Hamilton who arrived in Detroit November 9, 1775, to assume the duties of lieutenant-governor. A member of a Scottish family of royal blood, Hamilton saw extensive military service in Canada before going to Detroit. Although he was an army man, his duties as lieutenant-governor were more those of a civil administrator. He determined overall policy, but he did not command the garrison which for most of the war was in the capable hands of Captain Richard B. Lernoult. Because of Hamilton's part in planning and directing the raids, particularly against Kentucky, his name became one with which to frighten children and an abomination to generations of unforgiving Americans. Responsibility for all atrocities was laid at his door, and it was charged that he paid the Indians for each scalp they brought back. As a result American propagandists hung the label of "Hamilton the Hair-Buyer" on him. There is no real evidence that he paid for scalps; on the contrary, he frequently cautioned departing war parties not to make war against women and children. Oddly, the men like Hamilton, Girty, and Elliott, whose names for generations have been anathema in Detroit, are regarded today on the Canadian side of the river as great and true patriots. The sites of their farms and homes around Amherstburg are in some cases looked upon as national shrines and are marked by historical plaques. Their descendants, especially those of Simon Girty, are numerous in the area.

The British and their Indian friends had no monopoly of black deeds; the Americans indulged in a few themselves. One of the most dismal pages in American history concerns the persecution of the Moravian Indians in southeastern Ohio. These people, most of them Delawares, had been Christianized by Moravian missionaries from Pennsylvania. They had become industrious farmers and were as civilized as their white frontier neighbors. They had forsaken the warpath and all they asked was to be permitted to remain neutral and let alone. But that was not to be. They were molested from both sides, but the Americans, to whom the only good Indian was a dead one, became their worst persecutors. A group of American patriots, claiming that the Moravian Indians had been aiding the British, descended upon their little settlement at Gnaddenhutten, Ohio, and viciously massacred nearly a hundred in their church. The survivors, led by their white missionaries, were forced to seek protection of the British, and in 1781 they moved to Detroit and were provided land which is now on the outskirts of Mount Clemens. There they established a thriving little colony, but their Chippewa neighbors were unfriendly and suspicious, and after the war they were forced again to move in 1786. Some went back to Ohio; others went to Canada and built a new village, Moraviantown near Chatham, Ontario, where a number of their descendants live to this day. But before leaving the Detroit area they made one lasting contribution; they built a road from Mount Clemens to Detroit to get their produce to market. It is now Gratiot avenue.

In order to check the raiding parties from Detroit and hopefully to capture the place, the Americans organized an offensive in 1778 under General George Rogers Clark. With a force of Virginia and Kentucky frontiersmen, he captured the distant posts of Kaskaskia and Cahokia and, so it appeared, seemed ready to pounce upon Detroit. Alarmed by the threat, Lieutenant-Governor Hamilton gathered a small force of rangers and regulars and went to Vincennes, Indiana, to block Clark's advance. But Clark made an epic march across the flooded plains of southern Illinois and Indiana, and surprised Vincennes. Hamilton and his force were captured, shipped to Williamsburg, Virginia, and clapped into jail. There was a loud clamor from the Virginians to hang the hair-buyer, a proposition heartily endorsed by Virginia Governor Thomas Jefferson. But George Washington, who feared a quid pro quo if Hamilton was executed, interceded and eventually Detroit's first lieutenant-governor was exchanged. Ultimately, Hamilton was made governor of Bermuda and gave his name to the island's principal town. At Detroit he was replaced by Captain Arent Schuyler DePeyster, American born and a member of a prominent New York family.

Clark's planned advance toward Detroit was stalled by lack of manpower, but a new threat was posed. Daniel Brodhead with a small army of Pennsylvanians marched from Pittsburgh into Ohio and built a fort about ninety miles south of Sandusky. To Captain Lernoult an attack against Detroit appeared certain and imminent. Surveying his facilities for defense, Lernoult found much to be desired. The town, a tinder box with its wooden buildings, and the old stockade, a rickety thing, were vulnerable to any kind of artillery. Guns placed on the slight rise behind the town beyond the Savoyard would command the fort completely. In fact it was possible to stand on that rise and look down into the town. Only one thing was to be done, Lernoult decided. That was to build new fortifications. He assigned the task to his engineer officer, Captain Henry Bird. One late afternoon in November 1778 Bird paced off the outline of a new defense works, and the next day construction was begun. The new fort was placed on rising ground north of town. It covered an area of about two-and-a-half or three acres, its center being in what is now the intersection of Fort and Shelby streets. The site is now occupied by the Federal building, the Detroit Bank & Trust Company, the Federal Reserve building, the Manufacturers National Bank, and the western corner of the Penobscot building.

Lernoult and Bird were in a hurry and managed to erect the basic structure by February 1779. A good deal, however, still remained to be done, and the work was continued over a period of several years. Everybody was put on the job; the soldiers of the garrison pitched in, and a large number of civilians were employed—the French somewhat against their will because after the French-American alliance, many secretly favored the cause of the colonies. A party of masons was sent from Quebec to do the stone work.

The completed fort has been described as having earthen ramparts built up on logs, eleven feet high, twenty-six feet thick at the base, and twelve feet wide at the top of the parapet. Inside was a banquette, six feet off the ground, which served as a platform for riflemen and artillery. On the outside walls of the ramparts were placed rows of sharpened pickets projecting horizontally to a height of six feet above ground level and slanting outwards at an angle of forty-five degrees. At the exterior base of the ramparts was a dry moat, twelve feet wide and five feet deep, in which was planted a line of pickets twelve feet high. Beyond these was the glacis with an abattis, a row of tree trunks with sharpened limbs pointing outward. There was only one gate, on the south or town side. It was protected by a blockhouse tower and a drawbridge. A covered way connected fort and town for a while; later a subterranean passage was built. Lernoult and his successors stripped the old fort and the naval vessels on the river of their guns, and requisitioned more from Quebec. As a result there was artillery mounted on each of the bastions and along each wall, making a fairly formidable array. Inside a number of buildings were put up. These included barracks, commandant's and officers' quarters, blacksmith, armorer and other shops. Outside the wall was the stone powder magazine, moved from its old location behind the church. A deep well was dug, and a flag pole was planted in the new fort's center. A few years ago during excavations for a modern building, the stump of the pole was unearthed. Diggers have also uncovered some of the old pickets. As soon as the work was complete enough the garrison moved in and it was named

Fort Lernoult for the captain.

With the addition of the new fortification which dominated the town and commanded the river, Detroit had a formidable military establishment. Because of the need for strengthening the garrison after Pontiac's War, a new installation called the Citadel had been built in 1764. This consisted of a complex of barracks, a guardhouse which was also used as a civil jail, a washhouse, and other structures. It was located on the west side of the town and the pickets were moved to enclose it. It occupied the space which is now Washington boulevard and the land just west of it, and extended north almost to the Savoyard River, or close to the present line of Congress street. The Citadel accommodated from two to three hundred troops, and after Fort Lernoult was built, was used to house prisoners. At times during the Revolution it was filled to its capacity of three hundred and ninety-two persons. The Citadel was consructed of timber cut on Belle Isle by Colonel Israel Putnam of Connecticut. Putnam, it will be recalled, later served as a general of the American forces in the Revolutionary War. After the Pontiac troubles and during the Revolution when the British were determined to keep their supply lines open at all costs, a naval flotilla was added, consisting of nine vessels of varying size. Some of them were probably built in a shipyard on the River Rouge at a spot now part of Woodmere Cemetry, not far fom the giant Ford Rouge works. The royal dockyard was established at what became the foot of Woodward avenue and it served Detroit for many years as the principal wharf. Lately the location has provided the docking facilities for the popular Bob-Lo excursion boats.

With the completion of Fort Lernoult, a new line of pickets was erected in 1779. These extended from the corners of the new fort down to the east-west walls of the town. A little later the pickets were again changed so that the area enclosed, based on the present street plan, was as follows: from the eastern side of the old town up Griswold street to Michigan avenue, along Michigan to Washington boulevard, and south along a line between the latter and Cass avenue to the western limits of the old wall. This extension materially enlarged the area of Detroit. The enclosure took in the town proper and the Citadel on the south, and Fort Lernoult on the north. In between was an open expanse utilized by the military for a parade ground and a woodyard, and large plots were placed under cultivation as gardens for growing food for the garrison. The section around the fort on all sides and extending to Woodward avenue on the east has always been known and appears in the abstracts as the Military Reserve.

The fort continued to be called Fort Lernoult as long as the British occupied Detroit. When the Americans took over it was renamed Fort Detroit, and was so known until after the War of 1812 when it became Fort Shelby in honor of the governor of Kentucky who led an army of Kentuckians to the relief of Detroit. In 1827, no longer needed, the fort was dismantled, the earth from the ramparts was used to fill in the land below Jefferson avenue, and the Military Reserve was subdivided. It now comprises the heart of Detroit's financial district.

The Revolutionary War ended in 1781 with the surrender of Yorktown, and yet it did not end for Detroit. A formal peace treaty was signed in 1783, assigning all the Northwest Territory between the Ohio and Mississippi Rivers and the Great Lakes to the United States. This, of course, included Michigan and Detroit. To assert its sovereignty over the area as well as to provide for its orderly development, Congress adopted the Ordinance of 1787, better known as the Northwest Ordinance. A notable charter, the ordinance provided for the territory's division into five states when population warranted and laid down certain ground rules for a territorial form of government until the time for admission to the Union arrived.

But the transition was slow as far as Detroit was concerned. The British were loath to give it up. Under pressure from local and Montreal merchants who did not want to lose the rich Indian trade, British occupation continued. The excuse was that the United States had not yet fulfilled all its 1783 treaty obligations. Consequently Detroit existed in a sort of political limbo. Legally it was a United States possession, but the British continued to occupy it with troops and to govern it after a fashion. It continued to be the chief western base for the British Indian Department, and the British gave huge amounts of money in the form of gifts and subsidies in an effort to maintain control over the Midwest tribes. War parties still harassed Ohio and Indiana, and the authorities at Detroit winked at what was going on. Merchants complained because what amounted to military government was bad for business. A lack of civil courts made the collection of debts difficult. At this time nearly all Detroit business and property was owned by seventeen individual merchants or partnerships. To placate them, a semblance of civil law was established and in 1791, when Upper Canada, now Ontario, was separated from Quebec, Detroit, an American city, anomalously elected two representatives to the Canadian provincial council or parliament.

Obviously it was a situation the United States could not long tolerate. President George Washington sent an army into the Ohio country to subdue the Indians once and for all. After a couple of abortive campaigns, General "Mad Anthony" Wayne soundly trounced the confederated savages in 1794 at the Battle of Fallen Timbers near present-day Toledo. This victory placed a well-trained and effective American army on the doorstep of Detroit. The British position was untenable, and when Chief Justice John Jay negotiated a peace and commercial treaty with the British government in November 1794, he had no difficulty in securing an article that provided for the evacuation of Detroit. In the spring of 1796 the garrison of Detroit was withdrawn across the river, and the new British base Fort Malden was established at Amherstburg.

On July 11, 1796, a detachment of American troops arrived at Detroit. The fort was turned over to them and the Stars and Stripes were hoisted. Detroit became an American town at last.

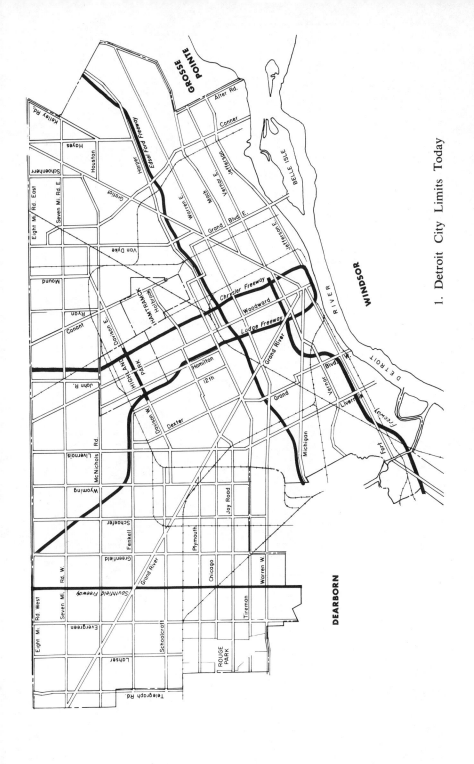

1. Detroit City Limits Today

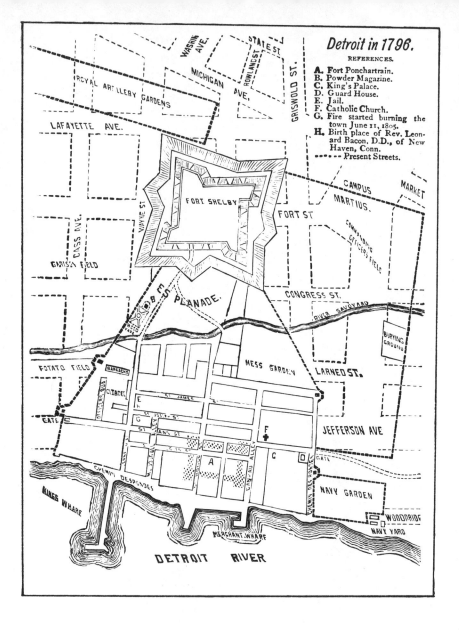

Detroit in 1796.

REFERENCES.

A. Fort Ponchartrain.
B. Powder Magazine.
C. King's Palace.
D. Guard House.
E. Jail.
F. Catholic Church.
G. Fire started burning the town June 11, 1805.
H. Birth place of Rev. Leonard Bacon, D.D., of New Haven, Conn.
----- Present Streets.

3. Statue of Cadillac

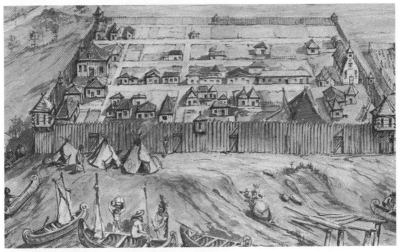

4. Fort Detroit about
1750

5. Henry Gladwin

6. "Mad Anthony" Wayne

7. Ribbon Farms in 1810

8. Pontiac's Siege

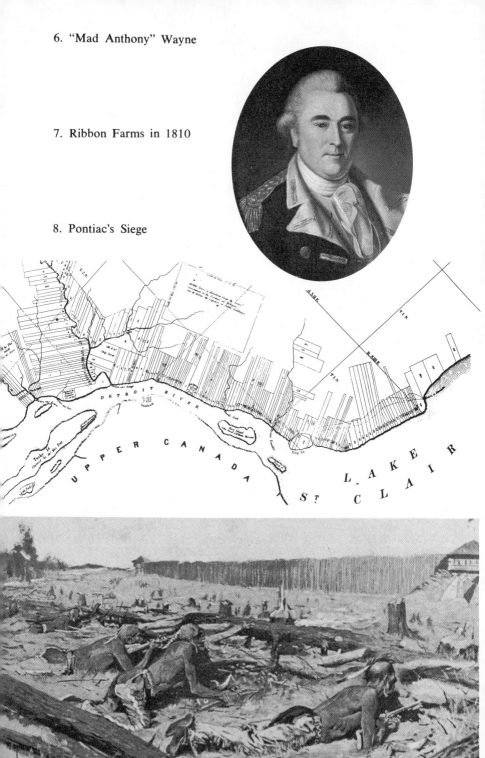

9. Detroit in 1794

10. Hull's Surrender

11. Father Richard

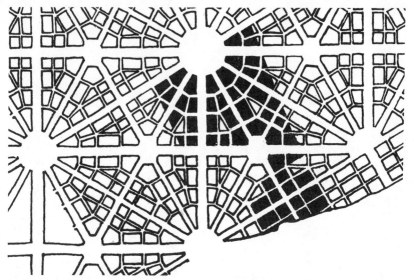

12. Detail of Woodward Plan

13. S.S. Walk-in-the-Water

14. Lewis Cass

15. Detroit in 1838

16. Citizens' Meeting in 1861

17. Election Scene in 1837

18. Second Regiment Troops in 1861

19. S.S. Philo Parsons

RALLY ROUND

THE UNION FOREVER

THE FLAG, BOYS!

100 MEN WANTED!!

For the 23d Mich. Infantry.

Enlist before April 1st, secure the Government Bounty of $300 00,

AND "KEEP OUT OF THE DRAFT!"

Government Bounty, $300; State Bounty, $100; Town Bounty, $100.

Apply to WM. SICKELS, St. Jrhns, or

O. L. SPAULDING,

Lieut. Col., 23d Mich. Infantry, Corunna.

March   , 1864.

["REPUBLICAN" PRINT, ST. JOHNS.]

20. Recruiting Poster

21. Michigan Central
    R.R. Depot

22. S.S. Frank E. Kirby

Special Grand

EXCURSION
FROM WYANDOTTE to TOLEDO
Sunday, May 11, 1902.
...STEAMER FRANK E. KIRBY...
THE FLYER OF THE LAKES.

Only 50c Round Trip.   –   About 4 Hours in Toledo.

Leaves Oak Street 10 A. M. City Time.   Home at 8:30 P. M.
Bicycles Carried Free.

ASHLEY & DUSTIN, MANAGERS,   -   -   -   DETROIT, MICHIGAN.

23. Excursion Announcement

24. S.S. Put-in-Bay

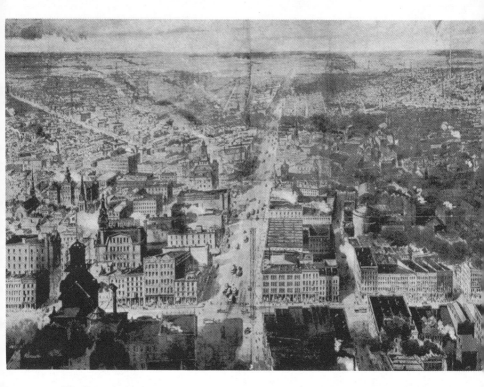

25. Detroit in 1887

26. Woodward Avenue in the Eighties

27. Fire Engine Co. No. 3 in 1871

28. Woodward Avenue in the Eighties

29. Ford Motor Co. in 1903

30. Early Horseless Carriage

31. Baseball Game in 1886
32. King's and Detroit's First Auto

33. Campus Martius in 1912

34. Seven Mile Road in 1914

35. Henry Ford in 1924

36. Liberty Bond Drive Parade in 1918

37. Depression Bread Line

38. Bootlegging

39. Stout Air Pullman

40. Ford Hunger March Aftermath

41-42. Before and During the Battle of the Overpass in 1937

43. Blind-Pig Origin of 1967 Riot

44. Aftermath of July 1967 Riot

45. Detroit in 1968

46. Ford Motor Co. River Rouge Plant

47. Ford-Lodge Freeway Interchange

48. Cultural Center

49. Thanksgiving Day Parade

50. McGregor Memorial Conference Center

4

Yankee Doodle Comes to Town

The Americans Arrive

The second article of the Jay Treaty stated that the British were to evacuate the western forts on or before June 1, 1796. The British were ready to keep their part of the bargain and moved most of their troops over to Fort Malden, leaving only a caretaking detail behind at Fort Lernoult. But the American army was not ready. General Wayne had his men strung out in three or four forts across northern Indiana and Ohio. Moreover, the general had the gout and was hurting. So he sent his aide Captain Henry DeButts to Detroit to confer with British Commandant Colonel Richard England, an appropriate name for the dignitary who was to preside over this small disintegration of the British Empire. DeButts was cordially received and with the help of Colonel England chartered three privately owned vessels which he sent to the mouth of the Maumee River to carry back the Americans.

The American army at that time was known as the Legion of the United States and Anthony Wayne was the commander-in-chief. The legion was divided into four sub-legions corresponding to regiments, although each was composed of infantry, artillery, and cavalry. The 1st Sub-Legion, which later became the 1st Infantry Regiment, was commanded by Lieutenant Colonel John Francis Hamtramck, a Canadian-born professional soldier who had served valiantly on the American side in the Revolution. The 1st Sub-Legion was the most advanced unit of Wayne's army and was assigned the duty of taking over Detroit. When DeButts' chartered sloops appeared, a detachment of sixty-five men under Captain Moses Porter boarded the *Swan* and sailed for Detroit. Owned by James May of Detroit, the *Swan* is said to have been the first vessel to fly the American flag on the Great Lakes. At any rate, Porter arrived, as we have seen, on July 11 and his soldiers disembarked at the King's Wharf which jutted one hundred and fifty feet into the river at the foot of Washington boulevard. Once the Americans had set foot on it, it ceased to be the King's Wharf and became the Government Wharf. Porter marched his men up the hill at noon and they presented arms while the British detail left the fort. It was all very friendly, very military, and very sporting. Two days later Hamtramck arrived with about four hundred men and discovered to his chagrin that there was not enough food on hand to feed them. The British, to show there were no hard feelings, sent over a few barrels of salt meat and other supplies, and amity reigned along the border. On August 13 General Wayne, gout and all, made a sort of triumphal entry which was celebated by a noisy but friendly Indian demonstration and a *Te Deum* was sung in the village church. Wayne moved into a house on Jefferson just east of Washington where the Pontchartrain Hotel now stands. It had been the home of Walter Roe, an attorney who elected to retain his British citizenship. Wayne set up headquarters and for the time being Detroit became the Pentagon of its day. Wayne remained in Detroit until November 15. Then he left for his home near Philadelphia but never made it. At Erie, Pennsylvania, he became seriously ill and died on December 15.

The arrival of the Americans posed a problem for some of the residents of Detroit, particularly those who were unwilling to give up their British citizenship. Among them were several of the more prosperous and influential merchants. The French did not care which flag flew over the fort so long as no one interfered too much with them. But the English businessmen had close trade alliances with Montreal; a change in sovereignty might disrupt their banking and credit connections, and force them to look to Albany or New York as their market place. Some solved the dilemma by packing up their worldly goods and moving across the river to Canada where they were already large landowners. Among those who made the move was John Askin who settled upriver near Belle Isle where he built a fine manor which he named Strabane after his ancestral home in Ireland. Tearing up his roots was not too difficult or costly for Askin. His daughter had married Elijah Brush. The Brushes remained on the old Askin farm where downtown Brush street is now. Thereafter known as the Brush farm it was the first one east of the town and the common. A sister-in-law of Askin was married to Commodore Alexander Grant who commanded His Majesty's Royal Navy on the upper Great Lakes. Grant had a palatial home at Grosse Pointe and did not want to leave it. He settled the problem by ignoring the change in government and stayed. Detroit was amused at the anomaly of the British naval commander directing his fleet from the United States. Grant continued to do so until his death in 1813.

Another family that crossed the river was that of

Angus MacIntosh, hereditary chieftan of the Clan Mac-
Intosh of Inverness, Scotland. The MacIntoshes were run
out of Scotland when some of the Highlanders became too
obstreperous to suit their British masters. Angus built a
fine house in Windsor and named it Moy Hall after the
ancient seat of the MacIntoshes in Inverness. Some years
later when the British were willing to forgive and forget,
the MacIntosh heirs went back to the old country and resumed their proper place as lairds of Moy and chieftains
of the clan, positions their descendants hold to this day.

One Detroiter named Park wanted no traffic with
the Americans at all. He had just built a new house, so he
tore it down and loaded the lumber on a barge which he
floated over to Amherstburg. There he reassembled the
house and it stands today, reputedly the oldest building
along the Detroit border. Simon Girty, who by reputation
had several Kentucky scalps hanging from his belt, thought
it a most provident thing to put the width of the river between himself and the Americans. There is a tradition that
when Captain Porter's troops hove into sight, Girty rode
his horse into the river and swam it across. At any rate,
he settled just below Amherstburg on a farm still in the
possession of his descendants. There is another tradition
that when old Simon died in 1818 he was buried under a
corner of a barn on the farm so vengeance-seeking Americans would not dig him up—for what purpose was never
explained.

Not all of the merchants moved away, however.
Several prominent ones accepted American citizenship,
families like the Macombs, Campaus, Abbotts, and Mays,
to mention but a few. They retained their businesses, their
wealth, and in some cases their slaves. Of the latter there
were about one hundred seventy-five in the town when the
Americans arrived. About half of them were Indians, the

rest were Negroes who had been brought to Detroit from Kentucky raids during the Revolution. There were a few Germans and a few Dutch in Detroit, too. Added to the French, English, Scotch and Irish, they gave the town a cosmopolitan flavor which it has always retained. Contributing to this cosmopolitan flavor was Commandant Colonel Hamtramck, Canadian born but of Luxembourg and French ancestry. He fell in love with Detroit and the romance was mutual; the people loved him. He bought a farm east of the city and when things progressed to the point that townships were laid out, one was named for him. Ultimately most of Hamtramck Township was absorbed by Detroit, but a northern section became a municipality in its own right. The city of Hamtramck, now one of Michigan's most populous towns and a major center of automobile production, has been engulfed by Detroit and with adjoining Highland Park is a municipal island, the two cities being completely surrounded by their larger neighbor. Colonel Hamtramck died in 1803 at the age of forty-five. A devout Catholic, he was first buried in Ste. Anne's churchyard. Later he was reinterred in Mt. Elliott Cemetery, but in 1962 the city named for him claimed his remains, he was reburied, and his grave was made a civic memorial at Joseph Campau and Dan streets in Hamtramck.

Americans are inclined to be uneasy unless they have things organized and the first-comers to Detroit were no exception. Accompanying General Wayne when he arrived was Winthrop Sargent, secretary of the Northwest Territory. Two days after he came to town, on August 15, 1796, he issued a proclamation organizing Wayne County. At that time the county consisted of quite a piece of real estate. It included all of Michigan's lower peninsula, part of its upper peninsula, and parts of present Wisconsin,

Illinois, Indiana, and Ohio. Among the localities then in
Wayne County were the sites of Milwaukee, Chicago,
Toledo, and Cleveland. Later, of course, boundaries were
revised and in 1815 Wayne County was shrunk to its
present dimensions. In 1799 the population of the Northwest Territory had increased to the point that an elected
legislature could be authorized. Detroit was entitled to one
representative—later increased to three. The people chose
Solomon Sibley, a young Connecticut Yankee who was
a comparative newcomer to town. Originally the capital
was at Cincinnati and later at Chillicothe. To carry out
his duties, Sibley was required to travel a long distance.
In 1803 when Ohio became a state, Michigan became part
of the Indiana Territory. This inconvenienced Michigan
because people who had business at the capital had to
travel all the way to Vincennes, a most inaccessible place.
This unsatisfactory arrangement caused much local grum-
bling and discontent. Congress heeded the protests of Detroiters. In 1805 Michigan was set off as a separate territory and provision was made for its government by a board
of appointed officers known as the Governor and Judges.
President Jefferson appointed the Revolutionary War veteran William Hull of Massachusetts as governor and Stanley Griswold of New Hampshire as secretary. The judges
were Augustus Brevoort Woodward, a native of New York
who at the time of his appointment was living in Washington, D.C., Samuel Huntington of Ohio, and Frederick
Bates of Virginia, who had been serving as Detroit's first
postmaster since 1802. Huntington declined the appointment and John Griffin of Virginia was made his replacement.

In 1802, prior to these developments, the legislative council at Chillicothe was persuaded by Sibley to adopt
an act for the incorporation of Detroit and to provide for a

slate of municipal officers, including a board of five trustees, a secretary, an assessor, a tax collector, and a marshal. The first meeting of the trustees was held in February 1802 in the tavern of John Dodemead on Jefferson avenue near Wayne (Washington boulevard). One of the first official acts was to adopt better ordinances for fire protection. The danger of fire was a bigger bugaboo to Detroiters than wild Indians. The old frame houses crowded on top of each other were tinder dry and made the town a veritable fire trap. Each householder was required to keep a ladder on his roof, to have fire buckets, and to cover his hearth fire every night. The town watch was instructed to report any house in which candles were seen burning later than usual. The town had a fire engine of sorts, a pump kept in a shed adjoining Dodemead's tavern.

Out of the Ashes

June 11, 1805, dawned like most other early summer days in Detroit. It was a market day for one thing. It was also a Catholic feast day. The French farmers came to town early and attended Mass at Ste. Anne's before spreading out their produce for sale on the common just outside the east wall of the stockade. Elsewhere the town was bustling as usual with the people going about their business. Then, suddenly, there was the dread cry, "Fire." Just how it started no one knows exactly. It has long been believed it began in the stable of John Harvey, the town baker, whose establishment was near the west end of the village. Some said that either Harvey or one of his employees knocked a live coal out of his pipe, setting fire to a pile of straw. In a matter of seconds the blaze engulfed the building and spread rapidly to adjoining structures. The alarm was sounded and men rushed to form bucket brigades. The fire engine was hauled out, but its suction hose was dropped into a cistern next to a hat maker's shop, and it became clogged with bits of felt and refused to work. Householders and merchants scurried back and forth with armloads of possessions, trying to get them safely to the commons or on board boats. Soldiers rushed down from the fort to lend a hand, but the flames got past them. Some-one carried the word to the church. Father Gabriel Richard hurriedly gathered up the vestments and sacred vessels, and carried them to the common between the north stockade and the fort while Father John Dilhet, his assistant, finished celebrating Mass.

The day was almost windless, but the fire created its own draft and swept across the town in all directions. The Citadel and the government store were consumed. The flames raced down Ste. Anne street (Jefferson avenue) devouring Dodemead's tavern, the stores of the merchants, the church, the Council House, and a couple of low dives, one of which was operated by the common-law wife of Harvey the baker, strictly for cultural purposes, of course. Soon Detroit was just a pile of hot ashes. John Askin, look-ing out the door of his home across the river, saw a huge pillar of black smoke rising from the town. He called his sons and servants and pushed off in a boat to give what help he could. But Detroit was beyond help. In less than three hours nothing remained of it except a warehouse near the river, a blockhouse, and a few fire blackened chim-neys, pointing like accusing fingers at the sky. Everything else was gone, and from the fort which remained untouched, observers gazed on a scene of indescribable desolation. People took refuge where they could find it: in the farm houses up and down the river, in the fort, and in tents and hastily constructed bowers of branches on the common. Father Richard set to work at once organizing relief and gathering food and clothing for the homeless. Surveying the scene, he was heard to murmur, "Speramus meliora; resurget cineribus" (We hope for better things; it will arise from its ashes). A few years later Detroit would put these words on its corporate seal and make them its official motto.

The fire of 1805 proved to be a blessing in disguise. As a result of Baker Harvey's over-cooking the town, Detroit got more than a handful of embers and a Latin motto out of the conflagration. It was rebuilt in the semblance of a modern city with more spacious lots, wider streets, and open areas for parks and public buildings. Of course this did not happen all at once, but a plan was prepared as a starting point. The town that was destroyed contained about three hundred buildings, including sheds, stores, outhouses, barns, and sties. The population was an estimated five hundred souls, not counting the soldiers in the fort. There were probably not more than one hundred dwelling places and the entire town, exclusive of government structures, was owned by sixty-nine proprietors.

For the first few days after the fire little could be done. The people were in a state of shock, despair, and uncertainty. None of the newly appointed officials of the territory was as yet on the scene except Judge Bates. Governor Hull and the other judges, expected momentarily, did not arrive until June 30. Some of the townspeople wanted to start rebuilding on their old lots, but Bates urged them to wait until the new government was in full operation.

As soon as Hull and the other judges arrived, they made the plight of the town their first order of business.

They rejected the idea of reestablishing the village within its former crowded and confined limits. Instead, they persuaded Congress to donate the commons west of the Brush farm and extending north three miles, plus an additional parcel known as the Ten Thousand Acre Tract. A surveyor was called in—he was borrowed from Canada—the land was measured off along the river and for a short distance back from the shore line, and laid out in lots. It was decided that a new lot of not less than five thousand square feet would be given to each person seventeen years or older who had been a resident at the time of the fire. The location of these properties was to be determined by drawing lots. The Ten Thousand Acre Tract was to be offered for sale in parcels of eighty acres or more, the proceeds to be used to build a jail, courthouse, and other public buildings.

It was left to Judge Woodward to decide how the new town above the strip of lots along the river was to be laid out. Born in New York City in 1774 and a graduate of Columbia College, Woodward had lived and practiced law in Virginia and Washington, D.C. He had formed a close friendship with Thomas Jefferson from whom he derived many ideas which, being advanced for a fairly primitive frontier society, caused him to be regarded in Detroit as an eccentric. Whether he was really an oddball or a genius years ahead of his time, there is no question that he was a most remarkable man. In Washington where he owned property, he had watched Major Charles L'Enfant lay out that capital city and adopted ideas for the new Detroit from L'Enfant's plans.

The Woodward Plan, as it came to be known, called for a system of north-south and east-west boulevards two hundred feet wide which at regular intervals would intersect at extensive circular plazas or circuses. From these would also radiate, like the spokes of a wheel, a series of secondary avenues one hundred and twenty feet wide. Then two boulevards and four avenues would be linked together by a network of sixty-foot wide streets in effect creating three concentric circles around each circus. Each of these circus-oriented systems would be a hexagonal unit which could be repeated and tied into others just like it, so that as the town grew in population it could be expanded in any direction. The grand circuses would be the sites of public buildings, churches, and schools. Lots of no less than five thousand square feet each would provide for spaciousness. Actually these large lots established a traditional characteristic of Detroit; with plenty of land available it became a city of single homes. For years, in fact, Detroit led the nation's big cities in the number of single owner-occupied homes. Conversely, it had no apartments or row houses in any great number to create a concentration of population. This ultimately produced problems such as a lack of effective transportation from which Detroit still suffers acutely.

But Woodward was concerned with 1807, not 1967. His plan was adopted and some of the principal streets were laid out according to his ideas. The main street was named Woodward, not in his honor the judge coyly observed, but because it ran "toward the woods." (Woodward actually planned Washington boulevard to be the main street, but the location of Fort Shelby prevented its extension south to the river.) In 1818 the Woodward Plan was abandoned and the city, then mostly hugging the river, found it expedient to go to something which more resembled a checkerboard layout. Yet in the central part of downtown remnants of the Woodward Plan may still be seen. Campus Martius, which marked a corner of the original hexagon, is one of the open plazas with streets like Woodward, Michigan, Cadillac Square, Fort, and Monroe radiating from it. Continuing up Woodward to Grand Circus Park, one can find a dramatic example of half of one of Woodward's projected circuses or large open spaces, and his radiating boulevards (Madison and Washington) and avenues are clearly discernible.

Detroit rebuilt slowly after the fire, but it rebuilt solidly. One of the chief benefits of the conflagration was some semblance of order in granting lots and confirming titles. Titles to the old French ribbon farms were confirmed by the governor and judges sitting as a land board. These are now known in the abstracts as the private claims. They take in much of Detroit east of Brush street and west of Cass avenue, and they extend back nearly to Grand boulevard on the north. Title to a large part of the remainder of the city derives from the Ten Thousand Acre Tract. Naturally when most of the people got around to building new houses they wanted to locate as close to the river as possible. As a result most of the town for the next twenty years was below the present Campus Martius. New streets conforming to the Woodward Plan were opened, and some of the old streets were widened and renamed. Thus Ste. Anne street became Jefferson avenue. The heart of the town centered between the river and Larned or Congress. The principal north-south streets were Wayne (now Washington boulevard), Shelby, Griswold, Bates, and Randolph. Building on these streets extended to about Lafayette and Monroe. West of Griswold building was discouraged by the federal government which wanted to keep a clear field of fire from the fort. The area generally between Congress, Michigan, Woodward, and Washington contained the fort and other military installations, and was held until 1827 as the Military Reserve. A few hardy souls ventured as far north as Grand Circus Park, and an occasional house or cabin stood along Woodward and adjacent streets in that area. North of Campus Martius, however, was mostly wide open space.

The new houses in the lower part of town were considerably better than the old ones they replaced. Many had stone foundations, although the upper parts continued to be frame. But they were made of sawed lumber and were not log cabins. Governor Hull added a touch of elegance to the town in 1807 when he built the first brick house in Detroit. It stood at the southeast corner of Jefferson and Randolph. Fifty feet square and two storied, the Hull house for its time was a real mansion. After Hull left in 1812 it was put to various uses. General William Henry Harrison made it his headquarters during the War of 1812; it became a hospital, a store, and frequently remodeled, a hotel. Today, just to show how the world has progressed, it is a dusty parking lot.

Across the street from Hull's home, on the southwest corner of Jefferson and Randolph, another important building was erected about 1807. This was the Council House where government business was transacted and visiting delegations of Indians were received. Constructed of stone and solidly built, it originally had but one story. Later a second floor was added and the upper chamber was used as a meeting place by Zion Lodge. Lectures were occasionally given there and sometimes on Sunday afternoons Father Richard would speak to the Protestants who had no regular churches of their own. In 1816 the Reverend John Montieth, the town's first settled Protestant minister, used it for services and the First Protestant Society, which became the First Presbyterian Church, was organized there. Once in a while the Reverend Richard Pollard, chaplain of the British garrison at Fort Malden, would paddle across the river and hold services for the Episcopalians. The Council House was destroyed by fire in 1848. After that the site

111

was occupied by Firemen's Hall, a large structure which was a combination of many things: a club for the volunteer firemen, but not an engine house; an auditorium for public meetings such as lectures and concerts. Eventually, after remodeling, it was used by the city of Detroit to house the offices of the Water Board and later the Welfare Department.

In the 1950s the site was cleared as part of the Civic Center development. Old Mariners' Church was then moved from its original location to the site of the Council House. Old Mariners' was built in 1849 on the west side of Woodward avenue between Jefferson and Woodbridge. As the years passed the chuch deteriorated into a run-down building used principally for commercial purposes. At one time its first floor was a post office; later it became a peanut vendor's stand patronized by river-boat excursionists. Restored and moved to its present park-like surroundings, this venerable Episcopal church now has a nondenominational character as a civic religious institution. It is one of the few fine salvage jobs that Detroit has done in preserving its landmarks.

The Woodward avenue lot on which Old Mariners' originally stood was next door to the tavern of Richard Smyth built shortly after the fire of 1805. Centrally located, Smyth's was a popular gathering place. On frequent occasion the governor and judges and city officials met there becaues it provided the opportunity to transact public business without interfering with the officials' drinking. Detroit of that period had several other inns and hotels built after the fire. The enterprising James May gathered up the chimney stones which were left and used them to build what was known as the Mansion House at the northwest corner of Jefferson and Cass. Judge Woodward bought the place from May but leased it for hotel purposes, reserving rooms for his own use. It became a famous hostelry and continued to be used until 1836. Cobo Hall today stands where the Mansion House once did.

Perhaps the most famous of all early Detroit's hotels was one built prior to 1812 by Ben Woodworth, brother of Samuel Woodworth, the author of *The Old Oaken Bucket.* Named the Steamboat Hotel, it stood at the northwest corner of Woodbridge and Randolph behind the Council House. This was an ideal location because it gave Woodworth first grabs at incoming travelers whose boats docked near the foot of Randolph. "Uncle Ben" Woodworth was a live number. He held several public jobs, including that of hangman when one was needed. His hotel was the place for upper-crust entertainment, such as public banquets and balls. It, too, was destroyed by a fire in 1848 which swept away most of the older structures south of Jefferson avenue. Today visitors to Canada pass over the place where Uncle Ben's Steamboat Hotel once stood when they enter the vehicular tunnel to Windsor.

After the American occupation and probably before the fire of 1805, the old king's dockyard at the foot of Woodward avenue was abandoned. A little later a long shed was built in the middle of Woodward. Divided into stalls, it was used as a public or farmers' market until 1835. Above it, at about the present intersection of Woodward and Jefferson, was the whipping post which was used until 1830 when it was taken down and corporal punishment was abolished. Another old landmark was the house of Joseph Campau built on the south side of Jefferson between Griswold and Shelby, the traditional site of Cadillac's home. The Campau house, one of early Detroit's showplaces, was erected in 1813 at a cost of $6,000, a staggering amount of money for that day. It stood until 1880 when so-called progress was responsible for its demolition. It was replaced by a commercial building which stood until the 1950s when it in turn was torn down for the Civic Center development. The site is approximately in front of the Veterans' Memorial building.

From the standpoint of business, things went on just about as they always had. Fur was the chief item of trade and swindling the Indians was regarded as good clean fun except by the Indians. They did not like it and developed a pure and undistilled hatred for the Americans. Moreover, they were deeply concerned by the Americans' insatiable hunger for free or cheap land. Emigrants from the eastern states poured into the Midwest, thickly settling Tennessee, Kentucky, Ohio, Indiana, and Illinois. Michigan was largely spared this influx because the pioneers were afraid of the Indians and reports had been circulated that Michigan land was unfit for cultivation. As a result Detroit's population did not increase materially. In 1812 it was not much more than one thousand persons, with another thousand living on adjacent farms. Dissatisfaction with the government's policies and unhappiness because of settler encroachment on their hunting lands caused the Indians to look to the British for aid and comfort. Fort Malden, headquarters for the Canadian Indian Department, became the source of all good things for the Indians. From all over Michigan and the Midwest the tribes made periodic treks to Malden where they were royally received and given lavish presents and subsidies. British traders— some say they were really British agents—circulated through Michigan and kept their redskin friends supplied with weapons and encouragement. The Americans in turn distrusted both the Indians and the British.

It was this distrust, plus the desire for more land, plus British impressment of American sailors on the high seas, plus a few more pluses that brought on the War of 1812. The portents were there for all to read long before hostilities erupted. Fearful of attack as early as 1807, Governor Hull strengthened the town's defenses and partially mobilized the militia. The Indians, on the other hand, were again raiding frontier settlements, and the Shawnee Chief Tecumseh was trying to form an alliance of the tribes. He was aided by his brother the Prophet who was preaching a holy cause to the Indians. In November 1811 Governor William Henry Harrison of Indiana led an army which destroyed the Prophet's village at Tippecanoe and the fat was really in the fire. Tecumseh openly allied himself to the British; war became inevitable.

Drums of War

Hull was called to Washington to confer with the president and other government leaders. He was offered a generalship and command of the Army of the Northwest. He was reluctant to accept because he could foresee only disaster unless the United States had naval control of Lake Erie and Lake Huron. The British had a small but effective naval force cruising those waters. Nevertheless, Hull was persuaded to accept the commission and in June 1812 took command of a scratch army of twelve hundred Ohio volunteers and four hundred regulars of the 4th United States Infantry. His chief lieutenants were Colonels Duncan McArthur, Lewis Cass, and James Findlay, all budding Ohio politicians, and Lieutenant Colonel James Miller of the 4th Infantry. Back in Detroit there was a single company of

regulars guarding the fort and a few hundred local militiamen who had little interest in getting involved in a war,
particularly if they had to do any fighting.

Hull led his motley collection of troops on a long
march from Dayton through a gummy swamp in northern
Ohio, being forced to build his own road all the way.
Around the first of July he reached the Maumee River.
There he loaded his baggage and personal papers, including orders and muster rolls, his sick soldiers and the band
instruments, aboard a couple of chartered schooners. Unknown to Hull, Congress had declared war on June 18
and the word was sent to him, not by special courier, but
simply in a letter by ordinary mail. Someone was more
thoughtful and informed the British at Malden who then
knew a state of war existed a week or more before Hull
did. As a result when one of Hull's schooners, the *Cuy-
ahoga*, sailed up the river it was quickly and easily captured. Hull finally learned he was at war on July 2 when
his army was still fifty miles from Detroit. However, he
pushed on and arrived on July 7.

Fort Malden was only lightly held, and Hull's orders were to take it immediately if possible and then move
against Niagara. There he was supposed to join up with
another American invading force. These combined armies
were then to advance against Montreal where they would
be joined by a third column coming up from New York
State. A quick and easy victory was expected, the war
would be over, and Canada would be a possession of the
United States. The British would be expelled, bag, baggage
and jack boots, from North America. That was the grand
strategy. Like most dreams, it did not come true.

At first Hull attempted to carry out his orders. On
July 12 he invaded Canada, crossing the river just below
Belle Isle and landing near a windmill on land now oc-

cupied by the Hiram Walker distillery. He marched down to Windsor where he set up headquarters in the new brick house of Colonel François Baby. That house, incidentally, still stands in the Windsor civic center as a historical museum. It is one of the oldest buildings along the border.

Once comfortably established in Baby's living room, Hull sent out patrols to probe the defenses of Fort Malden and a skirmish or two occurred. The first one, an engagement at the River Canard, resulted in the first bloodshed of the War of 1812. Had Hull thrown his whole weight against Fort Malden he should have been able to take it easily. Instead he delayed, and the delay was fatal. While he was marking time waiting for heavy siege artillery, Mackinac was captured and Hull began to have visions of a horde of Indians descending upon him. Also, he began to run short of supplies. Food and other essentials, including fresh beef on the hoof, were sent up from Ohio but they got only as far as Frenchtown (now Monroe, Michigan). Captain Henry Brush, commanding the supply train, was afraid to continue to Detroit because Tecumseh's Indians crossed the river at their pleasure and were prepared to attack him. Hull sent out two expeditions to escort Brush in. One was badly beaten; the other defeated some British and Indians but failed to link up with Brush. It dawned on Hull that his supply line was hopelessly blocked and on August 8 he evacuated Canada, returned to Detroit, and buttoned up his entire force of about twenty-five hundred men in the town and fort.

On August 13 General Sir Isaac Brock, commander of British forces in Upper Canada, arrived at Malden with a small reinforcement of regulars. A professional soldier to his fingertips, a man of daring and decision, Brock looked over the situation and made up his mind that Hull was dangling from the branch like a ripe plum ready to be picked. He was more correct than he knew. Hull was having nightmares about Indian attacks and atrocities, the Ohio colonels were on the verge of mutiny because of his inaction, and there was talk about relieving him of command and placing him under arrest. On August 15 Brock sent Hull a demand for surrender which was turned down. In one last effort to open his supply line, Hull sent four hundred Ohio troops under Colonels McArthur and Cass by a circuitous backwoods route to try to reach Captain Brush at Frenchtown. Brock countered by planting a battery in what is now Windsor's Dieppe Park and began to bombard Detroit.

The bombardment caused more noise than damage, but it threw the civilian population into a tizzy. Most of the people gathered up their possessions and ran to the fort; others sought refuge in a ravine on the Macomb farm. The principal casualty was a big pear tree which stood near the corner of Griswold and Woodbridge. The British gunners used it to sight on, and an American soldier was ordered to chop it down. Before he had completed his task a British ball struck the tree and smashed it to smithereens, thus saving the soldier some hard work. About this time Hull ordered the Ohio troops camped on the common behind the town into the fort.

That night Brock made his move. He assembled his troops, about seven hundred and fifty regulars and militia, and about five hundred Indians under Tecumseh, marched them up the river to Sandwich, and began to ferry them across to Springwells near present Fort Wayne. By morning they had all landed. The Indians were ranging through the woods near the town and Brock's troops were advancing slowly up the river road which is now West Jefferson. To throw an added scare into Hull by making his force appear more formidable than it really was, Brock disguised his militiamen as regulars by dressing them in red coats. Meanwhile, on the morning of the 16th the bombardment was stepped up. Several houses in town were damaged. Augustus Langdon and his family were sitting down to breakfast in their house at Woodward and Congress when a ball crashed through the roof, smashed the dining room table, and plunged through the floor into the cellar. The family escaped without harm and also without breakfast. Judge Woodward was just arising in his room at the Mansion House when a shot crashed through the wall, tore up the bed, and landed in the fireplace. The learned judge, unhurt, bounced out, probably in his long johns. Some other shots did more harm. One struck just outside the fort, killing two men; another hit the gate, killing two soldiers; and a third crashed into a building inside the fort, killing Lieutenant Porter Hanks, who had surrendered Mackinac a short time before, and two doctors, and injuring others.

That was enough for Hull. He ordered a white flag run up the flagstaff and at noon Brock marched in. Hull surrendered the fort, the town, all his weapons, and all his troops, including the detail under McArthur and Cass that was floundering around in the woods out near the River Rouge. An American battery planted in the middle of West Jefferson near Cass was forbidden to fire on Brock's column as it advanced, although the officer in charge later testified that he could have blown the British to kingdom come. Altogether it was one of the most dreary military fiascos ever suffered by American troops. It was made more so by the fact that with a numerically superior and well-armed force at Hull's command, not a single shot was fired in defense of Detroit. Almost immediately after the capitulation the American forces were evacuated. Hull and the regulars were taken to Quebec, the Ohioans were shipped to Cleveland under parole, and the local militia was disbanded and allowed to go home. Later exchanged, Hull was court-martialed and sentenced to be shot for cowardice, but President Madison pardoned him in view of his Revolutionary War services. The fault was not all Hull's. He had assessed the situation correctly in the first place when he said the United States could not hold Michigan without naval superiority on Lake Erie. Washington did not support him as it should have. A scapegoat was needed to distract attention from Washington's errors, and poor old Hull was a likely and convenient candidate.

A day or two after the surrender Brock left the Detroit area, leaving Colonel Henry Proctor in command. Local citizens were assured their private property would be respected if they behaved themselves, but were reminded they would have to live under semi-martial law. In this fashion Detroit won the dubious distinction of being the only major American city ever occupied by a foreign foe. The feeling of local shame persisted for a long time.

British occupation lasted just about a year, and during that time the Four Horsemen stabled their apocalyptic steeds in Detroit. Seldom has the city known bleaker times than during the War of 1812. At its best and most benign a foreign occupation is cause for the miseries, and the administration of Colonel (later General) Proctor was not at all benign. Proctor hated Americans and lived in fear of them, and he endeavored to cover that fear with a veneer of harshness. He did not directly interfere with the right of the people to enjoy their private lives and property; neither did he do much to protect it. Business, already badly disjointed by the war, suffered even more by the lack of civil law. All American civil officials except Judge Woodward moved out when the British moved in. Woodward remained as long as possible, acting as a sort of intermediary between the people and the military, but gained little for his efforts except some unmerited postwar charges that he aided and abetted the enemy. The town was overrun by Indians who helped themselves to just about anything that caught their fancy, and most merchants had their stores broken into and their merchandise carted away. Proctor refused to prevent these depredations. The Indians were fickle allies at best and he dared not risk offending them.

Almost immediately after the fall of Detroit the United States began to organize a relief expedition consisting of newly recruited troops principally from Ohio and Kentucky under the command of General Harrison. Late in 1812 he had advanced into northern Ohio and was contemplating an attack on Malden and the recovery of Detroit. At Erie, Pennsylvania, and Buffalo, New York, ships were being constructed or remodeled into armed vessels that could challenge the British on Lake Erie. At Frenchtown the settlers complained that Indians were harassing them. In January 1813 a strong column of Kentuckians under General Winchester marched to their relief and to establish a forward base for a later campaign against Detroit. But Winchester was an incompetent commander and allowed himself and virtually all his men to be captured in a surprise raid led by Proctor. Then, after Proctor's back was turned, some of the Indians went on a drunken spree and massacred about a hundred of the wounded Kentuckians. This dismal affair became known as the River Raisin Massacre and provided Kentucky with a new battle cry. After the war the bones of the dead were gathered up, taken to Detroit, and buried in the Protestant cemetery which by then was on the east side of Woodward avenue just south of Cadillac Square. In 1834 they were moved to a new cemetery which is now Clinton Park. There they remained until 1849 when a delegation of Kentuckians came to Detroit, took possession, and carried them back to Frankfort where they now repose.

Many survivors of the River Raisin debacle as well as other prisoners were taken by the Indians to Detroit where they were hawked through the streets like so many head of cattle being offered for sale. These unfortunate men were frequently mistreated in order to arouse the pity of the townspeople, thereby inducing them to shell out ransom money. Detroiters paid all they could; even some of the British officers dug down into their pockets and came up with ransom. Many of the leading citizens, including Judge Woodward and Father Richard, bitterly criticized Proctor for not stopping these outrages. But instead of heeding them and doing the humane thing by curbing the savages, Proctor exiled a dozen or more of his most outspoken critics from the city, including Woodward and Richard.

But Proctor's days were numbered as far as Detroit was concerned. On September 10, 1813, Commodore Oliver Hazard Perry with his squadron met and defeated the British flotilla off Put-in-Bay Island. Harrison immediately invaded Canada, captured Fort Malden, and sent a brigade across the river to reoccupy Detroit on September 29. Proctor retreated toward Niagara, but on October 5 Harrison caught up with him near Chatham, Ontario, and totally defeated him in the Battle of the Thames. Tecumseh was killed and Proctor fled ignominiously. While there would still be a few alarms and excursions along the border during 1814, the war in the Northwest was to all intents and purposes at an end.

The year 1814 probably marked a low point in Detroit's history. There was always the fear that the British would be able to mount a new offensive in the West. This time the United States took no chances and after Harrison's victory a large number of troops was stationed in the town. They were quartered in the fort and in log cantonments hastily erected just north of where the Citadel once stood. During the year an epidemic of some sort swept through the camps and the soldiers died by the dozens. Altogether, between four and seven hundred succumbed to the disease which has never been satisfactorily identified. They were buried in common graves at the northeast corner of Cass and Michigan avenues. To check the spread of what was called the plague, the troops were dispersed and quartered in small detachments up and down the river from Ecorse to Grosse Pointe.

The undernourishing hand of famine was also felt during the year. The war interrupted the planting of crops. The additional military population made that many more mouths to feed. It was difficult to get supplies from the East, particularly during the winter, and everyone was forced to tighten his belt. Shortages were so acute in some of the outlying districts that, as Judge Woodward reported to Washington, people were reduced to the grim necessity of subsisting on boiled hay. He made strong appeals to Washington for relief and when it finally arrived, Father Richard was put in charge of distributing it, thus becoming Detroit's first, if unofficial, welfare commissioner.

The farms were in bad shape. Houses had been plundered by Indians, soldiers and Indians had torn down barns and fences for firewood, and livestock had been stolen. For at least ten years after the war Congress was granting indemnities to those whose property had suffered. The Indians were a serious problem during 1814 and part of 1815. Accustomed to living off British subsidies and handouts, they were without means of support after Proctor departed. They roamed the woods and fields near Detroit, begging what they could and stealing what was left. They were in an ugly mood and frequently committed serious crimes. Early in 1815 General Cass, who had been appointed territorial governor to succeed Hull, organized a sort of police force and restored a semblance of peace and order. But before that happened the people lived in terror of the Indians and dared not venture far from the town.

On September 10, 1814, Ananias McMillan put his cows out to pasture at the north end of the commons. He lived at the corner of Bates and Congress across the street from where the bus depot stands today. Usually the task of bringing in the cows fell to Ananias's eleven-year-old son Archie, but because there had been reports of Indians in the vicinity, Ananias decided to accompany the boy. Near what is now the intersection of Woodward and State street they met three men who warned them not to go farther into the woods. But they continued on and at the present corner of Griswold and State they were jumped by a gang of Chippewas. Ananias was killed on the spot and Archie was carried off. The southwest corner of this intersection was later occupied by the fancy grocery store of Peter Smith, still later the building was taken over by the hardware firm of T. B. Rayl, and in 1966 it was a corner doughnut shop with offices above. Archie was taken by his captors to the Saginaw region where he was held for about a year. He and his descendants became prominent in business and public life in Michigan. The kidnapping of the boy and the murder of his father in what is now the heart of downtown Detroit was the last Indian atrocity committed in the city.

Detroiters got precious little out of the War of 1812 except an inferiority complex and a couple of souvenirs. Of course they did change the name of Fort Detroit again—this time to Fort Shelby—in honor of Governor Isaac Shelby of Kentucky whose citizen-soldiers liberated the town. As for the souvenirs, they were a brace of cannon said to have been used by Perry in the Battle of Lake Erie. In 1874 they were mounted on masonry pedestals and flanked the entrance to the City Hall on Woodward avenue in what is now Kennedy Square until its demolition in 1961. The guns were then moved to the Dossin Marine Museum on Belle Isle where they stand guard over a picnic ground. They would be valuable relics if there was any real proof that Perry ever saw them. Unfortunately, the evidence is strongly against that possibility.

The War of 1812 came to an end with the signing of the Treaty of Ghent on December 24, 1814. The peace pact was ratified by Congress with an audible sigh of relief on February 15, 1815, and the news reached Detroit a week or so later. Obviously some sort of celebration was called for and one was arranged. On March 29 the leading citizens of Detroit assembled at the Steamboat Hotel with their invited guests, the British officers from Fort Malden and civilian dignitaries from the Canadian side of the river. The fiddles played late into the night, glasses were filled and emptied time after time as the toasts to peace and brotherhood rang out. Uncle Ben Woodworth put on a feast that banished all remembrance of the famine of the year before. The banquet, billed as the Grand Pacification Ball, ended like all good stories should with everybody living happily ever after.

Or at least for a little while.

5

The New Breed

Meet Lewis Cass

The best thing that ever happened to Detroit and Michigan was Lewis Cass.

He appeared first in Detroit in 1812 as the colonel of a regiment of Ohio volunteers. He was a better public administrator than he was a soldier, although he did gain some distinction in the latter category. After the capitulation of Detroit, Cass was shipped home to Ohio on parole. Exchanged, he served under Harrison and returned to the city in 1813 when it was retaken from the British. Because of his services, both military and political, President Madison appointed him governor of Michigan Territory on October 29, 1813. He held that post until 1831.

Cass was more or less typical of the new breed of men who came to Michigan after the War of 1812. Whereas prior to that time under both the British and American regimes it was the military men who dominated the scene, conditions now changed and Detroit began to take form as a truly American city with democratic New England characteristics determining its destiny. Not all who came to Detroit in the two or three decades following the war were New Englanders, but the majority and certainly the most influential were.

Cass was born at Exeter, New Hampshire, in 1782, the son of a Revolutionary War officer who elected to remain in the army and went to the Ohio country where he held a commission in the legion. Young Lewis followed his father west, settling near Zanesville, Ohio. He studied law, got elected to the Ohio legislature, and started upon one of the most distinguished careers in American political history. When he finally relinquished the position of territorial governor after eighteen highly successful and progressive years, he went on to become secretary of war, minister to France, United States senator from Michigan, presidential nominee of the Democratic Party in 1848, and finally secretary of state on the eve of the outbreak of the Civil War. He died in Detroit in 1866.

No part of his public life was more fruitful than the years he spent as head of the territorial government. To him, more than to any other one man, can be attributed Detroit's development and Michigan's attainment of statehood. Of course he was not alone, and progress was not the result of his single-handed efforts. He was assisted by able men, some of whom, like William Woodbridge and Douglass Houghton, he persuaded to come to Detroit. Others came for various reasons of their own, mostly to get rich, but Cass was quick to recognize their worth and make use of their talents. Among them were such stalwart leaders as Charles C. Trowbridge and Henry Rowe Schoolcraft. A few were already in Detroit when Cass arrived—Judge Woodward, Father Gabriel Richard, and Solomon Sibley. For these, too, he found a place in his scheme of things.

Because the law required the governor to be a property owner—and because even a governor had to have a place to live—Cass bought the old Macomb farm immediately west of the town between present Cass and Third streets, and extending back from the river about three miles. It consisted of more than five hundred acres. The original house, built during the French period, stood on the river bank near the present foot of Second avenue. Behind it was an extensive meadow, sometimes called the Deer Park, which in the early days was used for public assemblies and picnics. In 1836 the house was moved back to Larned street near Second. It was torn down in 1882. But before that happened Cass built a splendid new home in 1842 at the northwest corner of Cass and Fort directly across the street from today's Detroit Club. This building stood until 1876. It was replaced by the brick residence of Governor Henry Baldwin which in its later years was used as the hall of Palestine Lodge and then as a tailor shop. It was torn down in the 1930s and today, like so many of Detroit's historic sites, is a parking lot. The Cass farm was sold to a syndicate of real estate promoters, subdivided, and in turn sold to home owners and business operators. That was in 1836 and Cass ultimately received more than half a million dollars for his property, making him one of the wealthiest, if not the wealthiest, man of his time in Detroit. He reserved two parcels of land which he donated to the city. One became the site of the old Cass high school, a building torn down in 1965 for the Fisher expressway development. The other was dedicated to public use as Cass Park.

At the war's end Detroit had a population of eight hundred and fifty persons, and that of Michigan Territory was less than five thousand. It was obvious to Cass that what was most needed were settlers. Immediately after the War of 1812 and with the Indian danger no longer serious, a great westward migration began. Citizen-soldiers from the eastern states had their first look at the West during the war and liked what they saw. Congress set aside vast tracts in the Old Northwest as bounty lands for ex-soldiers. But the rush of settlers by-passed Michigan. Instead they poured into Ohio, Indiana, and Illinois. One reason was the bad name Detroit and Michigan had gained in the war; more important was the adverse report of government surveyors, one of whom declared in 1817 that Michigan was "an interminable swamp." He and others circulated the story that not one acre in ten thousand was fit for cultivation. The fur trading companies, particularly the American Fur Company of which John Jacob Astor was the proprietor, encouraged and helped circulate these false reports. The fur men preferred beaver to settlers in Michigan. Still another reason for the lack of public enthusiasm for Michigan was its inaccessibility. To reach Detroit one had to haul a wagon across Ohio, an arduous pull which included traversing the Black Swamp, or across Canada, in the early postwar days regarded by many as hostile territory. The only other way was by slow, uncertain, and expensive passage from Buffalo or some other lake port on a sailing vessel.

Thus throughout the East, Michigan was given an undeservedly bad image. Cass realized this and set out to change it. He began a publicity campaign that would have done credit to modern Madison avenue. A capable writer himself, he wrote articles for major eastern publications; he urged residents of the territory to write letters back home to friends and relatives extolling the virtues and glories of Michigan. Visitors and tourists were invited to come and see for themselves. One who made the trip was Dr. Jedidiah Morse, the noted geographer. He had written "interminable swamp" across his maps of Michigan, a place he never saw until 1820. He was given the red carpet treatment and went away converted. Dr. Morse was accompanied by his son Samuel F. B. Morse, a portrait painter and later the inventor of the telegraph.

In 1817 President James Monroe was persuaded to visit Detroit, and other distinguished junketeers came from time to time. Their visits received considerable publicity in the East and helped change the bad image of Michigan. To dispel further what he considered foul canards against the fair name of his domain, Cass organized exploring parties that penetrated the interior and took a look at what lay beyond the thin fringe of civilization. Some of the places visited were no more than twenty or twenty-five miles from Detroit, but no white man had ever seen them before Cass and his friends investigated them. Some of the excursions were little more than weekend campouts; others were large-scale expeditions financed by the federal government, such as that of 1820 on which Cass led a group of scientists into the Upper Peninsula and to what is now Minnesota in search of the source of the Mississippi River.

There were also some events of national importance which helped start the flow of traffic to Michigan. In 1811 Robert Fulton successfully sailed his steamboat *Clermont* up the Hudson River from New York and almost immediately everybody began to think in terms of steam navigation. At Black Rock near Buffalo, Noah Brown, who had designed some of Commodore Perry's 1813 naval vessels, laid the keel of a one hundred thirty-five foot side-wheeler which was launched May 28, 1818, and named *Walk-in-the-Water*. The first steamboat on the upper Great Lakes, she excited much enthusiasm in the West. Detroit prepared for her arrival by building a new wharf at the foot of Bates street.

Walk-in-the-Water left Buffalo on her maiden trip on August 23, 1818. Her skipper was Captain Job Fish and she carried twenty-nine passengers. After stops at Dunkirk, Erie, Cleveland, Sandusky, and Venice, Ohio, she arrived at the mouth of the Detroit River late on August 26 and dropped anchor for the night. The following morning she puffed and wheezed upriver with a pause at Fighting Island to pick up a welcoming delegation of distinguished Detroiters including Judge Woodward. As she passed Amherstburg the Canadian shore was thronged with bug-eyed Indians amazed by this smoke-belching monster that moved against the current without the aid of sails. Cracker barrel wits solemnly assured them the vessel was being towed by a school of trained sturgeons, an explanation willingly accepted.

Lacking a whistle, *Walk-in-the-Water* signaled her approach to Detroit by firing a small four-pounder cannon carried on her forward deck. Everybody in town turned out to greet her and there was wild cheering as she headed into her berth with the not-so-dignified Judge Woodward astraddle her bowsprit and waving a bottle, his constant companion. Among her passengers was Mrs. Julia Anderson who, with her sister Charlotte Taylor, would later donate the land on which Old Mariners' Church was built.

Walk-in-the-Water continued in operation for three years. She charged a fare between Buffalo and Detroit of $18 first class and $7 steerage. She was capable of accommodating a hundred passengers and was soon on a biweekly schedule which continued until 1821 when she foundered in a gale on the Canadian shore near Buffalo. But she set the pattern for what was to come, for before long many more steamships were built. Among the most famous in the 1820s and 1830s were the *Charles Townsend, Superior, Henry Clay, William Penn, Niagara, Peacock,* and *Enterprise.* By 1831 Detroit could expect daily arrivals during the navigation season and in 1833 Oliver Newberry, an enterprising Detroiter, launched the *Argo*, the first steamboat built in the city.

Another thing that made Detroit happy was the offering of public lands in Michigan for sale to would-be settlers. One of the first things Cass did was to negotiate treaties with the Indians by which they were persuaded to cede virtually all of what is now the two peninsulas of Michigan to the United States government. A federal land office had been opened in Detroit as early as 1804 but it was not very active. Until Cass negotiated these treaties there simply was not much land to sell. But by 1820, after the surveys were begun and the first treaties effected, the story was different. The land office was located in the Council House. Land sold mostly in large parcels for from two to four dollars an acre. What was not sold at auction, mostly to speculators, was offered to the small fry, usually in eighty-acre lots at a dollar and a quarter an acre. Land office business gradually increased, and about 1826 the office was relocated in the basement of the Bank of Michigan building of 1806 at the northwest corner of Jefferson and Randolph. That site, too, is now part of the Civic Center. So brisk did the business become—it was truly a land office business—that on some days Jefferson avenue was thronged with hundreds of men queued up waiting to file their claims. During those busy days Detroit suffered acutely from land fever.

The third link in the chain of events which shaped Detroit's future was Clinton's Ditch, more properly referred to as the Erie Canal or the New York State Barge Canal. Planned by New York's Governor DeWitt Clinton as a waterway to connect the eastern seaboard and the Great Lakes, actual construction was begun in 1817 to the accompaniment of the grunts of immigrant Irish laborers and the scoffing of wiseacres who said it would not work. When completed in 1825 it stretched three hundred and sixty-three miles across New York State, running through the Mohawk Valley and skirting the Finger Lakes. With its eastern terminus at the Hudson between Albany and Troy, and its western outlet near Buffalo, the ditch was an average forty feet wide and four feet deep. It cost the then staggering sum of $20,000 a mile to dig but was a financial success almost from the beginning. It opened officially on October 25, 1825, with impressive ceremonies which included the booming of the cannon of Perry's fleet. The guns were placed at intervals across New York State, and as they banged out in succession from west to east, they announced the canal's opening in Albany in a matter of minutes. October is pretty late in the season for much navigation on the Great Lakes, but traffic started with a rush nevertheless. Big cumbersome barges, capable of hauling heavy loads and many passengers, were pulled across New York by horses at a rate of "a cent and a half a mile; a mile and a half an hour." At Buffalo, of course, the westward bound passenger or cargo could be placed aboard one of the new lake steamers and could be in Detroit in a matter of hours. Hailing the canal's opening, the *Detroit Gazette* of December 5, 1825, happily pointed out: "We can now go from Detroit to New York in five and a half days. Before the war, it took at least two months more."

The Easy Road West

The combination of better transportation and abundant cheap land worked wonders for Michigan and established for all time Detroit's position as the metropolis of the territory and the state. The steamboat and the Erie Canal tapped a large and restless population in New England and in eastern and central New York. As these people came west by the thousands in one of the most significant folk migrations in history, they brought with them their Yankee characteristics and colloquialisms, and their independence of mind. Along with their household chattels and farm implements which the new transportation facilities permitted them to carry, they also brought the virtues of morality, thrift, and religion, and the desire for education. Within a matter of two decades they transformed Detroit from a French wilderness outpost into a model of a New England town.

Detroit was the funnel through which the settlers headed for the interior of Michigan passed, and during the 1820s and 1830s the reception of new arrivals was the city's most important business. Detroit was the port of debarkation for thousands, most of whom paused only long enough to refresh themselves and get a line on some good land before pushing on to the oak clearings of the interior. Some did not go far. They established settlements where the land was fertile and the streams would turn millwheels. Years later when the country clubs were built these settlements became Detroit's bedroom suburbs. There were many villages, for instance, like Birmingham, Pontiac, Royal Oak, Plymouth, and Northville. Scores of these new Michigan towns bore the names of the New England places from which their first settlers came.

On a single May day in 1836 more than twenty-four hundred settlers poured into Detroit, and the arrival of from seven to ten steamboats daily was not uncommon. Observing this hustle and bustle, Charles C. Trowbridge wrote to Lewis Cass who was then in Paris:

The opening of navigation has brought us immense crowds of old fashioned immigrants with their wives and babies and wagons and spinning wheels, and a hundred dollars to buy an eighty acre lot for each of the boys. I have never seen more crowded boats. Yesterday [May 28, 1837] our arrivals were eight steamboats, one ship, three large brigs and nineteen schooners. The day before, seven steamboats arrived.

Detroit's growth, at first not spectacular, was nonetheless steady. In 1819 the population was only 1,110, not much more than at the end of the war. By 1830 it had doubled to 2,222, and from then on it began to boom. In 1836, it was 6,927; in 1840, 9,124; in 1850, 21,019; and in 1860, just before the Civil War, Detroit boasted the very respectable population of 45,619.

This growth was aided by the new transportation and the Erie Canal working in reverse. The immigrants, mostly farmers, had produce to sell off their new farms and the canal opened up a market for Michigan crops. The eastern cities, particularly New York, became good customers for Michigan corn, wheat, and pork. The canal even broadened the horizon beyond New York. In 1857 the bark *Kershaw* loaded with Michigan produce cleared Detroit for Europe, and after that a regular trade with foreign ports was maintained. And that, it may be noted, was long before anybody gave a thought to the Great Lakes—St. Lawrence Seaway development. Commenting on the economic benefits of the Erie Canal even before it was finally completed, the *New York Spectator* declared: "A barrel of potashes, flour or any produce can be transported from Detroit to Buffalo with as little expense through Lake Erie, as a like quantity can be transported by land in the western part of this state to the canal from places which lie twenty-five or thirty miles from the canal route." This obvious fact quickly manifested itself in rising land values in Michigan, while those in parts of New York State declined.

Making of a State

With all this activity going on around them, Detroiters began to get ideas about their own importance. The new breed, being Yankees or of Yankee stock, found it intolerable to live under a form of government such as that of the governor and judges in which they had no voice in affairs. Not to be able to stand up in meeting and speak his piece was more than Brother Jonathan could bear. Governor Cass, who came out of the same barrel as his constituents, appreciated the people's desires and did something about it. Largely through his efforts Michigan Territory was granted the right in 1819 to elect a delegate to Congress. The first man sent to represent the territory was Cass's close friend William Woodbridge. He sat in the House of Representatives with a voice but without a vote. He was succeeded by Solomon Sibley, another Cass associate. When his term ran out the French element decided it was their turn and in 1825 elected Father Gabriel Richard. It did not matter to them that on election day Richard was locked up in the county jail, having been arrested on a body writ by one of his parishioners who complained that Richard had slandered him. Speaking from his pulpit, Richard had called attention to the fact that this particular member of his flock was living with a woman who was not his wife. But Richard finally made bond and went off to Washington to become the first and only Roman Catholic priest ever to sit in the halls of Congress.

The next step in governmental advancement came in 1824 when the autocratic rule of the governor and judges ended and a representative form was instituted through an elected legislative council. This was not quite democracy as the Yankees would have liked it, for they elected a list of eighteen members from which the president chose nine to serve. But it was better than the old system. In the same year Detroit reorganized its municipal government and for the first time elected a mayor, a clerk, and aldermen. The first mayor was John R. Williams, nephew and business partner of Joseph Campau. In 1835 Detroiters wanted to honor the mayor by naming a couple of streets after him. The first was easy enough, Williams street, but what name for the second? The people solved that knotty problem by calling it John R. street, a name that has baffled later citizens and visitors alike.

Taking stock of things, the citizens with the help of their political leaders decided there was no point in having a legislative council unless there was a suitable place for such an august body to meet. Besides, the people were saying, Michigan was twice as good as Ohio and Indiana with Illinois thrown in for good measure, and if those wastelands could be states in the Union, Michigan could too. They knew the time was not far off and before long they would need a state house. Meanwhile it would adequately shelter the legislative council.

So a capitol was built. Under the Woodward Plan of 1807 such a building was supposed to have stood in Grand Circus Park. But that was still too far out in the country in 1824. Another site was selected, the small triangular plot of ground fronting on State street and the head of Griswold. Just opposite the spot where a few years earlier Ananias McMillan met his doom, it is known today as Capitol Park and serves a very useful purpose as a bus loading station and a haven for pigeons with digestive difficulties. The building progressed slowly, not being completed until 1828. It cost $21,000 and was financed largely by the sale of lots in the Ten Thousand Acre Tract. When it was finished it was a wonder to behold. Its ground dimensions were sixty by ninety feet; it had two stories and was topped off by a graceful tower one hundred and forty feet high, to the top of which citizens and visitors climbed for a breath-taking view of the town, river, and countryside. The building was of classic design with lofty pillars across the front. It could have been a large Congregational church in some out-of-the-way New Hampshire valley.

The Old Capitol, as it eventually came to be called, was not without its faults and was the target of criticism. Pompous councilors insisted it was an unbearable hardship to walk to sessions held away out in the wilds from Woodworth's or some other downtown tavern. At the time it was built it was in the fields. Griswold street had not then been opened north of Michigan avenue.

In 1835 Michiganians rose up on their hind legs, adopted a constitution, and declared themselves a state. Nobody else in the nation paid the slightest attention to them, and when they sent senators and representatives to Washington, those dignitaries were allowed inside the Capitol only as spectators. It was not until 1837 that Michigan, having settled its boundary dispute with Ohio, was finally admitted to the Union as the twenty-sixth state. The building on State street continued to serve as the capitol until 1847 when Lansing became the capital city. Legislators objected to Detroit because the cost of living amid the sin and splendor of the metropolis was too high.

After Detroit ceased to be the center of state government, the Old Capitol stood idle and empty for many months. Then it was taken over by the board of education and converted into a union school. In 1863 it was remodeled and the upper floor was used by the city's high school. In 1865 the first public library was opened in one of its main floor rear rooms. It was again remodeled in 1875, this time extensively with a brick front added. All vestige of the old building disappeared at that time. It continued to be used as the town's high school until one cold morning in January 1893 when it was completely destroyed by fire. The flames consumed all the academic records. That was the happy part of the disaster because a whole generation of young men immediately graduated and dared anyone to prove otherwise. After the debris was cleared away the place became a park. High school classes were transferred to rented quarters in the Biddle House, a hotel at Jefferson and Randolph where Governor Hull's house originally stood. The Biddle House served until 1896 when Central High School—now Wayne State University's Old Main Hall—was completed at Cass and Warren avenues.

Before Michigan could be admitted to statehood there were a few items of unfinished business to be disposed of. One involved finding a successor to Cass who left for Washington and a cabinet post in 1831. A year before his departure President Jackson appointed Virginia aristocrat John T. Mason to be secretary of the territory. Mason did not care much for the job. He was eyeing lusher pastures in Texas. When he came to Detroit he was accompanied by his son Stevens Thomson Mason, an engaging young man who attracted the favorable attention of Cass. When John Mason resigned after a few months he prevailed upon Jackson, with the endorsement of Cass, to name his nineteen-year-old son Stevens T. as his successor. For the next several years the young man was the outstanding civic figure in Detroit and the future state of Michigan.

At first Detroiters did not take kindly to the idea of a government leader who was still not dry behind the ears, but young Mason quickly charmed them and won their full support. After Cass's departure George B. Porter of Pennsylvania was made the new governor of the territory, but he did not work very hard at the job and was frequently absent from Michigan for long periods. That meant that Stevens T. Mason filled in as acting governor most of the time until statehood was attained. He did a creditable job.

His first big task was in 1832 when the western frontier broke into flames with a new Indian uprising led by the Sauk Chief Black Hawk. Most of the activity was confined to northern Illinois and Wisconsin, but some Michigan Indians joined the party, and while there were few actual incidents or atrocities, the West was thrown into panic. Mason acted promptly and called out the militia which marched toward Chicago to do battle. They had not gone far when they were recalled. Danger to the settlements, it was apparent, was greatly exaggerated and Cass, as the new secretary of war, rushed enough regulars west to handle the situation. Unfortunately, the soldiers did far more damage to Detroit than Black Hawk and his braves.

On July 4, 1832, the steamer *Henry Clay* out of Buffalo, carrying about three hundred troops, arrived at Detroit en route to Chicago. Some sickness was reported aboard and local health officials investigated. They diagnosed the malady as Asiatic cholera which at that time was prevalent in some eastern cities, having been imported by European immigrants. The *Henry Clay* was ordered to move away from the city. She proceeded to Belle Isle where she anchored for a few hours and then pushed on to Fort Gratiot (Port Huron). By the time she arrived there more men had come down with the disease and most of the others, terrified, jumped ship and started back to Detroit on foot. Many made it, although several died in the bushes along the way. Those who finally reached the city were cared for in improvised hospitals, but the damage was done. The cholera swept through the town and scores came down with it. Many citizens in fear for their lives fled the city, but when they tried to enter nearby surrounding towns, they found the roads barricaded and were turned back by armed guards. A party of refugees traveling by stage was halted at Ypsilanti. When they tried to force their way into town their horses were shot.

Many devoted Detroiters pitched in and did what they could for the sufferers. Father Gabriel Richard obtained a cart and daily made a circuit of the city, collecting the dead for burial. He also nursed the sick until September 13, 1832, when the epidemic was on the wane, he took the cholera and died. Altogether ninety-six Detroit citizens succumbed.

Two years later the disease struck again, and this time with added horrors. During a twenty day period in August 1834, one hundred and twenty-two persons died of cholera. Large kettles of pitch were burned at night in front of various houses and at intervals along the streets. The Capitol was turned into a hospital and so was Most Holy Trinity Church which then stood on the northwest corner of Bates street and Cadillac Square. Father Martin Kundig tore out the pews and set up litters, and men and women of his parish acted as nurses. Detroit suffered, altogether, four cholera outbreaks; the third was in 1849. The fourth and last epidemic occurred in 1854.

There was one big stumbling block to Michigan statehood in 1835 and Mason endeared himself to the public in his attempts to surmount it. As has been stated, Michigan declared herself a state in 1835 and elected

Mason governor although he was then only twenty-four years old. What prevented the new self-proclaimed state from being given its star in the flag was a dispute over the Ohio-Michigan boundary line. Michigan claimed the line should run far enough south to include Maumee Bay and Toledo. Ohio wanted its northern line pushed far enough north to take in Toledo. The argument was over a stretch of land called the Toledo Strip, and the resulting fuss has come down in history known as the Toledo War.

Neither Michigan nor Ohio would yield an inch. Ohio proclaimed possession and attempted to hold court in Toledo. Governor Mason called out his militia and marched into Toledo to hold it by force and arrest the Ohio judges. Ohio's militia was then summoned. Both armies glared at each other and engaged in a few barroom brawls, but never got to the point of shooting except, as legend has it, for the killing of an Ohio pig by Michigan soldiers. They no doubt were more interested in pork chops than boundary lines. The most sensational incident was the arrest by Michigan troopers of Ohio Colonel Benjamin Stickney and his son Two Stickney. Both were shortly released and nobody would have remembered the incident had it not been for the colonel's practical custom of naming his offspring numerically in the order of their arrival. Thus Two Stickney became famous; One Stickney, who was not involved, failed to gain any notoriety.

The posturing and counter-marching continued for about a year until finally President Jackson became disgusted. A presidential election was coming up in 1836 and he wanted Ohio's support and electoral votes for the Democratic Party. Michigan, still lacking official commonwealth status, had no electoral votes, so it is easy to see who won. The decision was in Ohio's favor. She got Toledo and later generations of Detroiters have felt that it served her right.

As a sop to her injured feelings, Michigan was given the western half of the Upper Peninsula which turned out to be a pretty good bargain when copper and iron were discovered there. With the matter settled, Michigan was at last given statehood on January 26, 1837. Mason, the idol of his people, continued to be governor until 1840. He died in New York on January 4, 1843, at the age of thirty-one and was buried in Trinity churchyard. In 1905 his bones were brought to Detroit and reburied in Capitol Park. Elaborate civic ceremonies were held on that occasion, and one of those who attended was his 92-year-old sister Miss Emily Mason. Three years later a heroic statue of the Boy Governor, as he was fondly called, was erected over the grave.

Detroit was the center of some other exciting events within a year after Michigan became a state. The people of Canada were seeking governmental reforms and a revolt, known as the Patriot's War, broke out in 1837. The rebel leaders were chased out of Canada and based their operations in border cities in the United States. Detroit was a natural place and became one of their headquarters. Many Detroiters in sympathy with their aims joined the movement. In 1838 a mob seized a quantity of arms stored in the Wayne County jail and in the federal arsenal which, after Fort Shelby had been demolished, was built on Michigan avenue in Dearborn. Governor Mason and other officials did their best to prevent an armed invasion of Canada by the Patriots. But despite their efforts, a band of insurgents crossed to Windsor where they were promptly defeated by the loyal local militia. Several of the invaders were killed in the skirmish and a few others were summarily hanged. What might have been a serious international incident had the effect of hastening governmental reforms in Canada, leading to the establishment of the dominion, the centennial of which Canadians celebrated in 1967.

During the 1838 excitement a group of over-zealous Detroiters seized one of the ubiquitous city hall cannons and prepared to bombard Windsor. They were thwarted by General Hugh Brady in command of United States troops in Detroit. He ordered the cannon broken up and an attempt was made to do so. The gun, however, proved stronger than the wrecking crew and its only damage was a chunk of iron chipped out of the muzzle. If one is a cannon fancier, he may gaze on that blemish today and know how it got there. The cannon is one of the pair now in front of the Dossin Marine Museum on Belle Isle.

There is another reminder of the Patriot's War in the Detroit area, a gravestone in the yard of St. John's Anglican Church in Sandwich. It bears these words:

Sacred
To the Memory of
John James Hume, Esquire
M.D.
Staff Assistant Surgeon
Who was infamously murdered and his body
afterwards brutally mangled by a gang of armed
ruffians from the United States styling themselves
Patriots
who committed this cowardly and shameful outrage
on the morning of the 4th of December, 1838; having
intercepted the deceased while proceeding to render
professional assistance to Her Majesty's gallant
militia engaged at Windsor, U.C., in repelling the
incursion of this rebel crew more properly styled
Pirates!

6

Light in the Wilderness

School Days

When the Yankees came to Detroit they introduced some newfangled notions. Some called these ideas culture; others called it civilization. The old conservative French who were still around had their own terms for such things, and they were not complimentary. For a long time the French were less than enchanted with their new neighbors. They had a name for them. A Yankee was a *cochon Bostonnais* or Yankee pig. The Yankees, on the other hand, considered the easy-going French to be shiftless and backward. There was a definite rift which healed slowly. That it healed at all was due in great part to Father Richard. He clearly saw that unless the French met Yankee competition, they would remain a minority group. He urged them to learn to read, write and speak English, to participate in public affairs, and to adopt the modern viewpoint.

In order to help them—or push them into the mainstream of American life—Richard realized that education was needed more than anything else. During the British regime and the early days of the American period there were occasional tutors and private schools in Detroit. But only the children of the prosperous could attend. The wealthy sent their young ones east for their education. As early as 1804 Richard organized what might be called a parochial school; his idea was to train boys who might later be sent to a seminary and be trained for the priesthood. His efforts were not notably successful.

His next attempt at education began about 1808. Detroit had been burned out, Ste. Anne's Church was gone, and Richard established new quarters at the Spring Hill farm, a ribbon farm west of the city near the present Fort Wayne. There he lived and conducted services. But he had a lot of room and worked out a plan to utilize it for a vocational school for white and Indian children, both boys and girls. They would be instructed in the elements of reading and writing, and also in farming, carpentry, blacksmithing, printing, weaving, cooking, and other household arts.

Naturally he had no money for such an undertaking, but that did not stop him. He set out to raise it. Detroiters showed little enthusiasm for his plan—why try to teach Indians?—so he looked elsewhere. Judge Woodward was sympathetic and aided him by introducing him to President Jefferson. Along with others, Jefferson made a cash contribution, but more important, the president arranged for him to obtain some government funds. With that help, modest as it really was, Richard was in business and his school opened. He personally trained four young women of his parish as teachers who conducted what actually amounted to private schools in the nearby French communities. The Spring Hill school was not a brilliant success and was always mired in poverty, but it struggled along until 1810 when the government, which had rented the land to Richard, sold the farm at public auction to Judge James Witherell for five thousand dollars.

After the War of 1812 the newly arrived New Englanders were not satisfied with makeshift educational arrangements, although they were forced to put up with them for many years. In 1827 Governor Cass recognized the need and was influential in having an act adopted which provided for the establishment of common schools as a public responsibility. It was the obligation of the community, he pointed out, to furnish education for the children of the poor. Under the act of 1827 a school was opened, but not for long. The original Michigan constitution, and all succeeding ones, acknowledged in the strongest terms the need for free public schools and offered a financial base from the sale of state lands. In 1837 Detroit was divided into seven school districts, each district being autonomous. The result was that some districts organized schools while others did not. District No. 1 occupied the second floor of a building on Woodbridge near Shelby. It stood on piles over the river and the first floor was Prouty's grocery store. District No. 4 school was held in the basement of the First Methodist Church at Gratiot and Farmer. District No. 6 kept school in a private residence at Jefferson and Beaubien.

None of these schools was wholly free, none was satisfactory, and only about one child out of three in Detroit was able to attend. In 1842, however, things improved somewhat. A new law was adopted, making Detroit into a single school district, creating a board of education, and giving the city the power to levy a tax for school support. Fundamentally the same system that was written into the 1842 law applies today. The Board of Education promptly bought a building, the first publicly owned schoolhouse, in 1843. It was at Park Place (now Times Square) near Grand River. Naturally it was an old-fashioned one-roomer and cost $540. Those were bargain days where education was concerned. A lady teacher was paid $18 a month. Men came higher; they got $30. Negro pupils were sent to separate schools until 1869 when the school system was integrated. Up to 1850 all schools were in rented or purchased structures, but in that year the Board of Education built its first schoolhouse, the Barstow School on Congress at Riopelle. It was in use until a very few years ago.

Cass and several other leading citizens had young daughters. There was no satisfactory finishing school where they could learn the social graces, such as enunciating "prunes and prisms" through nicely pursed lips. In 1830 these fathers banded together, wangled a free lot at the corner of Woodward and Michigan, and erected a three-story brick building called the Detroit Female Seminary. The location was the future site of the City Hall which is now Kennedy Square and an underground parking garage. The seminary operated only from 1836 until 1842. After that, but before the City Hall was built in 1871, the building was used for various purposes, including an armory, supreme court chambers, and a second-hand store.

Not everything that was done in Detroit reflected sound Yankee conservatism, but the results, if not always practical, were frequently spectacular. That applies even to education, such as the time in 1817 when a university was established although there were no schools to supply it with scholars. Even without facilities for teaching the three Rs, the local moguls went blithely ahead and founded an institution of higher learning that, by comparison, would have made Harvard at the time look like a trade school for left-handed mechanics. This university has generally been considered the brain child of Judge Woodward, although he had several collaborators, among them Governor Cass, Father Richard, and the Reverend John Montieth.

Everyone, except possibly the French, was thinking and talking about the need for a school system in 1817. Being for the most part politicians, Woodward and his friends decided anything could be accomplished if only a law was passed. As the territory's chief justice and generally considered, at least by himself, as the most erudite person in these parts, the task of writing the law was assumed by Woodward. He came up with a beauty. To give him his due, though, he was genuinely interested in education. He had talked many times with Thomas Jefferson about founding a national university; he had examined the educational systems of other nations, particularly France where Napoleon had established a national university. In addition Woodward was interested in natural science; in 1816 he wrote a book entitled *A System of Universal Science* in which he sought to classify all knowledge. He even went further and created a terminology which would apply to all branches of learning, and hopefully, would be universally adopted. He called this the Epistemic System, and one of his terms was *encathol* which meant universal or all-inclusive.

What better way was there to give his epistemic system practical application than by using it as the outline or framework of a system of universal education? And that is exactly what he did. The law he wrote called for a university with thirteen departments, including just about every known discipline from medicine to military science. But his idea, which was then and is now but vaguely understood, went beyond that. It called for lower level schools, academies, libraries, museums, and all the paraphernalia of teaching. And this was designed for a territory that contained more bears than people and had not a single elementary or public high school.

Woodward named his creation the Catholepistemiad

149

or University of Michigania. Strange as this may sound, it had a reasonable ring to his colleagues who adopted the law which created it without a murmur of dissent on August 26, 1817. Montieth was appointed president at a salary of $25 a year and Richard was made vice president at $18. The thirteen departmental professorships were divided between the two of them. Taxes were provided to pay for it and a lottery was approved to give additional financial support. On September 24 the cornerstone for a building was laid on the west side of Bates street between Larned and Congress directly across the street from the present bus terminal. Of course the site is a parking lot today. The building stood until 1858 when in the name of progress or something it was torn down.

Not surprisingly, there were no scholars available when the Catholepistemiad's doors opened. Instead, the building was used as a classical academy and a primary-elementary school for a number of years. But the university idea did not die. In 1821 the legislative council abolished the Catholepistemiad and in its place created the University of Michigan which was a definite forward step because everybody could pronounce and spell the latter. It was placed under the control of a board of trustees, very similar to the board of regents which runs it today. Even after 1821 and with a new name the university did not begin to function immediately. In 1837 it was moved to Ann Arbor. And finally in 1841, after faculty residences and a classroom building were erected, the University of Michigan opened its doors to two professors and six students. But aside from the weird language and the impracticability of the Catholepistemiad, Woodward's plan was not as outlandish as the scoffers liked to make it appear. In principle Woodward was on sound ground, and the present great University of Michigan is proud to date its origin from the act of 1817.

In 1967 it celebrated its one hundred and fiftieth anniversary.

The Church Bells Ring

During the formative years of Michigan, Detroiters had almost as much trouble going to church as they had going to school, except for the Catholics. The latter were well provided for by Ste. Anne's and by new parishes as the city grew. After the fire of 1805 the Catholic community did fall on hard times for a while. Father Richard conducted services temporarily in the Meldrum warehouse, one of the two buildings which escaped the flames. Then, as we have seen, he set up a chapel at the Spring Hill farm, and there was another in the upriver area to take care of parishioners who lived out Grosse Pointe way. Meanwhile he dreamed and planned for a new church, and finally in 1818 a new Ste. Anne's was begun on Larned street between Bates and Randolph. The lot is now occupied by the bus terminal directly across the street from the City-County building. Donated by the government, it was a deep lot running all the way back to present Cadillac Square. Construction of the new church proceeded slowly, but the first services were held in the basement in 1820 before the upper part of the structure was completed.

The church was finally consecrated in 1828 and for early Detroit it was an imposing building. Its frontage on Larned street was sixty feet and its length was one hundred and sixteen feet. It was surmounted by a dome in the center and twin spires soared loftily from each corner of the front. These spires could be seen for miles and for years helped mariners on the river to get their bearings. On the extensive grounds surrounding the church were a small arbor suitable for quiet contemplation, a vegetable garden, and in time several smaller buildings for the rectory, a school, a hospital, and other purposes. This Ste. Anne's eventually outlived its usefulness and in 1886 it was sold and torn down. The parish moved to a new church on Howard at Nineteenth, now Ste. Anne street. Some of the interior equipment of the old church, such as an altar and pews, was installed in the new one, and by remaining in use today helps provide a link with the past. The tomb of Father Richard also was moved and placed under the main altar of the new Ste. Anne's. Sadly, in 1967 this Ste. Anne's appeared to be doomed, although Detroiters of many faiths were busy trying to raise funds to prop up the sagging roof and walls. The archdiocese promised, however, that if the efforts failed and it was necessary to tear down the old church, it would be replaced by a new one.

The Catholic Church kept pace with the growth of Detroit. Originally the city was a part of the diocese of Quebec. After American independence it was transferred to the see of Baltimore, and then came under the jurisdiction of Bardstown, Kentucky, and Cincinnati. At an early date it was planned to make Michigan a separate diocese but that was not done until 1832. Father Richard had been made bishop designate, but died before he could be officially appointed by the Vatican. Instead, Detroit's first bishop was the German Frederick Rese who arrived in 1834.

Most Holy Trinity was the city's second parish. It was organized in 1834 to minister to the Irish and its first building was purchased from the Presbyterians. In 1849 the parish moved from Cadillac Square to the edge of Cork-

town. The present Most Holy Trinity Church was built in
1866 at Porter and Fourth streets. Other parishes followed
quickly to take care of the growing population and the
ethnic groups who moved in on the tide of immigration.
Among the earlier churches was St. Mary's, established in
1843 at St. Antoine and Croghan, now Monroe. Its congregation was principally German. SS. Peter and Paul's was
built in 1848 at Jefferson and St. Antoine; St. Patrick's at
Adelaide and John R. dates from 1862. Ste. Anne's, SS.
Peter and Paul's, and St. Patrick's all served at one time or
another as the cathedral. In 1937 Detroit was designated
an archdiocese and the new Church of the Most Blessed
Sacrament at Woodward and Belmont became the cathedral. The distinguished churchman Edward Mooney was
made archbishop in 1937 and in 1946 he was elevated to
the cardinalate.

It was much more difficult for the less numerous
Protestants to go to church. The British garrisons usually
had chaplains and presumably their services were available
to civilians who needed them. Itinerant preachers and circuit riders came through occasionally, a missionary stopped
off now and then, and there was always the self-ordained
evangelist. As has been said, the Reverend Richard Pollard
of Sandwich sometimes paddled across the river to hold
services for Detroit Episcopalians, and Father Richard occasionally gave informal Sunday afternoon discourses to
Protestants in the Council House.

But there was no settled Protestant minister in Detroit until the Reverend John Montieth arrived on June 30,
1816. A native of Gettysburg, Pennsylvania, and fresh out
of the Princeton Theological Seminary, he was induced to
come to Detroit by a group of civic leaders which included
Cass. Montieth was at the disposal of all Protestants, and
his services in the Council House and sometimes in the uni-

versity building were under the auspices of the First Evangelical Society formed in 1817. In 1821 its name was changed to the First Protestant Society. Its membership included Methodists, Baptists, Episcopalians, Congregationalists, and Presbyterians.

The Presbyterians were the majority and in 1819 they began to raise funds for a church of their own. The governor and judges obligingly gave them the old Protestant cemetery on Woodward between Larned and Congress and in 1820 the First Protestant Society built a church at the northeast corner of Woodward and Larned. In 1825 the Presbyterians took it over as the First Presbyterian Church and continued to use it until 1834 when a more elaborate building was erected on the same lot. That one was destroyed by fire in 1854. The lot was then sold, half the proceeds going to the First Presbyterians and half to part of the congregation which wanted a new church on the west side. The First Presbyterians built on the corner of State (now Gratiot) and Farmer on land now covered by the J. L. Hudson Company department store. The church remained there until 1891 when the present one was built at Woodward and Edmund. The offshoot of the First Presbyterian Church was a new west side church built in 1849 as the Second Presbyterian. The site was the southeast corner of Lafayette and Washington, the site of the present Federal building. In 1855 a new edifice was erected at the southeast corner of Fort and Third. Still in use and a city landmark, it became known as the Fort Street Presbyterian Church.

The Methodists were active in the Detroit area before any other Protestant denomination. As early as 1818 they built a log church on the banks of the River Rouge in what is now Dearborn. It continued in use until about 1823. It was the first Protestant church in Michigan except for one near Mount Clemens erected by the Moravians in 1782. In Detroit the Methodists were allied with the First Protestant Society until 1823 when they broke away and established their own church at the southeast corner of Gratiot and Farmer where Crowley's department store is now. In 1834 they moved to a new location on Woodward at the northeast corner of Congress street. They remained there until 1849 when a new church was built farther up Woodward at the southwest corner of State street. The Congress street church meanwhile continued to be used until 1864 when the two congregations merged and built a fine edifice at the northeast corner of Woodward and Adams which has been occupied ever since as the Central Methodist Church.

The Episcopalians left the First Protestant Society in 1824 and created St. Paul's parish. The first St. Paul's was built in 1827 on a donated lot on Woodward just north of and adjoining the Presbyterian church. This St. Paul's remained in use until 1852 (its site is now occupied by a burlesque theater) when a fine Gothic building was put up on Congress street at the northeast corner of Shelby. This location is now the rear of the main office of the Manufacturers National Bank. In 1845 a second parish was organized and Christ Church was built at Jefferson and Rivard. The present building dates from 1863. In 1860 St. John's was built at Woodward and Vernor (then High street, now Fisher freeway). By 1896 business was encroaching on St. Paul's and its parishioners had moved away from the lower part of the city. The church building was dismantled stone by stone and reerected at the corner of East Grand boulevard and East Lafayette and became the Church of the Messiah. A new St. Paul's—actually a chapel—was then established at Woodward and Hancock. The present Cathedral Church of St. Paul was consecrated in 1911.

Michigan originally was part of the Episcopalian diocese of Western New York, but in 1832 the diocese of Michigan was created with Detroit as the see. In 1836 Samuel McCoskry, a Pennsylvanian and a graduate of West Point, became the first bishop.

The First Baptist Church had its building on Fort at Griswold where the Dime building is now. It stood there from 1830 until 1872 when it moved to Cass and Bagg (now Temple). In the early 1900s it was relocated out Woodward at the northwest corner of Blaine. Later it was sold to an interdenominational group.

The Second Baptist Church, organized in 1836, was Detroit's first Negro church. For several years its services were held in rented buildings, but in 1857 a church on the north side of Croghan (now Monroe) at Beaubien was purchased from a Lutheran parish. It is still at that location, one of the oldest of Detroit's churches.

The Congregationalists were generally affiliated with other denominations until 1844 when they began to hold services in the Old City Hall on the east side of Woodward at Campus Martius. In 1845 a building was obtained at the southeast corner of Jefferson and Beaubien, and in 1854 the Congregationalists moved to a new church at the southwest corner of Fort and Wayne (now Washington). They remained there until 1892 when the present First Congregational Church was built at Woodward and Forest.

The first Germans who came to Detroit were Catholics, but in the years prior to 1850 when immigration swelled the local German colony, many of the newcomers were Lutherans. They organized first in 1833 and held their services in a carpenter shop at Woodbridge and Bates. Later they were granted use of the Presbyterian session hall which stood next door to the church at Woodward and Larned. The Lutherans built their own St. John's Church in 1837 at the northeast corner of Monroe and Farrar (now Library). The parish occupied a new building in 1877 at Russell and Antietam streets. In the years immediately following the founding of St. John's the influx of Germans resulted in the establishment of several new Lutheran churches, most of them in the lower east side district.

The First Christian Church in Detroit was organized in 1838, and in 1863 it purchased the former Congregational Church on Jefferson. In 1871 a church building was purchased from the Presbyterians on Washington boulevard; it has long since been torn down. A Unitarian Church was organized in 1849 or 1850. Its first home (1853) was on Lafayette at Shelby. In 1883 it moved to Woodward and Selden. One of the most famous downtown Detroit churches was the Universalist Church of Our Father. Organized in 1879, its first building was erected on Park between Bagley and Adams. It remained there until the Tuller Hotel was built on the site in 1914 when the church moved to the corner of Cass and Hancock.

Detroit's Jewish community began to grow about the same time as that of the Germans and by mid-century there were enough members to form Congregation Beth El, organized in 1850. For the first few years meetings were held over a drug store on Cadillac Square near Bates street, but in 1860 a former Methodist church on Rivard between Lafayette and Monroe was purchased and converted into a synagogue. Seven years later Temple Beth El found new quarters at Washington and Clifford, remaining there until 1903 when a splendid new Temple Beth El was built at Woodward and Erskine. In 1922 the congregation moved to its present building at Woodward and Gladstone. The Woodward-Erskine building was remodeled into a theater as the Bonstelle Playhouse which for several years was the home of Jessie Bonstelle's repertory company. It is now owned and operated for theatrical purposes by Wayne State University.

Detroit's second Jewish congregation Shaarey Zedek was organized in 1861 and at first used the same rooms on Cadillac Square which had been the home of Temple Beth El. In 1864 a former Episcopal church was purchased at the southeast corner of St. Antoine and Congress, but it was soon outgrown. In 1876 it was torn down and a new synagogue was built at the same location, but financial difficulties were encountered and the building reverted to the contractors. After a brief period in which services were held in rented halls, the contractors leased the new temple to the congregation and Shaarey Zedek occupied it until shortly before World War I. At that time a new structure was built on the northwest corner of Brush and Willis, a location now part of the new medical center. Congregation Shaarey Zedek recently moved to suburban Southfield.

Detroit Goes to Press

In Detroit's early days the people threw their garbage into the river and caught their own fish. There was no need whatever for newspapers with which to wrap either of those commodities. Besides, until the Yankee migration began, not many people were able to read. If anyone felt an irresistible urge for a newspaper, he could usually get hold of one from Pittsburgh, Baltimore, Philadelphia or New York. Little did it matter that it was likely to be several months old and the news older. But an enlightened community without a newspaper exists in a vacuum. The remarkable Father Richard realized this and on one of his fund-raising trips to the East in 1809 he bought a printing press and a font of type, and brought the equipment back to Detroit where he set it up at his Spring Hill farm. He shortly obtained the services of printer James M. Miller of Utica and started a newspaper.

It was named the *Michigan Essay or the Impartial Observer*, a title almost as big as the paper itself. The first issue appeared August 31, 1809; it was small in size and one and a half columns were in French, the rest in English. Whether it was avidly read or not is a question. Apparently it was received with indifference, because as far as is known there never was another issue. Nevertheless, the Richard Press continued to be busy, turning out several books, one of which was a schoolbook Father Richard undoubtedly intended to use in his own Spring Hill school. Today imprints from the Richard Press are valuable rarities.

The next newspaper publishing venture was more successful. At the suggestion of Governor Cass, who wanted a political organ as well as something to inform the people on public affairs, John P. Sheldon and Ebenezer Reed began the weekly publication of the *Detroit Gazette*. The first issue bore the date of July 25, 1817. Although crude compared to later newspaper standards, the *Gazette* was lively and informative, and can be read today with interest. As Detroit's first real newspaper, it remained in business until its plant on Atwater near Wayne was destroyed by fire in 1830.

After that there was a brief period in which Detroit was without a Democratic party organ. There were a couple of Whig papers, but like that party itself, they faded away. A Jacksonian voice was needed. John R. Williams and his uncle Joseph Campau bought a press and some type from a floundering paper in Pontiac and on May 5, 1831, published the first edition of the *Democratic Free Press and Michigan Intelligencer*, a name that was soon shortened to the *Detroit Free Press.* Its first office was on Jefferson near Shelby, but in the ensuing years fires and growth caused it to occupy several locations. These were in buildings at Jefferson near Washington, Jefferson at Woodward, Jefferson at Griswold, Woodward near Congress, Griswold at Woodbridge, and Shelby and Larned. In the early years of this century the paper moved into a building on Lafayette just west of Griswold. Now known as the Canadian National-Grand Trunk building, for a long time it was called the Transportation building. The paper remained there until shortly after World War I when it moved into its present quarters on Lafayette between Washington and Cass.

The *Free Press* claims to be the oldest continuous newspaper published in Michigan, although it has had almost as many different owners as it has had locations. It attained great prestige and influence at one period of its existence. In fact, it had an international following. In 1881 and for a short time thereafter it published a special edition in London which was widely circulated in the British Isles. During its more than one hundred and thirty-five years its columns have been graced by many distinguished writers and editors, not the least of whom was the late newspaper poet Edgar A. Guest.

Detroit's giant in the newspaper field, the afternoon *Detroit News,* was founded by James E. Scripps, a member of a great newspaper family that has been a virtual dynasty in American journalism. Its first issue was on the street on August 23, 1873. In many respects the *News* represents a series of newspaper mergers and absorptions, and its ancestry can be traced back to the *Northwest Journal* of 1829.

Some of the papers it has taken into its fold include the *Detroit Advertiser, Detroit Tribune, Detroit Journal,* and William Randolph Hearst's *Detroit Times,* purchased in 1960. The *News* originally had its plant on Shelby between Congress and Larned, but in 1917 it moved into a new home at Lafayette and Second. At that time the new building was considered the finest newspaper plant in the world.

Over the years Detroit has been a veritable newspaper graveyard. The number of papers which flourished briefly and then died of poor circulation or hardening of the editors' arteries number in the hundreds. Today the morning *Free Press* and the evening *News* have a monopoly of the daily field, a monopoly which is not likely to be challenged by any new competitor in these days of high publishing costs. The *News* has branched out into other fields. It established and still operates radio and television stations WWJ and WWJ-TV. The radio station, licensed in 1921, was the first in the United States to broadcast regularly sponsored commercial programs. An indirect offshoot of the *News* is the Cranbrook complex consisting of a church, private schools, an art school, and a science museum. Located in suburban Bloomfield Hills, it was established in the 1920s by the late George G. Booth, son-in-law of Scripps, and his wife Ellen Scripps Booth. For many years Booth was publisher of the *News.* The *News* also displayed a pioneer interest in aviation and was among the first American newspapers to utilize planes and radio in gathering news.

7

Their Brothers' Keepers

Charity Begins at Home

One sound New England tenet was that it was moral, patriotic, and comfortable to get ahead in the world. That explains why so many New Englanders moved to Detroit and Michigan. Of course not all of them made it big. There were always the poor, the sick, and the unfortunate, and they became the responsibility of their more fortunate neighbors. Organized charity in Detroit dates from 1817 when a group of ladies of the First Protestant Society formed the Moral and Humane Society. This was a kind of sewing circle endeavor whose lofty aim was "to suppress vice and to report any poor children destitute of education." The society existed for only three years and its total expenditures were $64.37. But a little vice could be suppressed and some destitute children could be helped for that money in 1817. So at least it was a beginning.

The Catholic community went ahead of its Protestant counterpart in providing aid to the sick and poor.

After the cholera epidemics of 1832 and 1834 there was much distress in Detroit; the disease left behind many impoverished widows and orphans. To take care of them a county poor farm was established on some farm land at what is now Gratiot and Mt. Elliott avenues. Father Kundig, the German pastor of an Irish parish, became the first officially appointed superintendent of the poor. Probably at his instigation the Catholic Female Association was formed in 1836 for "the relief of the sick and poor." An orphanage was built adjoining the poor farm and was operated by the Catholic Female Association. In 1839 the poor farm was moved to a new location at Michigan and Merriman roads and is now known as Eloise. Two buildings on the property had been an inn, the Black Horse Tavern. Ultimately this developed into a huge complex which includes the Wayne County Infirmary and the Wayne County General Hospital.

With this shift of location in welfare activity it became necessary to make new provisions for the children. In 1851 an orphanage was built on the south side of Larned just west of Randolph on ground now occupied by the City-County building and adjacent to Ste. Anne's Church under whose supervision it was operated. About the same time the name of the sponsors was changed from the Catholic Female Association to St. Vincent's Female Orphan Asylum. The St. Vincent Society and a St. Vincent's Home were still doing their good work, although at a different location, in 1967.

The Ladies' Protestant Orphan Asylum, an offshoot of the First Presbyterian Church, was organized in 1836 to care for children in a donated house on Beaubien just south of Fort. It was soon moved to specially constructed quarters on Jefferson at Adair. These remained in use until comparatively recent times. It is now in Grosse Pointe.

Obviously it would be impossible to record all the

charitable undertakings of early Detroit. There were many and a number of them still function effectively. Some, like the St. Andrew's Society, came into existence to help newly arrived immigrants. Founded in 1835, St. Andrew's was for the purpose of alleviating the pains suffered by Scots who had left their native heath and heather for the more lush pastures of America. Their hall was at the southwest corner of Woodward and State, a site now occupied by the B. Siegel Company store.

Another interesting early institution was the Industrial School established as a charitable enterprise in 1857. Its purpose was to provide education, clothing, and at least one good meal a day for poor children. It first opened its doors at Monroe near Randolph, but about 1863 it moved to a rented building on the north side of Grand River at Washington. It continued to operate until the early years of this century when improved public school facilities made it no longer needed. The school building gave way in the 1930s to an interurban bus terminal which was in turn replaced by the inevitable parking lot.

In time the philanthropic causes became so many and the demands and solicitations so frequent and often overlapping, that local leaders felt something better should be worked out. People began to feel that there was a drive for some different charity every day, and managers complained that constant solicitation interfered with factory production and office routine. The result was the pooling of all needs and resources into a common fund with distribution to each institution or organization on the basis of its proved need. The necessary money was raised by a single united campaign. This method had the further merit of reducing the proliferating fund-raising costs, thus conserving more for actual charity. Known as the United Foundation, this central agency first began to function in 1949.

The results were spectacularly successful and the idea was widely adopted by communities throughout the United States. In recent years the United Foundation's give-once-for-all campaigns have regularly exceeded their quotas. Covering the entire metropolitan area, it annually raises in excess of $20,000,000 from both large and small subscribers, many of whom contribute painlessly through payroll withholding plans.

Aches and Pains

Over the years Detroiters have probably been no more prone to disease than people in other large cities; in fact modern Detroit has frequently been cited by public health authorities as one of the healthiest places in the nation. Nevertheless, Detroit has had its share of aches and pains. Aside from the cholera visitations, physical ailments have come for the most part from endemic rather than epidemic sources. The earliest affliction which laid everyone low at some period of his life was the shakes, more professionally known as the ague. Breeding in stagnant swamps and pools, the malaria-bearing mosquito buzzed happily and bit deeply. Described as the "bane of the pioneer," the ague was celebrated by the ditty:

> Don't go to Michigan, that land of ills;
> The word means ague, fever and chills.

It struck with such regularity, it was said that "the justice of the peace entered suit on his docket to avoid the sick day of the party or his own." The prescribed nostrum was whiskey in copious quantities. It did not cure, but it made the disease bearable. The ague persisted in Detroit until the surrounding area had been drained and by the time of the Civil War it was much less of a nuisance. Still, local hospitals reported occasional cases as late as the 1890s.

Many Detroiters until recent times were afflicted with goitre due, it is said, to an iodine deficiency in the water. This has been corrected by adding the necessary ingredients to ordinary household salt. Even more serious was diphtheria which for some reason was prevalent in Detroit and Michigan. It was common until about the time of World War I when effective vaccines were developed. For many years in the 19th and early 20th centuries the death rate from diphtheria was appalling; the Michigan mortality rate was the highest in the world. Fortunately, the disease has been virtually eliminated.

From the earliest times Detroit has had its quota of doctors—good ones and quacks. The first medical society was organized in 1819. In the latter part of the last century many of the doctors had their offices on West Lafayette street near Griswold, a circumstance which caused Lafayette to be known as pill alley. For a long time the sick were treated at home, the early maternity ward was a room off the kitchen, and the dying met their Maker in the same bed in which they had been born. Cadillac maintained what was called a hospital in his village, although it was more properly a barracks or dormitory in which sick soldiers and civilians could be isolated. Later military forces frequently had buildings set aside for the care of the sick. But for civilians there was nothing until 1845 when four nuns converted a log building on the grounds of Ste. Anne's at Larned and Randolph to hospital purposes and called it St. Vincent's Hospital. Within a short time the institution was moved to a new building on Clinton at St. Antoine on a lot donated by Mrs. Antoine Beaubien. The name was changed to St. Mary's Hospital. Another new building was put up in 1879 on the same site, but facing on St. Antoine. In 1948 St. Mary's was sold to a group of doctors and became Detroit Memorial Hospital.

Agitation was begun as early as 1829 for a government hospital in Detroit to care for sick and injured Great Lakes seamen, but it was not until 1854 that the United States Marine Hospital was built at Jefferson and Mt. Elliott. It continued in use until the 1920s when a new one was built in Grosse Pointe. The original hospital buildings were then turned over to the Immigration Service. Some of them, or parts of them still in use, are among the oldest structures standing in Detroit.

Harper Hospital was opened in 1864 for the care of Civil War wounded. It stood on land at Woodward and Martin Place donated by Walter Harper, a recluse and eccentric, and his housekeeper Nancy Martin. The Harper-Martin trust was under the direction of the First Presbyterian Church. After the war the government turned the barracks-like buildings back to the trustees and Harper became a civilian hospital. It did not use all the buildings on the grounds; one was used by the Detroit Medical College when it was organized in 1868. This school was the forerunner of the present Wayne State University College of Medicine, thus enabling Wayne State to date its origin from 1868. In 1884 the wooden barracks were disposed of and a new hospital was constructed on John R. at the head of Martin Place. This venerable building is still in use. In 1928 the present main unit of Harper was built facing Brush street.

Harper's neighbor Grace Hospital dates from 1888 when it was established at John R. and Willis by a group of homeopaths who were barred from practice at Harper. In 1901 Grace became a dual hospital open to regular practitioners as well as homeopaths. While the old buildings are still in use, Grace opened a fine new modern branch at Meyer and West Seven Mile in 1941. It is known as the Grace Northwest Unit.

Providence Hospital, long one of the area's leading Catholic institutions, dates from 1869 when it opened as a maternity hospital for unmarried girls. It stood on Fourteenth street at Dalzell. Later it became a general hospital and new facilities were built at West Grand boulevard and Fourteenth. In 1964 the boulevard property was given up and Providence followed the crowd into the suburbs with completely new facilities. It is now in Southfield near the huge Northland shopping center.

The present Henry Ford Hospital at West Grand boulevard and the John C. Lodge expressway (formerly Hamilton avenue) began in 1911 as the Detroit General Hospital privately owned and operated by a group of doctors. One of its backers was Henry Ford; in 1915 when the institution ran into financial trouble, Ford took it over. Construction of the present main building was begun in 1917 and completed in time for use immediately after World War I as a convalescent hospital for veterans.

Detroit has two municipal hospitals. Herman Kiefer Hospital at Taylor and Hamilton dates from 1893 when it was the pest house for the care of contagious diseases. Receiving Hospital on St. Antoine adjoining old St. Mary's was established in 1915 to handle emergency cases. Its name recently was changed to Detroit General Hospital.

About 1956 the grand concept of a medical center was proposed for the area occupied by Harper, Grace, and other hospitals. Some two hundred and fifty acres of land were acquired through the urban renewal program and considerable progress has been made toward completion of the center. Eventually it will include not only Harper and Grace, but also Hutzel (formerly Woman's Hospital) and Children's Hospital. Hutzel dates from 1868 and Children's from 1887. The center also will include the Wayne State University College of Medicine, research and library facilities, and proposed specialized hospitals, including one for the aged. The area is bounded by Mack, Woodward, Warren, and Chrysler freeway. Most of the section has been cleared, including land being developed as housing for doctors and for other medical personnel and services.

A Dash of Culture

While Detroiters were doing soothing things to their aching joints and salving their bruises, they were also improving their minds—an infinitely more difficult thing. Detroit winters were long and until the advent of the railroad, the close of navigation meant almost complete isolation from the rest of the world. A man could die of boredom during the iced-in season. Even business ran to the slack and a young clerk, made idle of necessity, could become a willing recruit of the devil, which of course was not considered respectable. So to promote healthy minds and noble thoughts during the annual ice-age, upward and onward societies were formed to entertain, enlighten, and elevate. The first was the Lyceum organized in 1818. It was a lecture society and study group, but it lasted only three years. A more permanent organization in the same year was the

Detroit Mechanic's Society. Not a labor union as the name might suggest, its membership was composed of merchants, businessmen, and craftsmen—a sort of 19th century cross between a board of commerce and Rotary Club. It met first at Smyth's tavern, but by 1828 had become affluent enough to afford a clubhouse on the southwest corner of Griswold and Lafayette, and continued in existence until about 1886.

In 1831 the more highbrow Detroit Athenaeum was organized with Lewis Cass as its president. This was a serious lecture group and it brought some distinguished speakers to Detroit. One was Dr. Douglass Houghton of Troy, N.Y. A young physician-scientist, Houghton remained in Detroit to become a mayor, a founder of the school system, and the first state geologist who helped develop the salt and copper mining industries.

Largely through Houghton's influence the Athenaeum was merged in 1832 with the newly formed Young Men's Society, a major force in Detroit public affairs for the next half century. Everybody who was anybody, or expected to be, became a member. It was chartered by the state legislature, and membership was open to everybody of good character who could pay his five dollars annual dues. The society bought a lot in 1850 on Jefferson between Bates and Randolph where it put up a building. It later erected a larger one on Woodbridge at Randolph in the rear of what had once been Governor Hull's residence. This hall seated several hundred persons and was long used for public meetings and concerts, and as a social center. The Young Men's Society lasted until 1882.

A third organization was the Fire Department Society, the purpose of which was to provide entertainment, recreation, and cultural exposure for the young men who made up the city's volunteer fire companies. Organized in 1840, the Fire Department Society was also a strong civic influence. In 1851 it built Firemen's Hall on the site of the former Council House. This hall had an auditorium which seated upwards of fifteen hundred persons, and was the scene of many concerts and entertainments where the great stars of the day performed. The Fire Department Society began to wane when a professional fire department was created in 1861 and in 1883 disbanded entirely.

There were several other early organizations which had an impact on Detroit and endeavored to raise its citizenry above the level of ignoramuses. For instance, there was the Michigan Historical Society founded in 1828 with Cass as its first president. Its membership included the town's most distinguished men and early meetings were held in the old Capitol. The society collected many important documents pertaining to early Detroit's history; for the most part these have been preserved and now belong to the Detroit Public Library. The Detroit Historical Society was not founded until 1922. Through municipal support and public contributions, the Detroit Historical Commission has been able to build or acquire three local museums: the main Detroit Historical Museum at Woodward and Kirby, a neighbor of the Public Library and the Institute of Arts, a military museum at Fort Wayne, and a museum of Great Lakes history on Belle Isle.

The Young Men's Christian Association was first established in Detroit in 1852. After a somewhat uncertain early existence it finally took firm root about 1882. It had several locations, but in 1887 it acquired ownership of a building at the northeast corner of Griswold and Grand River. In 1909 it moved to its present downtown headquarters at Witherell and Adams facing Grand Circus Park. There are, of course, branches in many parts of the city.

Most of the early societies such as the Mechanic's, Young Men's, and Fire Department had reading rooms and libraries for the use of their members and eventually most of their books found their way to the shelves of the Public Library which was officially created in 1865. Prior to that Detroiters had to buy their own books or borrow them from one of the subscription libraries of which there were several. The first was the City Library Association incorporated in 1817. It had rooms in the old university building on Bates street. The Public Library was given quarters in Capitol High School from 1865 to 1877 when its own building was erected in Centre Park on Gratiot between Library and Farmer streets. The present main library at Woodward and Kirby was opened in 1921 and was substantially enlarged in 1963. The Centre Park library became the Downtown Branch. Its present building dates from 1932.

The Detroit Institute of Arts started out as a private institution, really an outgrowth of the Detroit Scientific Society, part of whose collection of oddities it inherited. Detroit has had a number of famous artists including Alvah Bradish, John Mix Stanley, Julius Rolshoven, Robert Hopkin, and Gari Melchers. Interest in good art was general. In 1885 the Detroit Museum of Art was organized and in 1888 it opened a new building at the southwest corner of Jefferson and Hastings, the site of the former home of General Hugh Brady, commandant of United States troops stationed in Detroit. Its name was changed in 1919. In 1927 a much larger and more adequate museum was opened on Woodward facing the Public Library. This building was turned over to the city upon completion and its support became a municipal obligation. The museum was materially enlarged by the addition of a south wing opened in 1966 and the construction of a north wing was begun the same year.

The Detroit Symphony Orchestra, which had to depend largely on public contributions, has had a career as bouncy as a polka. The first concert, which resulted in its permanent organization, was given in 1914 in the old Detroit Opera House then fronting on Campus Martius a few steps east of Woodward. Ossip Gabrilowitsch, son-in-law of Mark Twain, became the first permanent conductor and under his baton the orchestra thrived. In 1919 its own concert hall, Orchestra Hall, was built at Woodward and Orchestra Place. Hard times followed later and Orchestra Hall was abandoned except for occasional concerts and use as a recording studio. Today it stands as a slum monument which nobody seems to know what to do with. Later the orchestra was resurrected through the efforts and money of German-born chemical tycoon Henry Reichhold and it entered a new era of prosperity. Its performances were given in Music Hall, formerly the Wilson Theater on Madison avenue, or in the Masonic Temple auditorium. In 1956 the Ford Motor Company and its dealers presented Detroit with the Henry and Edsel Ford Auditorium as a memorial to the two automotive leaders. The second structure to be erected in the Civic Center near what had been the foot of Bates street, the Ford Auditorium has been the home of the Symphony Orchestra ever since.

The Lively Arts

For many years Detroit was a garrison town and much of its life centered around the waterfront, two circumstances which gave the city a gamey flavor. Streets along the river were lined with saloons and other interesting establishments which catered to soldiers and seamen, and those who by inclination or economic status were more or less aloof from high-mindedness. As the Yankees moved in they observed such goings-on with more than mild distaste and tried to apply corrective measures. These took the form of blue laws which sought to prohibit Sunday markets (this made the French angry), Sunday horse racing (which made them even angrier), and other forms of outdoor amusement, as well as some of the indoor types. In 1817 the town marshal, acting under one of those Sabbath laws, arrested a whole platoon of soldiers who were doing nothing more sinful than fishing from the municipal pier. Enforcement of Sunday quiet persisted for a long time. It was not until 1886, for example, that the Public Library was permitted to be open on Sunday afternoon. Even then the issue brought down thunder from the pulpits. One preacher declared that after opening the reading rooms (no withdrawals were at first permitted) the next inevitable step would be the sale of beer in the parks on the Sabbath. Nobody took that danger too seriously because no earnest Detroiter was ever known to have died of thirst on Sunday. Saloons were supposed to be closed, but enough saloonkeepers had lost their keys so that one did not have to look hard or far for an oasis. Some of the drinking spots along the river became famous, some for sin, other for *gemütlichkeit*. Among the former was the establishment of Billy Boushaw who controlled politics in the lower precincts and became known as the boss of the "first of the first." Translated, that meant the first precinct, first ward. Billy could predict the exact vote for his favored candidate right down to the last ballot. If, just before the polls closed, it appeared there might be a slight deficiency, Billy would round up enough floaters or repeaters to make his predictions come true. Billy's saloon and sailors' flophouse was located at the northwest corner of Beaubien and Atwater streets.

Another noted spot in the more genteel category was Schweitzer's at Atwater and Schweitzer Place (formerly Hastings street), still doing business one hundred and two years after its opening. Still run by the same family, it never blew out its lamps, even during the drear days of prohibition.

In time sin moved uptown and flourished along Croghan and Rowland streets where conditions became so bad that eventually, to recapture a slight degree of respectability, their names were changed to Monroe and Griswold. Rowland street was the short street bordering Capitol Park on the west. Other streets underwent similar metamorphoses in order to preserve or restore property values. The dens of iniquity sometimes became too much for the public to stand and were sternly dealt with. In 1841 the Common Council could get no court action against a particularly seamy joint at Randolph and Cadillac Square, so it adopted a resolution calling on the marshal to tear the place down. Aided by a joyful posse, he proceeded to carry out orders. The proprietors of this "evil resort" were a pair known as T. Slaughter and Peg Welch. They later sued the city for damages and recovered. For many years Detroit had a thriving red light district on the lower east side which continued to operate until about the time of World War I.

Prior to 1865 Detroit's laws were enforced by constables, each ward being responsible for keeping its own backyard clean. Under that arrangement few backyards ever were cleaned up. The city or metropolitan police department was not organized until 1865. Because the waterfront was the most troublesome area, the central police station was located on Woodbridge just east of Woodward. Although long unused, the red brick building stood until a few years ago when the Civic Center improvement resulted in its demolition. The first police department headquarters was built in 1883-84 in East Park, a triangular plot bounded by Farmer, Randolph, and Bates. The site is now occupied by the municipal Water Board building. The present police headquarters on Beaubien between Macomb and Clinton dates from 1922.

Gallows Song

The story of Detroit's jail has, as a climax, an illustration of how far advanced this pioneer community was in its social attitudes. The first jails were the guardhouses in which civilian prisoners were deposited in custody of the military. Later, after the American occupation, blockhouses were rented from private owners for lockup purposes. The first one, which escaped the fire of 1805, was at the northeast corner of Jefferson and Cass; in 1815 the jail was in a wooden building on the north side of Jefferson near Shelby; and in 1817 a two-story rented blockhouse at Jefferson and Randolph housed the wayward. It was used only until 1819 and was torn down in 1826. In 1819 a new jail was built in Centre Park facing Gratiot between Farmer and Library. It was built with proceeds from the sale of land in the Ten Thousand Acre Tract. Its ground dimensions were forty-four feet on Gratiot by eighty-eight feet in length, and for its day it was quite an imposing structure. As a jail, however, it was not a huge success, chiefly because it never had many occupants. Whether Detroiters were law abiding or whether judges were lenient, it is hard to say. Most of the jail's boarders, like Father Richard, were

176

locked up on body writs in civil cases or for non-payment of debts. These people could hardly be classed as hardened criminals. Drunken Indians were occasionally tossed in the tank and there were white offenders from time to time. The jail finally was torn down in 1847 and a new one was built at the corner of Beaubien and Clinton. Ever since, this has been the site for the Wayne County Jail. The present building, several times enlarged, was erected in the fall of 1928 and is considerably more crowded than its predecessors.

The old Centre Park jail had its finest hour in 1830 when Stephen G. Simmons of the village of Wayne was hanged for murdering his wife in a drunken rage. The event created quite a stir for no white man had been executed in Michigan under American law since the British evacuation in 1796. A few Indians had been hanged, of course, but they did not count. Simmons received a fair trial before a jury and three territorial judges sitting *en bloc*. But carrying out the sentence proved difficult. Sheriff Thomas G. Knapp flatly refused to be a hangman and gave up his office. Uncle Ben Woodworth allowed he would do the job in the interests of preserving respect for the law and was appointed sheriff in Knapp's place. The whole community stirred with excitement and Woodworth erected a grandstand in the jail yard in anticipation of a full house of spectators. The gallows was constructed on Gratiot just across the street from Crowley's store which, of course, was not there then. Early on the morning of September 24 the crowd of Detroiters as well as whole families from surrounding farms and villages began to arrive. They came on horseback and in their farm wagons, bringing their children and picnic baskets. One citizen whose house overlooked the jail yard was one of the few who reversed the proceedings. He took his youngsters and went elsewhere for the day, but before he left he was swamped with requests from friends to be allowed to occupy his windows. He refused in disgust. To add a festive touch, Woodworth invited the garrison band to be on hand and toot a few lively tunes to keep the spectators amused.

At noon Simmons was brought out of the jail and mounted the scaffold. He was a big, florid, and handsome fellow; but not popular because when drunk he was a quarrelsome bully. Nevertheless, he conducted himself bravely and his appearance won the crowd's sympathy. He listened quietly while the death sentence was read. Then he made a touching and eloquent speech admitting his guilt, confessing remorse, and vividly pointing to the evils of drink. Then he sang a couple of verses of a hymn in a loud and firm baritone. When that was completed the trap was sprung. Woodworth had built his gallows well and Simmons died instantly.

Sobered and apparently ashamed of the holiday mood in which they had come to see Simmons off, the spectators dispersed quietly. Just as Simmons was the first white man to be hanged, so was he the last. The entire community was conscience stricken and no one else ever was sentenced to pay the extreme penalty at the hands of the state of Michigan. In 1846, the recollection of the Simmons execution still vivid in mind, the legislature passed a law which for all time abolished capital punishment.

Detroit had another notable prison, the Detroit House of Correction built in 1860 at Russell and Wilkins. A great gray fortress-like structure, it stood grim and foreboding, brooding over a dismal section of the city which became one of Detroit's first and worst slums. Today the Brewster public housing project occupies its site. The House of Correction was for the custody of violators of city ordinances and short term offenders, including vagrants who regularly got themselves sent up for ninety days when the cold weather arrived. Supposedly a correctional institution, it made a pretense of rehabilitation by operating some industry such as a chair factory within its walls. By contract it also accepted the overflow from state penitentiaries and federal prisons. There was a block for women when there were neither state nor federal reformatories for them, and at times it housed some really charming girls. One who graced its halls was the hard-bitten Belle Starr, a notorious horse thief and bad man's moll from Oklahoma, a character straight out of the horse operas. Time has softened the image of Belle, and dime novels and television have transformed her into a heroine of the Old West, something she never was. The old House of Correction was torn down in 1931 when a new municipal prison was built outside of suburban Plymouth.

Freedom Road

A strong anti-slavery and abolition sentiment developed early in Detroit; probably it grew out of the New England conscience, but part of it must also be attributed to the fact that slavery simply was not good economics here. Slavery was proved by trial and error to be unprofitable, although slaves were still owned in Detroit as late as 1830. They belonged to owners who had lived in Detroit during the British period and the transfer of sovereignty guaranteed the right to retain private property. No new slaves were acquired under the American regime.

In 1833 Detroit was given an opportunity to go

on record regarding its attitude toward the slavery problem. A slave named Thornton Blackburn and his wife escaped from their owner in Kentucky and made their way to Detroit. For two years they lived here unmolested; then they were traced and claimed by their owner. With a court order to back him up, Sheriff John M. Wilson arrested the Blackburns and held them pending their return to Kentucky. Public opinion was strongly on their side and large crowds, mostly Negroes, surrounded the jail on Gratiot. A woman obtained permission to visit Mrs. Blackburn and once inside, changed clothes with her, enabling Mrs. Blackburn to escape to Canada. A day or two later while Blackburn was being escorted to a boat to start his journey back south, the crowd rushed the sheriff and severely manhandled him. Blackburn was spirited away and joined his wife in Canada. The town was in such an uproar that it was necessary to order troops from Fort Gratiot to restore order. Such incidents as that involving the Blackburns eventually led to the establishment of the metropolitan police force.

From that time on Detroit became an important last station on the Underground Railroad. Thousands of slaves—no one knows the exact number—escaping from the South were passed along established routes which took them through Ohio, Indiana or Illinois into Michigan and to Detroit. En route they were hidden at night or by day, as circumstances demanded, in the cellars or barns of sympathetic farmers and townspeople who guided them from one station to another. In Detroit they were usually hidden in the livery barn of Seymour Finney's Temperance House. The hotel was at the corner of Woodward and Gratiot where Kern's department store stood until 1966. The stable was a block away at the northeast corner of State and Griswold across the street from the old Capitol. A bronze plaque on the wall of the Detroit Bank & Trust Company branch office now marks the location. After hiding in the barn until the way was clear, the fugitives were escorted across the river to Canadian sanctuary. Large numbers of Negroes in Windsor and southwestern Ontario trace their ancestry back to passengers on the Underground Railroad.

In 1854 a group of prominent Detroiters, including Zachariah Chandler, a wealthy drygoods merchant, decided some political action was needed to offset the obnoxious Fugitive Slave Law of 1850 and other governmental measures truckling to the southern slavocracy. Chandler and his friends held an informal conference in the newspaper office of the *Tribune* and then called a mass meeting in the City Hall. The latter meeting issued a call for all interested parties to attend a rally of similar committees from around the state at Jackson on July 6, 1854. The result was the organization "under the oaks" of the Republican Party.

The noted Negro orator and abolitionist Frederick Douglass was in Detroit to give a lecture in 1859. By design or coincidence, a fiery fanatical abolitionist of the direct action school arrived in town the same day. He was John Brown. He brought with him fourteen escaped slaves from Missouri—fifteen actually, because one was born along the way. After they had been delivered to the Underground Railroad conductors for transfer to Canada, Brown went out to the home of William Webb, a local Negro leader who was entertaining Douglass. There Brown laid out his plan for an armed insurrection to free the slaves. He received promises of help from some of those present and then moved on to Chatham, Ontario, to recruit a band of followers. His next stop was Harpers Ferry. The Webb house where his preliminary plans were discussed was on the north side of Congress street near St. Antoine.

Of course there were those who opposed abolition for various reasons and with varying degrees of intensity.

Perhaps the most outspoken foe of the abolitionists was Wilbur F. Storey, the eccentric editor of the *Detroit Free Press.* On the eve of the Civil War he warned that if Michigan troops marched against the South, they would receive "a fire in the rear" which would compel them to abandon a campaign against the Confederacy. But the voices of Storey and the *Free Press* were minority voices. The great mass of the people loyally supported the Union, although many were dubious about emancipation.

Civil War

The battlefields of the Civil War were far away and did not touch Detroit directly; the city's role was that of the home front. Having been a French, British and American outpost, Detroit always maintained some military tradition, although this became less pronounced after Fort Shelby was dismantled in 1827 and the stockade enclosing the town was torn down the year before. To accommodate troops that continued to be stationed here, the Detroit Barracks were built at Gratiot and Mt. Elliott in 1830 and remained in use until about 1855. Shortly before that Fort Wayne was completed in 1851 on the west side river front in Springwells Township. For its time it was a formidable work covering sixty-six acres. Its establishment was inspired in part by the border raids growing out of Canada's Patriot's War and as might be suspected, as a pork barrel measure to make local congressmen happy. It was almost, but not quite, continuously garrisoned until just prior to World

War II. During and after both world wars it was used as a storage and quartermaster depot, a reserve training center, and a Selective Service induction center. It never fired a shot in anger. Recently the works were acquired by the city for a military history museum. The rest of the reservation has been declared surplus property by the federal government and at this writing the city is negotiating for it to be used for enlarged museum, recreational or housing purposes.

Another military installation, almost unknown to Detroiters themselves, was Fort Croghan or, as it was often called, Fort Nonsense. It was built in 1806 at what is now Park and Vernor. It consisted of an earth embankment ten feet high surrounded by pickets and protected by a few pieces of artillery. It was used primarily to safeguard cattle which grazed on the nearby commons. Its use was discontinued after the War of 1812, but for many years it was a favorite playground for boys. Remains of the earthworks were still visible until after the Civil War.

Detroit sent a total of about six thousand soldiers to the front during the four years of the Civil War. When President Lincoln announced a state of war on April 17, 1861, and called for volunteers, a wave of patriotic fervor swept the city. A citizens' mass meeting was held on April 18 in front of the post office and custom house at the northwest corner of Griswold and Larned streets. Constructed in 1860, the building continued to be used for government offices until 1964 when it was torn down and the site became a parking lot.

First to answer Lincoln's call was the First Michigan Infantry composed of militia companies drawn from Detroit and other Michigan towns. The Detroit unit, Company A, consisted of the Detroit Light Guard, an organization which has provided the nucleus of the local militia and national guard down to the present time. Trained at Fort Wayne, the regiment was presented its colors in a ceremony in Campus Martius for which nearly all Detroit turned out. The First Michigan was the first western regiment to arrive at Washington. It was badly mauled at Bull Run after which, being a three months regiment, it was disbanded. Another distinguished Civil War regiment was the Twenty-fourth Infantry composed almost entirely of Detroit and Wayne County volunteers. It trained at the old fair grounds, then at Woodward and Canfield avenues, and arrived at the front in time to take part in the battle of Antietam, after which it was incorporated in the famous Iron Brigade. It opened the battle of Gettysburg on July 1, 1863, and was almost completely destroyed while holding up the Confederate advance until the mass of the Army of the Potomac could get into position. Its casualty rate was the highest of any Union regiment in the battle.

The recruiting of the Twenty-fourth was tarnished by a deplorable race riot in March 1863. The regiment had no part in that affair which was largely a protest against conscription, and disenchantment with emancipation and war policies generally. Violence against the city's Negroes reached the riot stage during the morning of March 6 when a mob of hoodlums swept through the lower east side along Brush and Beaubien streets between Monroe and Congress. It was in that area that most of the Negroes lived. City officials were slow to respond to the crisis and by late afternoon the disturbance reached fever pitch. Many Negroes were beaten and some were killed; many more were forced to flee their homes. Some crossed to Canada for refuge. A large part of the district was burned, and damage from fire, looting, and vandalism was extensive. Order was not restored until nightfall when federal troops were brought in from Fort Wayne and Ypsilanti.

On September 19, 1864, Detroit got the scare of its not-so-young life. That morning a band of Confederate agents working out of Canada boarded the packet steamer *Philo Parsons* at her dock near the foot of Woodward avenue and bought tickets for Sandusky, Ohio. The *Philo Parsons* regularly made the Detroit-Sandusky run with stops at Put-in-Bay and other Lake Erie islands. After leaving Detroit she stopped at Sandwich and Amherstburg where more southern agents, disguised as ordinary travelers, went on board. As the vessel entered Lake Erie they produced arms and took over the boat. Their purpose was to free three thousand Confederate prisoners held on Johnson's Island in Sandusky harbor. The island was guarded by the *U.S.S. Michigan*, a gunboat mounting fifteen guns. Part of the conspiracy was to capture the warship; then with the liberated prisoners to raid Great Lakes ports and cause as much commotion and disruption in the Union rear as possible.

Fortunately, the plot failed because federal counterspies learned of the plan and the captain of the *Michigan* was alerted. After terrorizing the regular passengers and capturing a second small inter-island steamer the *Island Queen*, which was scuttled, the Confederates realized they could not take either the *Michigan* or Johnson's Island. After cruising around aimlessly all night they returned to Sandwich, scuttled the *Philo Parsons*, and made their escape into Canada. Some were caught and at least one of the ringleaders was executed. When the full impact of what might have happened hit Detroit the citizens wore apprehensive looks for a long time.

Throughout the war Detroit supplied munitions and food for the Union armies; the city was a principal distribution point for supplies from Michigan towns and farms. In 1862 a new cantonment was built on Clinton between Joseph Campau and Elmwood avenues just opposite the present entrance to Elmwood Cemetery. Barracks for ten thousand men were erected. It was used as a recruiting and replacement depot, and later for the discharge of returning soldiers. The provost marshal headquarters was there also. Toward the end of the war it was used for the care of slightly wounded convalescents. The post was known as Camp Backus and disappeared soon after the war ended.

On April 16, 1865, following the assassination of President Lincoln, virtually all of Detroit turned out for a memorial mass meeting in Campus Martius. It was said to have been the largest assemblage of people in Detroit up to that time. In 1872 the city dedicated the Soldiers' and Sailors' monument on Woodward at the head of Cadillac Square. In 1901 a veterans' hall, known as Memorial Hall or the GAR building, was erected at the intersection of Cass and Grand River. The gray fortress-like structure continued to be the meeting place for Civil War veterans until the last surviving one died about the time of World War II. It was then taken over by the city as a recreational center for youths and elderly citizens. In 1891 Detroit was host to the GAR national encampment and thousands marched in the biggest parade Detroit had seen until the American Legion met here in 1931.

Detroit has a sentimental attachment to the Civil War, tenuous perhaps, but nonetheless real. Falling into the distinguished citizen category, it pertains to the residence here from 1848 to 1851 of an army lieutenant who commanded the old Detroit Barracks. His name was Ulysses S. Grant. He did not make any great splurge in the city's social life, although he did get around, and the presence of Lieutenant and Mrs. Grant at balls and parties was occasionally reported. Mrs. Grant, it was recalled, was a gay young woman who enjoyed the dances at the National

Hotel where she was sought after as a partner. Her husband, definitely not the dancing type, stood around looking glum and bored. Twice Lieutenant Grant was in the public notices; once when he slipped and fell on the icy sidewalk in front of Zachariah Chandler's store. He unsuccessfully sued the merchant who later became his secretary of the interior when Grant ascended to the presidency. On another occasion Grant was fined for riding his horse too fast through the streets. He might have been hurrying to the grocery store of Hiram Walker on the east side of Woodward just below Jefferson. It would not have been groceries the lieutenant was after, but another choice commodity distilled at the rear of the premises, which became world famous a few years later when Walker established a great distillery on the Canadian shore at Walkerville, now part of Windsor. Tradition says that Grant was a good patron of the Walker product. It may be true because, to put it delicately, Grant had a problem.

The Grants lived first in a small frame house typical of the workingman's home of that day at 253 East Fort street. It was on the north side of Fort between Russell and Rivard. Later he moved into a double house at the northeast corner of Jefferson and Russell. The latter, long ago demolished, became the site of the home of United States Senator James McMillan, and still later the premises of the University Club. Several years ago the Fort street house was acquired by the Detroit Historical Society. Moved to the present State Fair Grounds and furnished in the style of the period, it is a popular attraction for visitors.

Another Detroit resident from 1857 to 1861 was Captain George Gordon Meade who was in charge of the Corps of Engineers Great Lakes topographical survey. Meade was transferred to Philadelphia on the eve of the Civil War in which he won fame as the victor at Gettysburg.

He was Grant's strong arm in the later stages of the war as commander of the Army of the Potomac. While in Detroit, Meade lived at 3 Aspinall Terrace which was at the corner of Bagley and Clifford.

8

Men at Work

First Order of Business

The existence of copper in the upper peninsula of Michigan was known from the earliest times. The French heard about it from the Indians, and the exploration of the upper Great Lakes was due in part to the expeditions sent out to locate copper deposits. It was not until about 1841, however, that extraction and refining of copper ore began on a commercial basis. The enterprise quickly developed into a major industry, supported by large injections of local and eastern capital.

The discovery of substantial deposits of iron ore came in 1844, about the time the copper industry began to boom. Within a decade Michigan became the leading producer of both minerals and a new industrial era dawned for Detroit. Located on a water route accessible to the ingredients—ore and limestone—for making pig iron and steel, Detroit took on new importance as a center of heavy industry.

This importance was enhanced in 1855 when the St. Mary's River ship canal was opened. It made the transportation of raw material to Detroit mills and foundries easier, faster, and more economical. Industrial development was greatly accelerated as a result of the Soo canal. By the time of the Civil War it appeared as though Detroit would be the great iron and steel producing center of the United States, a position which was eventually preempted by Pittsburgh and the Chicago area.

Prior to the mid-1840s Detroit retained many of the characteristics of a river front trading post. From the time of its founding in 1701 until well into the 19th century business was almost exclusively concerned with the fur trade and its handmaiden the Indian trade. But by 1830 fur was no longer a major factor in Detroit's economic life. The Michigan wilderness was being opened up for settlement; game was disappearing and the fur trade shifted west, centering in St. Louis. Instead of Michigan swamps, ponds, and streams, trappers were ranging the headwater country of the Missouri and its tributaries for beaver. Detroit had become a commercial town, a town of wholesale and retail establishments supplying the needs of the settlers rapidly filling up the interior. It also did a fairly large freight handling and forwarding business. Grain, fish, and some meat, mostly pork, were being shipped out to eastern and even foreign markets where Michigan wheat was held in high esteem. Many slaves on southern plantations ate dried fish caught in nearby Great Lakes waters. Whitefish, herring, and other varieties were in demand. As late as the first decade of this century a commercial seine was operated at the head of Belle Isle and at night its creaking reel could be heard over much of the eastern part of the city as it pulled in its nets loaded with whitefish from Lake St. Clair. Pollution and the lamprey eel joined forces to bring commercial fishing on the Great Lakes to a near end, although efforts are being made to revive it with some hope of success.

The change from a fur to a commercial economy brought a new merchant class to replace the earlier tycoons whose wealth derived from Indian trade goods and pelts, although there continued for many years to be some activity in the processing of furs and the manufacture of fur hats, gloves, and other articles of apparel. Commerce remained concentrated around the river front, the principal streets being Atwater, Woodbridge, and Jefferson. Above Jefferson was the residential district extending north about to Adams, with Second or Third the western boundary and St. Antoine the eastern. Gradually some of the more prosperous citizens began to discover the delights of living on East Jefferson and built their homes farther and farther out. A few of the old houses dating from the 1830s still stand on East Jefferson. Others moved up Woodward; as business encroached north of Jefferson, the residential area pushed north of Grand Circus Park. But for a long time West Lafayette and Fort streets continued to be where the fashionable lived.

These solid citizens were of the professional class or were well-to-do merchants, many of whom were to do even better in the years ahead. What little manufacturing there was prior to the 1840s consisted mostly of light industry. The shops and factories turned out small products for household or farm use.

Trails of Mud and Iron

Detroit's growth as a mercantile center can be attributed to several factors, but the prime ones were the settlement of the interior and the development of transportation. For more than a century after its founding Detroit and Michigan were sadly lacking in the transportation department. The French needed no roads; the British were not going anywhere in particular that could not be reached more easily by water. They had no real reason to construct roads. The early Americans never got around to it. There was of course the River road, an extention of West Jefferson avenue which ran down to the Maumee, the site of present-day Toledo. Sometimes called Hull's road, it was vulnerable to attack by the British as Hull learned to his dismay in the War of 1812. In 1817 the military commanders sought an alternate route and a new road to Toledo, or at least part way, was built by soldiers. Really the extension of Detroit's Fort street, it was the first important road-building undertaking in this area.

Governor Cass and his associates, ardently desirous of populating the interior of Michigan, realized that it was of little use to urge settlers to stake out farms in the wilderness if there was no way for them to get there. He and some friends were interested in developing real estate around what is now Pontiac. To make it possible to reach there, the Pontiac road was authorized but was not completed all the way through until 1824. It is now Woodward avenue.

It took Father Richard to get a real road-building program started after he became territorial delegate to Congress. In 1825 he was successful in obtaining an appropriation for surveying and building a road connecting Detroit and Chicago. The route selected was the age-old Great Sauk trail which begins in Detroit as Michigan avenue and ends in Chicago as Michigan boulevard. Cutting across the southern part of Michigan, it is now U.S. highway 112, or approximately that. As the state's first federal road it did as much as anything to open Michigan for settlement and helped to account for the heavy population soon established in the southern tier of counties. About the same time roads also were built to Port Huron, Saginaw, and Grand Rapids. These became Gratiot road; an extension of the Pontiac road from that city to Saginaw Bay; and Grand River road. The latter was built with an 1832 federal grant.

These highways, while extremely useful, hardly merited the designation of roads. Actually they were no more than cleared tracks through the woods. The traveler in a wagon or on horseback had to weave around stumps left standing, mud holes were frequent and almost bottomless, and bridges were virtually non-existent. Travel over the roads was a slow and painful process for man and beast.

People began to demand something better and in 1848 the maintenance of the principal roads—Michigan, Woodward, Grand River, Gratiot—was turned over to chartered companies. Private enterprises proceeded to plank or corduroy these highways and were permitted to collect tolls. Each of the plank roads had a toll gate at the city limits. The one on Woodward, for example, was at Adams avenue where the R. H. Fyfe shoe store was built later. There was another in Highland Park at Church street; the old toll house still stands as part of a remodeled residential structure. Naturally there were toll gates at intervals all along the way. The plank roads were an improvement but were far from satisfactory. A few years after they were constructed the toll companies adopted the Canadian practice of filling and grading the roads with gravel. Toll roads remained in existence in a few instances until 1895 when their franchises were bought up and they were taken over by the city.

Detroit began to get the benefit of railroad transportation almost as early as it got highways and for several years the railroads were vastly superior as a means of getting around. The first lines were state owned and financed, a situation which led to considerable confusion and loss to the taxpayers. Nevertheless, the state got them going and kept them going—at least occasionally—until 1846 when private interests took them over.

The first line out of Detroit was the Detroit and Pontiac Railway which began operation on May 19, 1838, with twelve miles of track completed to the vicinity of Royal Oak. The cars were drawn by horses for the first year, but in 1839 a steam locomotive was obtained. The line ran out Dequindre on the same right-of-way the Grand Trunk uses today. The original depot was at Dequindre and Jefferson, but it was soon moved to Gratiot and Farmer, the line being extended from Dequindre to Gratiot. The site of the station is across the street from the J. L. Hudson store. Behind the depot facing Campus Martius on the approximate site of the old Detroit Opera House, was Andrews' Railroad Hotel which was connected with the station.

East side residents opposed having the rails on Gratiot with trains running past their homes, spewing sparks, and scaring their horses and cows. One dark night a group of irate citizens tore up the track, for which twelve of them went to jail. But the protests were too strong to be ignored and in 1852 the route was changed. The trains ran from Dequindre to Atwater and then east to Brush street where a new depot was built. That venerable structure still stands and handles north side commuter as well as Canadian National traffic today. The Detroit and Pontiac gradually reached out to Pontiac and eventually to Grand Haven where it had car ferry connections with Milwaukee. Its name was changed to the Detroit and Milwaukee, and ultimately it became part of the Grand Trunk system.

The Michigan Central was the second railroad. Organized in 1837 as the Detroit and St. Joseph, it began op-

erations in 1838 when the line was completed to Dearborn
and then to Ypsilanti. Kalamazoo was not reached until
1846. That same year track was laid through to New Buffalo on Lake Michigan and ferry service was available from
there to Chicago. The Michigan Central finally entered
Chicago in 1852.

The Michigan Central line ran down Michigan avenue to Griswold street. Its first depot was on the site later
occupied by the City Hall (now Kennedy Square). A spur
track was extended down Woodward to Atwater to serve
the businesses in that area. However, the citizens objected
to the nuisance, just as they did to the Detroit and Pontiac
on Gratiot, and in 1848 a new depot was built near the foot
of Third street. It or a later adjacent terminal was used
until 1913 when the present station at Fourteenth and Vernor was built. The Third street buildings were destroyed by
a series of fires, the last one in 1966 sweeping out of existence the old freight house which stood approximately
where the first depot was built.

The great desire of the people of Detroit during the
1840s and 1850s, particularly the business community, was
for closer connections with the East. The Michigan Central
built and operated a fleet of luxurious lake steamers which
carried passengers and freight between Detroit, Cleveland,
and Buffalo. But with the winter shutdown of lake navigation, the fleet was useless. So in 1854, partly with the help
of Detroit capital, the Great Western Railroad was built
across the lower Ontario peninsula with its western terminus
at Windsor. That opened the East and a traveler from Chicago using the Michigan Central could make connections
on the Great Western to the Niagara River where he could
board the New York Central for Albany and New York.
Unfortunately, the Great Western's gauge was different
from that used in the United States and for several years it

could not handle American cars. Partly for that reason a new line, the Chicago and Canada Southern, was built in 1873 and became part of the New York Central-Michigan Central systems. In 1882 the Great Western was taken over by the Grand Trunk Western system. For many years through passengers and freight were carried across the Detroit River on car ferries—the Canadian National still operates some—but in 1910 the railroad tunnel under the river was completed. After that there was no interruption to fast through service.

Other lines were built into Detroit later. Among the more important were the Wabash, Pere Marquette, and Pennsylvania. They used the Fort street or Union Depot at Fort and Third which was built in 1893.

No record of local transportation would be complete without mention of the better known steamship lines which operated out of Detroit and have, alas, vanished into the same limbo of forgotten things as the horse and buggy. The most famous of the steamship companies must be the Detroit & Cleveland Steam Navigation Company which operated a fleet of fast and luxurious side-wheelers between Detroit, Buffalo, Cleveland, Mackinac Island, and way ports. Organized in 1850, the D. & C. lines with their Detroit terminal at the foot of Third street led the world in freshwater service. The great black-hulled vessels were in reality floating hotels, and their overnight service to Buffalo was an experience in convenience and pleasant living. In their later years of operation it was possible for the tourist to put his car aboard at a low cost. That was when the roads across Canada left something to be desired. The D. & C. gave up the ghost in 1950, the victim of a combination of the automobile, good highways, air service, and the high cost of operation, due in large part to labor union requirements.

The Ashley-Dustin line was a contemporary of the
D. & C., also dating from the 1850s, although its antecedents could perhaps be traced back even further. It, too,
operated famous vessels—the *Put-in-Bay* and the *Frank E.
Kirby* particularly. The line connected with Sandusky and
the Lake Erie islands, hauling both passengers and freight.

Another line dear to Detroiters was the White Star
which ran such swift and graceful ships as the *Tashmoo,
Waketa, Greyhound,* and *City of Toledo.* Established in
1873, it served the ports from Detroit north to Port Huron
and south to Toledo, with stops at such once famous recreational and vacation spots as the St. Clair River flats, Tashmoo Park, and Hickory and Sugar Islands. The Ashley-
Dustin and White Star Lines succumbed to the same malady
as the D. & C. and at about the same time. The White Star
gave up in 1933; the Ashley-Dustin a few years later.

Getting back and forth to Windsor was always a
problem and ferry service of sorts, usually consisting of a
canoe or rowboat, was available from the earliest times.
Later, steam ferries went into service and in the 1850s,
through a series of mergers and consolidations, the Detroit,
Belle Isle & Windsor Ferry Company emerged. With departures at ten-minute intervals from the foot of Woodward avenue, a nickel (later a dime) would buy an international trip. Until the first Belle Isle bridge was built in
1889, the ferry was the most popular way to reach the
island park. For many years riding the Belle Isle ferry was
a favorite Detroit pastime. One could go aboard in the
morning and ride back and forth all day for ten cents.
During the warm summer days mothers would pack a picnic
basket, take the children and ride all afternoon. Then dad
would appear on the dock after leaving his downtown office,
join the family, and enjoy the basket supper during a few
more turns up and down the river. The Detroit, Belle Isle

& Windsor service was discontinued about the time of World War II when the line was no longer able to compete with the Detroit and Windsor vehicular tunnel, completed in 1930, and the Ambassador Bridge, opened in 1929. With the exception of a single excursion line still running to Bob-Lo (Bois Blanc), a downriver amusement park, and a single cruise ship, Detroiters these days have to own and navigate their own craft to enjoy the river. It might be added that thousands do exactly that.

It would be expected that the Great Lakes shipping activity centered in Detroit would naturally be complemented by drydocks, shipyards, boiler and engine works, and ship suppliers and chandlers. It was. There were several firms in each of these categories and the east side waterfront in the neighborhood of Hastings and Orleans streets was lined with yards and shops. Perhaps the outstanding shipbuilder and repairer was the Detroit Dry Dock Company founded in 1852. Its drydock, a huge affair, was at the foot of Orleans and the company later acquired another yard in Wyandotte. Detroit Dry Dock built some of the most notable freight and passenger steamers on the lakes. Today's shipyards are more concerned with servicing and repair than with shipbuilding. The major yards and drydocks are now located downriver near the mouth of the River Rouge.

The Money Men

Industry and commerce require a financial base and that is something Detroit was a long time getting. All during the French and British regimes hard money was a rare commodity; most trade was by barter or, in the case of the bigger merchants, on credit with Montreal, Albany or New York factors. In the first years after the American takeover there was still very little specie around. Bank notes, most of them issued by eastern institutions, were viewed with suspicion. Currency of a sort was devised by Detroit merchants, consisting of signed slips of paper with the denominations of a few cents to a few dollars written in. Sometimes they were good, frequently they were worthless, and there was always the danger of counterfeiting, an art which flourished. However, they were all the town had. A bank, it was felt, was sorely needed.

In 1806 a group of fast-talking promoters from Boston came to town and persuaded the governor and judges to grant them a charter for a bank. Their request was approved despite the fact that the governor and judges had no legal authority to do so. Anyway, the Detroit Bank opened for business in a brick building it constructed at the northwest corner of Jefferson and Randolph. Today the location is a parking lot behind the City-County building where the mayor and lesser municipal dignitaries park their automobiles. The public never has had much use of the site even when it was occupied by a bank. As fast as deposits were made, the hard money was carted off to Boston and replaced by paper money of little or no value. The bank lasted two years and Boston won every round. For a long time after that Detroiters were skeptical of banks and kept their money under their mattresses.

The next attempt at a bank was in 1818 when the Bank of Michigan was lawfully chartered. It occupied the old Detroit Bank building until 1831 when it moved to a building on the south side of Jefferson near Woodward. In 1836 the Bank moved to a new building at the southwest corner of Griswold and Jefferson. This structure was the first in Detroit to be built of dressed stone. It did the best it could, served the community reasonably well, and then went out of business in 1842, but without loss to its depositors. Since then Detroit has had a whole directory full of banks, some good and some not so good. In the former category was the Detroit Savings Fund Institute established in 1849 at the northeast corner of Griswold and Woodbridge, now part of the Civic Center. After a few years it changed its name to the Detroit Savings Bank and thrives today, Michigan's oldest banking institution, as the Detroit Bank & Trust Company. Its present main office at Fort and Cass sits on what was once Fort Lernoult.

Today Detroit banks are included among the largest in the nation, but generally speaking and with two or three important exceptions, the present banking structure dates from the depression of the 1930s when new banks were organized to replace others closed by government edict.

Heavy Industry

Detroit always had its sawmills, but it was never a lumber town in the sense that Saginaw, Bay City, Muskegon, and other Michigan cities were. There was little actual lumbering around Detroit; in fact, even before the Civil War cordwood had to be imported from other areas of Michigan and from Canada. Nevertheless, much Detroit capital went into the lumbering industry and the city acquired its share of sawdust millionaires. These included such well-known names as Alger, Newberry, Murphy, Cutler, Ward, Whitney, and Stevens. Most of these men along with others who amassed substantial fortunes from lumbering were engaged in other enterprises also, and it was their capital which helped finance much of the local industry in the latter part of the 19th century, as well as the automobile industry in the early 20th.

The availability of good hardwood in Michigan, however, did lead to a flourishing woodworking industry or businesses in which wood and skilled woodworkers were required. Wagon and carriage building was one, and of course shipbuilding was another. Furniture was also made in Detroit, but like carriage building, the industry was not extensive here. However, the carriage and wagon business, even if comparatively small, employed a number of highly skilled workmen whose craftmanship proved valuable and essential when the making of automobile bodies, frames, and wheels began.

Detroit's first real heavy industry was the manufacture of railroad cars, wheels, and other equipment. It had its beginning around 1840. At that time there were no rail connections beyond the state's borders and most of what Michigan needed in the form of rolling stock and equipment it had to produce itself. Along with rail equipment shops, a number of foundries and machine and boiler works sprang up, furnishing boilers and engines for the new mining industries, sawmills, and ships.

A physician, Dr. George B. Russel, provided the first major impetus to railroad equipment manufacturing in 1853 when he organized a company which became the Detroit Car & Manufacturing Company. Starting with a small plant on Gratiot, operations soon expanded to larger shops at the foot of Beaubien and then on Monroe street. Competitors entered the field, such as the Michigan Car Company in 1865 and the Peninsular Car Works in 1885. In 1892 several of these concerns merged, including the Russel interests and Michigan Car, and in 1899 they were taken over by the American Car & Foundry Company.

In 1871 George Pullman bought a plant in the area bounded by Monroe, St. Aubin, Macomb, and the railroad, and for eight years Detroit was the main center for the manufacture of the Pullman sleeping car. In 1879 chief operations were moved to Chicago, but cars continued to be built here until 1893. In 1868 Detroiter William Davis invented the refrigerator car and interested local meat packer George H. Hammond who provided him with capital. An enterprising man, Hammond also founded the Hammond-Standish Company which became the largest meat packer in Michigan. The first shipment by refrigerator car was made from Detroit to Boston in 1869, and Detroit gained a new industry and a couple of new millionaires. These industries naturally encouraged other inventions and many new railroading ideas and improvements of a mechanical nature came out of the Detroit shops. Not the least of these was the railroad track cleaner and snow plow, the invention of Augustus Day.

Railroad equipment and other metal products which rolled out of Detroit factories in increasing quantities required a basic metals industry which Detroit was quick to provide. Behind this local enterprise was the figure of a most remarkable man—a real giant of industry. He was Eber Brock Ward, born in 1811 in Ontario of Vermont stock. The Ward family settled at Marine City soon after the War of 1812 and when Eber was about twelve or thirteen years old he shipped as a cabin boy and deck hand on the river trading schooner of his uncle Captain Sam Ward. Through shrewdness and hard work Eber Brock Ward prospered and became one of the developers of Michigan industry. His interests were broad. They included the ownership of timber and ore lands, newspapers, railroads, steamship and insurance companies, glass manufacturing, and banking. He was one of the promoters of the Soo canal and one of the first to take advantage of it.

With a group of local financiers Ward organized the Eureka Iron and Steel Works in 1853 on a 2,200-acre site in Wyandotte. There a big furnace and a tremendous plant were erected. It was an ideal location: northern ore and limestone could be brought in cheaply by water—mostly in Ward's bottoms; extensive beech forests were nearby to supply the charcoal with which most steel was then made; and it was close to a growing market which eventually became nationwide. It was in the Eureka furnace in 1864 that the first commercial steel was produced in the United States by the Bessemer process.

The company prospered and Ward prospered with it. He was probably Detroit's richest man and its first millionaire. He lived in a palatial home at Fort and Nineteenth (now Ste. Anne) streets, then a suburban area. After his death the Ward house was taken over by the Catholic diocese and became the House of the Good Shepherd. Long a familiar west side landmark, it stood until comparatively recent years.

After Ward's death in 1875 the officers of Eureka seemed to lose their nerve. The use of charcoal in steel production gave way to coke which was more easily available close to the eastern and Illinois coal fields, a depression discouraged company officials and stockholders from modernizing the plant, and ultimately the business petered out. In the early 1890s the Eureka works were razed except for part of the furnace and the administration building. They remained for many years as a reminder of how close the Detroit area came to being the steel producing center of the United States.

Less spectacular than Ward's iron and steel operations, but in the long run more durable, were the fairly extensive copper and brass industries. Necessitated to a large extent by steamship and logging engine manufacture, copper and brass became important factors in the local economy in the 1850s and continued to be to the present. Under the impetus of the automobile industry iron and steel have made a comeback and local production is substantial. The Ford Motor Company built its own furnaces and foundries at its Rouge plant. Other huge works at River Rouge, Ecorse, and Detroit, most of them divisions of national steel corporations, supply the local market and again make Detroit a major steel producer.

Paints and Pills

Other important industries established about the time of the Civil War included paints and varnish, tobacco, drugs and chemicals, stoves and shoes. Why Detroit became a center for paint manufacturing is difficult to explain, but it did. Possibly shipbuilding, furniture making, and woodworking had something to do with it; certainly the Civil War era of Midwest expansion and settlement caused thousands of new city homes, farmhouses, and barns to be built, and they had to be painted. Perhaps, though, the best explanation is that men with a knowledge of paint-making settled in Detroit and went into business. The two Berry brothers were the first. They opened a small shop in 1858 and mixed their first batch of paint in a thirty-gallon vat.

Soon their production had increased many-fold and their paints and varnishes were sold all over the world. Many Detroiters now living have fond recollections of Berry Brothers as the kindly firm which as an advertising gimmick gave away to small boys highly-varnished wooden wagons with high sides and red wheels. They were as familiar on the streets then as the Hondas and hot rods of today, and much safer.

Other well-known paint concerns established in the 1860s and '70s were Boydell Brothers, Detroit White Lead Works, and Acme White Lead and Color Works. Some of these companies are still producing under different names or as divisions of larger corporations which have absorbed them. In time the automobile industry increased Detroit's importance as a paint and finish producing center.

Along with paint, Detroit shops turned out large quantities of soap. Probably the best-known was the Queen Anne soap advertised by a huge sign on the east side waterfront, for years a local landmark. Queen Anne wrappers could be redeemed and a store full of choice merchandise was long maintained by the company on lower Woodward near the river.

Of great importance to Detroit's economic past and present was the drug and pharmaceutical industry which gained a firm foothold here. The manufacture of drugs was the outgrowth of backroom activity in some local drug stores where the pharmacists of the day rolled their pills and concocted their own tonics and ointments. There was a great demand for these products; physicians were neither numerous nor proficient, particularly in the rural communities, and people had to doctor themselves and their livestock. The result was not only drug manufacturing, but a large wholesale drug business also.

As an industry it started in 1845 when Jacob Farrand began to make pills in his combination drug and grocery store on Woodward near Jefferson. Eventually he expanded and as Farrand, Williams & Company became one of the Midwest's leading wholesale drug firms. The company continued in business until a few years ago.

In 1865 Frederick Stearns opened a drug store on Jefferson near Brush street and before long was doing a substantial business in the manufacture of not only regular pharmaceuticals, but also so-called patent medicines, toothpaste, perfume and other toilet articles. After outgrowing several plants Stearns built a large factory and laboratory on East Jefferson at Bellevue. Stearns became immensely wealthy and is still remembered for his generous support of the arts. The Frederick Stearns Company was merged with a national drug firm in 1947. The Jefferson avenue plant, now a health clinic, still stands.

The bright star in Detroit's pharmaceutical diadem is Parke, Davis & Company which dates back to 1867. It was founded by Dr. Samuel Duffield, a member of a distinguished local family. His father the Reverend George Duffield was minister of the First Presbyterian Church for thirty-one years. Dr. Duffield began making drugs over a drug store at Cass and Henry and the building soon was taken over completely as a factory. Duffield was joined by two partners, Hervey C. Parke and George S. Davis. Then he withdrew from the management and the firm became Parke, Davis & Company. In 1873 a new location was selected on the river near the foot of Joseph Campau, a site the company's greatly expanded plant still occupies. With branches all over the world, Parke, Davis & Company is one of the leaders in the drug field and one of Detroit's best known as well as one of its oldest businesses.

Some druggists went in different directions. Theodore Eaton, for instance, entered the wholesale drug business in 1855 and then branched into the field of chemicals which the company still produces. James Vernor, on the other hand, liked to mix soft drinks in his drug store and concocted a ginger ale. As a result the ginger ale business soon overshadowed the drug store and for a century Vernor's ginger ale has been a household item enjoyed by generations of children and adults. The business remained in the Vernor family, which held the formula for the beverage as a closely-guarded secert, until 1966 when it was sold to a national bottling company.

The Warming Spot

Long before Detroit put the world on wheels it was warming the nation's backsides and keeping its coffee hot. For years the city was the world's foremost manufacturer of stoves and kitchen ranges.

The industry started about 1830. At that time most stoves were made at either Albany or Troy, New York. When a cast-iron part of a stove broke, or did whatever it was that made stoves inoperable, a new part had to be ordered from the East. That was time consuming, inconvenient, and in winter resulted in cold feet and other portions of the anatomy. The Hydraulic Iron Works in Detroit got the idea of making parts for the local market and was successful enough to branch out into the production of complete stoves. A young lad from Brooklyn, Jeremiah Dwyer got a job as an apprentice with Hydraulic and after a while decided he wanted to learn more about the business. He spent a few years in an Albany stove works, then returned to Detroit in 1861 and set up his own business. He did well and three years later, Charles A. Ducharme and George Barbour, well-known names in Detroit industry, put up the necessary capital, and Dwyer's small operation became the Detroit Stove Works and in 1871 the Michigan Stove Company. Other companies, notably the Pensinular Stove Company, also entered the field in the 1870s and '80s, and for fifty years or more stove manufacturing was Detroit's leading industry.

The Michigan Stove Company was probably the best known. Its plant on the south side of Jefferson at Adair was familiar to every Detroiter as the home of the Garland range. The location became a landmark because on the property there stood a huge model of a Garland range as large as a house. It was built originally for display at the Chicago Columbian Exposition of 1893. After the fair closed the stove was brought back to Detroit where it became a must for sightseers as an industrial wonder of the world. No visitor to Detroit did right by his friends and family back home unless he sent them a picture postcard of the "Detroit stove." In 1927 the stove was moved to a pedestal near the Belle Isle bridge, but several years later progress of some sort demanded the land upon which it stood. The announcement that it would be torn down was answered by roars of outraged public fury. So the stove was moved to the Michigan State Fairgrounds in 1965 and there it stands as a permanent monument to one of Detroit's first great manufacturing industries, warming the hearts if not the rumps of the people of the city.

As is so often the case, the vigor of the stove industry died when its founders died. Central heating and modern kitchen equipment—fields invaded by the automotive and big electric appliance companies—offered competition which the old concerns were too tired to meet. The Detroit-Michigan Stove Company ceased production in 1957. Only one of the pioneers the Peninsular remains.

Weed and Seed

There is an affinity between a red-hot stove and a well-aimed squirt of tobacco juice, so it must be considered inevitable that when Detroit began to make stoves, it also had to make the other ingredient of a soul-satisfying sizzle. Although Detroit did (and still does) roll a lot of cigars, the basic product was pipe tobacco, and even more basic, good old fashioned "eatin' " tobacco. It was not until about the time of World War I that a "he man" would be caught dead smoking a cigarette. Tobacco chewing was one of life's comforts. Men laboring in factories or lumber camps had no time to keep lighting pipes, and besides, smoking was usually a forbidden hazard. Pipes were for swells, or for a quiet hour of contemplation on the front porch of a summer evening, or down behind the furnace in the cold of winter. Cigars were too expensive for the ordinary working man; they were only to celebrate births, weddings or elections. But a man could literally get his teeth into a cheek-swelling chaw, and it would carry him through a long ten-hour day at the mill, with no greater problem than what to do with it when its final succulence had been extracted. One had to be careful where he stepped in those days.

So the production of tobacco products, particularly chewing tobacco, became one of Detroit's early leading industries. There were several firms, but two men in particular made their marks in the field. One was John J. Bagley; the other was Daniel Scotten. Both served apprenticeships in the first tobacco business established in Detroit in 1840 by George Miller who had a store and factory on the west side of Woodward just below Jefferson. Dan Scotten and his brother Oren went into business for themselves in 1856, their most famous product being Hiawatha, a chewing tobacco. Bagley started three years earlier, and made and sold a toothsome delight known as Mayflower which kept the jaws of his customers working all over the United States. Both Bagley and Scotten were astute businessmen. Scotten proved his shrewdness just before the outbreak of the Civil War. With all the capital and credit he could lay hands on he bought southern tobacco until his warehouse bulged. Bagley became a leader in philanthropic activities and was twice elected governor of Michigan. That was in the 1870s. Had women then had the vote he probably could not have been elected dog catcher. Dan Scotten loved the good things of life and in 1888 built the Cadillac Hotel at Michigan and Washington. Rebuilt in the 1920s, that famous hostelry became the Book-Cadillac and then the Sheraton-Cadillac.

No account of Detroit's business activity would be complete without reference to the seed industry which was established largely by Dexter M. Ferry who supplied the entire nation with everything from onions to nasturtiums. His packets of seeds, grown on his own seed farms in or on the outskirts of Detroit, made farms and gardens bloom all across the land. Ferry came to Detroit from Rochester, New York, in 1852 and found work as a clerk in a book and stationery store. In 1867 he entered the seed business, taking over the small concern of Miles T. Gardner who operated a farm and nursery on Michigan road near Eloise. Ferry established his own farm of three hundred acres at Grand

River and what is now West Grand boulevard, the land on which Northwestern High School now stands. He also built a large warehouse and office building on downtown Brush street between Lafayette and Monroe. This building was completely destroyed in 1886 by one of the city's most spectacular fires. It was rebuilt, however, and the structure still stands, used for storage and office purposes. In later years D. M. Ferry & Company acquired a new and larger farm near Rochester, Michigan, and as the result of a merger, the firm became the Ferry, Morse Seed Company. After World War II most of its operations were transferred to California. Ferry and his son were and other members of the family continue to be leaders in the community's business, philanthropic, and social life.

For a while toward the end of the last century Detroit gave promise of becoming an important shoe manufacturing center. But the most important company in the field was built largely by the drive and genius of one man —Hazen S. Pingree. When he died the industry locally pretty much died with him.

There were two important shoe companies in Detroit prior to Pingree's entering the business. They did some custom shoemaking but were chiefly wholesalers and retailers. The earliest was the pre-Civil War firm of Henry P. Baldwin who not only was a successful business leader, but also was twice elected governor of Michigan. The other was the company of Richard H. Fyfe. An employee of Baldwin, Fyfe branched out for himself and opened a store on Woodward avenue. In 1918 the R. H. Fyfe Company erected a tall building at the northwest corner of Adams and Woodward facing Grand Circus Park. It was hailed as the largest shoe store in the world. In 1965 the upper part of the building was remodeled into luxury apartments while the R. H. Fyfe Company continued to do business on the ground floor. Today Fyfe's is one of Detroit's oldest firms.

Pingree, who became more important himself to Detroit than his shoe business, was a native of Maine, a typical down-east Yankee. At twenty-two he enlisted in the Union army and was in several major Civil War battles. Captured by Mosby's Raiders, he was imprisoned at Andersonville. There he met several Michigan men who were so loud in their praises of their state that Pingree decided to make Detroit his home. Upon release from Andersonville he came to Detroit, found employment as a cobbler with Fyfe and Baldwin, and in 1866 opened his own factory in partnership with Charles A. Smith. Before long their plant at Woodbridge and Griswold employed more than seven hundred people, many of them women. Until a few years ago, long after the company had gone out of business, there was an association of elderly women, former employees, who proudly bore the name of the Pingree Girls. More will be heard about Hazen S. Pingree in another part of the Detroit story.

9

The Old Home Town

Where Life was Worth Living

By the time the Gay Nineties rolled around Detroit had lost most of its small town characteristics and had become a real city, big and bustling, and with a charm that, unfortunately, has all but disappeared. The population had increased to 206,000; the boundaries had been pushed out north, east, and west as the new residential sections were planted in what only a short time before had been corn fields and wood lots. Huge elm, maple, and chestnut trees shaded the streets, and gracious homes, most of them frame and painted either white or dark green, gave the newer residential areas an air of comfort and well-being. The Board of Commerce coined a new municipal slogan, "Detroit, where life is worth living," which was not far wrong. City boosters sagely predicted that almost any time now Detroit would surpass Cleveland in population and wealth.

All the tools of civilization were available. Omnibuses, private carriages, and even shank's mare had given way in 1863 to the first horse-drawn streetcars on Jefferson between Dequindre and Third. Soon there was a network of lines and in 1893 the first electric streetcar clanged its

way out Woodward. Shortly thereafter high-speed interurban lines began to connect Detroit and other Michigan
and Ohio towns. The interurban terminal long stood on
Bates street just south of Jefferson. The telegraph had
reached Detroit in 1847, the first line running to Ypsilanti.
The local telegraph office then was in the rear of a building
at the northeast corner of Jefferson and Cass. The telephone
came in 1878; the first exchange was in the basement of a
building on Griswold near Jefferson. As the number of subscribers increased, the telephone company erected a building on Clifford at Washington. In 1966 it was remodeled
into a luxury apartment house. The present Michigan Bell
offices at Cass and State street were built in 1918.

Detroit's streets were first lighted by gas in 1851;
electric street lighting began in 1884. That year seventy-
two towers, 104 to 150 feet high and carrying powerful
arc lights, were erected throughout the city. These stood
until 1918 when the last one at Ferry and St. Aubin was
taken down. Those towers were not very effective, but they
were spectacular. It was an awesome sight to watch a daring man ascend to the top in a little bosun's chair elevator
to clean the lamps.

Homes and other private buildings began to be
lighted by gas soon after 1851, the Detroit Gas Light Company being the supplier. A short time later a rival company
was organized, and the Detroit Gas Light Company was
given the west side of the city as its exclusive territory. The
Mutual Gaslight Company was given the east side. The two
companies merged in 1893, thus establishing what is now
the Michigan Consolidated Gas Company. The first gas
works were on Woodbridge between Fifth and Sixth.

Electricity for home lighting began in 1893. The
present Detroit Edison Company was incorporated in 1903,
although its predecessor, the Edison Illuminating Company,

had been operating for several years prior to that. The first Edison office and generating plant was on Washington at State. In that building, still used as a branch office, a young stationary engineer was employed at the turn of the century. His name was Henry Ford. The public was first supplied with water by private companies, beginning in 1825. The city took over the waterworks in 1836, and in 1853 the Board of Water Commissioners was created and has operated the system ever since.

The first paving in Detroit was cobblestone, laid in 1825 on Jefferson. Later there were more cobblestone streets, and then brick was used extensively. But most of the streets, both business and residential, were paved with round cedar blocks. They were quiet and aromatic, and reasonably satisfactory on residential streets, although they had a tendency to float away in a heavy rainstorm. About 1892 asphalt began to come into use, but it was not until about the time of World War I that it covered most streets. Sidewalks of this era were usually ten-inch boards, laid on stringers set on a cinder base. They were rough on youngsters' bare feet and no good at all for roller skating. They began to give way to cement in the early 1900s.

Gradually over the years Detroit acquired other refinements of a civilized society. One of these was a City Hall where politicians roosted inside and pigeons outside, and the taxpayers were in jeopardy coming or going. Detroit's first City Hall was built in 1835 on the east side of Woodward at Cadillac Square. Behind it was the public market; in fact, the first floor of the City Hall was occupied for many years by hucksters' stalls. Prior to its construction the mayor and council met wherever they could find a place—in the Council House, in old military buildings adjoining the fort, in taverns or the back rooms of stores.

The growth of the city eventually outmoded the

215

first City Hall, and something more spacious and elegant was needed. Plans for a new one were discussed beginning about 1860, and building might have started then had not the Civil War interrupted public works of that nature. As it was, Detroit had to wait "until the boys came home." The site selected for the new City Hall was directly across Woodward from the old one, on the parcel of land bounded by Woodward, Fort, Griswold, and Michigan, a part of the old military reserve. There, it will be recalled, stood the Female Seminary and the Michigan Central Depot in earlier days.

The new building was completed and occupied in 1871, with the mayor, aldermen and other dignitaries, impressive in their high hats and their whiskers combed for the occasion, parading solemnly across Woodward to take possession of the new citadel of public virtue and justice. (Or so the guidebooks described it.) There immediately arose a great hulabaloo about what to do with the Old City Hall. One faction wanted to convert it into a public library. But there were stronger voices from the veterans of Antietam, Gettysburg, and Chickamauga. Money had already been subscribed for a war memorial and the foundations for it had been laid in east Grand Circus Park. But why, people asked with admirable second thought, put it so far out in the fields? Why not in front of the brand new City Hall? Reason prevailed as it invariably does if the lobby is strong enough; the foundations were dug up and transplanted in Woodward avenue. In 1872 the Soldiers' and Sailors' Monument, designed by Randolph Rogers of Ann Arbor and Rome, was unveiled. With that noble pile of granite and bronze hurling eternal defiance at the late Confederacy and assuring one and all that the South would not rise again, the Old City Hall looked pretty dowdy. A full view of the monument was obstructed, so down it came.

The new City Hall across the street was a thing of beauty in the eyes of Detroiters and a wonder to behold. It was big and imposing, and was surmounted by a high clock tower which on occasion tolled the right time. For many years the tower was used by the fire department as a fire watch station. The building's picture appeared on postcards, souvenir plates, spoons, and pillows, and its image was seen around the world. The first place visitors to the city were taken was downtown to see the City Hall. Their hosts were offended if their guests were not overwhelmed by the grandeur of the building. Actually, it was an impressive structure, made more so in 1884 when four statues were placed in corner niches. Donated by Bela Hubbard and the work of the celebrated sculptor Julius T. Melchers, they depicted Cadillac and La Salle, and Fathers Richard and Marquette.

In 1957 the city fathers finally abandoned the City Hall in favor of more luxurious surroundings in the new City-County building at Woodward and Jefferson. For the next several years public controversy again raged about what to do with the Old City Hall, but in the end it went down in a cloud of dust under the wrecker's ball. The name of the site was changed from City Hall Square to John F. Kennedy Square. In the early months of 1967 an underground parking garage was completed and the surface was in the process of being landscaped and beautified. The four corner statues were salvaged, and after lying on a scrap heap at Fort Wayne, were given to the University of Detroit which planned to reerect them on the campus at West Six Mile and Livernois.

When the city offices were moved into the new City-County building they were joined by the county offices and courts. Detroit was a long time getting a courthouse. Like the municipal officers, the judges originally met wherever

217

they could find a place to sit and accommodate a few lawyers and litigants. Sessions of the courts were held at various times in the Council House, private homes, hotels, and spare chambers in the City Hall. There even is a record of sessions being held out of doors under the trees in good weather. One early city directory notes that "places in the city of Detroit where these Courts are held are subject to change at the convenience of the Justices." Justice, one may assume, was sometimes obliged to slip her blindfold in order to find out where she was expected to appear.

In 1845, however, a courthouse was built at the southeast corner of Griswold and Congress streets, a site now occupied by the towering Guardian building. It remained in use until 1872 when it was torn down and the courts and county offices were given space in the then new City Hall. The county, however, had to have more room, and in 1895 a block was purchased at the east end of Cadillac Square, facing at a distance the City Hall. The boundary streets are Randolph, Brush, Congress, and East Fort. Construction was started in 1896 and the Wayne County building was occupied in 1902. It was (and is) an imposing structure of better than average "courthouse" architecture. The interior of the five-story building was done in a dozen varieties of foreign and domestic marble, and fine examples of woodwork went into embellishing the courtrooms. Now possessing a slightly down-at-the-heels appearance, the Old County building as it is now called houses the Detroit Traffic Court and some administrative departments which could not be squeezed into the new City-County building.

Every self-respecting city has to have a post office and Detroit is nothing if not self-respecting. It has had a dozen or more over the years. Prior to 1860 the location changed each time a new postmaster was appointed. Nobody knows where the first two were located. In 1806 James

Abbott was made postmaster and kept the post office in a log building he used as a storehouse at the southwest corner of Woodward and Woodbridge. After 1831 when Abbott turned in his mail pouches the offices were at various places along Jefferson in the present Civic Center area. In 1849 quarters were found on the first floor of Mariners' Church. As noted above, in 1860 a new building was put up by the United States government at the northwest corner of Griswold and Larned. This was Detroit's first Federal building. It also housed the United States district court, the marshal, and the collector of customs. It served until 1897 when a new Federal building was raised in the block bounded by Fort, Shelby, Wayne (now Washington), and Lafayette. That site was once occupied by Fort Lernoult. This second post office and federal building was razed in 1930 and replaced by a modern structure at the same location. It in turn continued to be the main post office until 1961 when a new one designed for the age of automation was built farther out Fort street at Eighth. The downtown office now has only branch status, but the building continues to house the federal courts and other offices. Not for long, however. Plans are well advanced for the construction of a new federal courthouse on urban renewal land in the vicinity of Michigan and First.

The Merchant Princes

Victorian-era Detroit witnessed another phenomenon experienced by many large American cities. This was

the emergence of the merchant princes and their establishment of the big department stores. The first one in Detroit
was Christopher R. Mabley who started in a small way in
Pontiac. Aware of greater opportunities in Detroit, he
moved here in 1870 and opened a clothing store on the
east side of Woodward about mid-block between Congress
and Cadillac Square. The site would be just a few doors
south of the present First National building. Mabley combined the talents of showman, gambler and merchandiser,
and resorted to such unheard of practices as buying a full-
page ad in a local newspaper to tell about his bargains.
This was the first time such an ad had ever been placed
in a newspaper and the idea was almost more than local
journalistic enterprise could cope with. It took several meetings, much strong language on the part of Mabley, and even
the threat of a lawsuit before the advertisement was run.
From men's clothing Mabley branched out into other lines
of merchandise by opening other stores on Woodward. Finally, however, about 1876 he built a new store on his original site and several adjoining lots. There he displayed all
kinds of merchandise from clothing for men and women to
notions and appliances, all under one roof. Thus was Detroit's first department store created. Like many another
great enterprise built by the genius of one man, this one
began to languish after Mabley's death in 1885, although
Mabley stores operated by the Mabley-Goodfellow Company continued to serve Detroit, but on a much smaller
scale, until 1929.

Another of the major department stores, still well-
remembered, was the Newcomb-Endicott Company located
on the east side of Woodward between Gratiot and Grand
River where the J. L. Hudson Company store stands today.
Cyrenius A. Newcomb and Charles E. Endicott formed a
partnership and opened a dry goods store in 1869 in the

Merrill block where the present City-County building is to-day. A year later the partners moved into the Detroit Opera House building facing Campus Martius just off Woodward. Then in 1879 another move was made, this time to the building on Woodward constructed especially for them by D. M. Ferry the seed king. As a minor social note it might be recalled that for delivery service Newcomb-Endicott used a fleet of light horse-drawn panel wagons brightly decorated in red and gold. They were the delight of small boys who, after the first snowfall, would attach their sleds to the rear axle for a fast hitch-ride.

Among all others the Detroit merchant prince to attain the purple was Joseph Lowthian Hudson whose J. L. Hudson Company is today among the nation's leading department stores. English-born, Hudson became, as did his father before him, an employee and limited partner of Mabley stores in Ionia and Pontiac, Michigan. After a first unsuccessful attempt to make it on his own, Hudson moved to Detroit in 1877 as manager of Mabley's clothing department. In 1881 Hudson again struck out for himself, establishing the J. L. Hudson Company in the Opera House building recently vacated by Newcomb-Endicott. Six years later he moved to the Henkel block on the west side of Woodward between Michigan and State. The business remained at that location until 1891 when Hudson moved into his own new building at the corner of Farmer and Gratiot where the First Presbyterian Church had been. The Farmer street corner was the first unit in the entire block the company now occupies. In 1907 additional frontage was taken on Farmer and in 1911 an annex was acquired on Woodward next door to the Newcomb-Endicott store. Then in 1927 Hudson's bought out their neighbor and the huge department store covered the entire block except for a small corner on Woodward at Gratiot, the home of Sallan's jewelry store. That parcel was finally incorporated into the main building in 1946 and the Hudson empire was firmly planted on the entire square bounded by Woodward, Farmer, Gratiot, and Grand River. With the acquisition of Newcomb-Endicott, Hudson's became the third largest department store in the United States, running close behind Macy's in New York and Marshall Field's in Chicago.

The shopper who came downtown on the horse or electric car to visit Mabley's, Newcomb-Endicott or Hudson's had a number of other stores in which to spend his money. After 1893 he could have gone to the People's Outfitting Company or to Partridge's which in 1908 became the Crowley-Milner Company. Beginning in 1897 the Ernst Kern Company was available on Woodward. Kern's was established in 1893 in a small store on St. Antoine near Fort and in 1894 it moved to Randolph street. Three years later Kern opened his store on Woodward at Gratiot. In 1919 a new and larger building was put up on the site where once Seymour Finney's Temperance Hotel stood. Kern's went out of business in 1959 and in 1966 the building was razed in the urban renewal process.

A Walk into the Past

Had the downtown visitor in 1890 started at Jefferson and worked his way north on Woodward, he would have passed many business landmarks, some of which are still there. On the east side of the street was the Merrill block, an office building which gave way to the present

City-County building. Before the Merrill block was built the site was occupied by Smart's Scotch store, a thriving general-store type of enterprise which gave the intersection the name of Smart's Corner by which it was long known. The rest of the block between Jefferson and Larned consisted of small shops, one of which was the jewelry store of Adolph Enggass, a firm which remained in business until about 1965. Across Woodward was Fyfe's shoe store which in time would move to Adams and Woodward. Between Larned and Congress on the east side of Woodward were congregated the offices of the various express companies. Across Congress on the northeast corner was T. B. Rayl's hardware store, later moved to Griswold and State. Next was Mabley's main store, and beyond, on the corner of Cadillac Square stood the Russell House.

The Russell House was Detroit's leading hotel for about half a century. Built in 1857, it replaced the National Hotel on the same site beginning in 1836. The Russell House took the place in the city's life that had been filled earlier by Ben Woodworth's Steamboat Hotel. It was the scene of almost every social and civic event of any importance; among its guests were virtually all the distinguished visitors of the era, including statesmen, theatrical figures, and businessmen. It even entertained royalty; the Prince of Wales, later King Edward VII, was a guest in 1859. The Russell House was replaced in 1907 by the Pontchartrain, probably the most famous of all Detroit hotels. The Pontchartrain bar and grill became the real financial center of the city; it was in that room that much of the infant automobile industry's financing was arranged. The Pontchartrain was torn down in 1920 and replaced by a large office building which housed the First National Bank, and later the National Bank of Detroit until the latter institution moved to its present location across Woodward. So fond were Detroit memories of the old Pontchartrain that when the city's newest hotel was completed in 1965 at Jefferson and Washington, it was the natural thing to name it the Pontchartrain.

Across from the Russell House on Woodward at Fort was the grocery store of G. & R. McMillan which catered to the best families of Detroit for a hundred years. It was a common sight to see the streets on which the store fronted filled with the gleaming carriages in which the grand ladies from Jefferson avenue and north Woodward came downtown to lay in their supplies of choice foods and liquors. Of course these grand dames were accompanied by liveried coachmen and footmen to carry their shopping baskets.

Nearby was the Bagley Memorial Fountain, provided for in the will of J. J. Bagley, built in 1887, and moved in 1925 to its present site in the Campus Martius north of the Soldiers' and Sailors' Monument. It is the only structure designed by famed architect Henry Hobson Richardson remaining in Detroit.

Behind McMillan's on the corner of Fort and Griswold was the ten-story Hammond building erected in 1889. It was Detroit's first skyscraper. Next door on the corner of Griswold and Congress was the Union Trust building. The entire square block is now occupied by the main office of the National Bank of Detroit erected in 1959.

Continuing the march up Woodward at Cadillac Square, across Woodward from the City Hall, was the Soldiers' and Sailors' Monument which has previously been described. Just north of the monument was the Wright, Kay Company, jewelers, in the Coyl building at the northeast corner of Campus Martius. Wright, Kay are still in business, their present store being at Woodward and John R. On the northwest corner of Woodward and Michigan were a couple of nondescript buildings, which in 1896 were replaced by the Majestic building, for many years Detroit's tallest structure. The Majestic building was begun by Mabley-Goodfellow who wanted their store housed in Detroit's most impressive building. But before it was completed Mabley-Goodfellow ran out of money and finishing the job was left to others. The capstone bore the letter M intended to mean Mabley. For the sake of economy the capstone was retained and the name was changed to Majestic. The Majestic building was torn down in 1962 and was replaced by the lofty new headquarters of the First Federal Savings & Loan Association.

Next door to the Majestic building site was the candy and ice cream store of Fred Sanders. He set up business in 1875 on the Majestic building site but moved a few feet north a couple of years later. Sanders made a notable contribution to American culture by inventing the ice cream soda. Still run as a confectionery and baked goods business, the company today operates a chain of stores including that early one on Woodward which still does a thriving trade.

A few doors up the street at the southwest corner of Woodward and State was a comparatively new building dating from 1884. It was where St. Andrew's Hall had been. In 1890 the place was occupied by Heyn's store, but before long it would be taken over by the B. Siegel Company organized in 1881. Siegel's is still there more than seventy-five years later. This distinctive building is one of the oldest on Woodward avenue.

If the thirsty pedestrian required something more robust than a Sanders chocolate soda, all he had to do was cross Woodward to the east side where Kern's later stood. There he would find Churchill's bar, a high-class oasis which catered to an elite clientele. Besides its liquid refreshments, it was known far and wide for the depiction

225

of a voluptuous reclining nude painted by Julius Rolshoven which hung over the bar and now graces the grill room of the Detroit Athletic Club.

Staggering out of Churchill's (which of course no Detroit gentleman ever did), the Woodward avenue perambulator would find himself in the State-Gratiot to Grand River block. East Grand River in those days was Wilcox street. Here he was enticed by the Lorelei of the department stores, Newcomb-Endicott, and on the west side by the Taylor & Woolfenden store. A few years later, becoming Elliott, Taylor & Woolfenden, the firm made a bold move north to the corner of Henry and Woodward, and for the convenience of customers ran an omnibus downtown. The experiment did not work out and E-T-W quietly gave up the ghost in the early 1900s.

Back across Woodward next to Newcomb's and where Hudson's later took over, was Macauley's book store, a place for quiet browsing. Modern Detroit has nothing to compare with it. In an adjoining store later appeared the notions business of Kresge and Wilson established in 1897. A short time later, after Sebastian S. Kresge bought out his partner, the business was moved across Woodward where a wide variety of merchandise was offered in the attractive price range of five to ten cents—"nothing over ten cents." This store, still in operation but considerably enlarged, became number one in the nation-wide Kresge chain.

If a new thirst began to develop about this time, it could have been assuaged in this block in the ice cream and confectionery shop of J. C. Kuhn at the southwest corner of Woodward and Grand River. In later years Kuhn's moved into the old Bell Telephone building at Washington and Clifford, and survived as a tea room until after World War II.

The next block from Grand River to John R. and Clifford was lined with small shops. On the east side, for instance, was that of D. J. Healy who began business as a dyer but branched out into women's clothes. A few doors above was the music store of Grinnell Brothers who in 1967 were still tooting their horn, but in a newer building on the west side of Woodward. On the west side in 1890 was the Keenan & Jahn furniture store which was destroyed by fire in 1894. Most of the employees were trapped inside when the fire started, and while none lost their lives, more than a dozen were scarred and crippled for life.

At the southwest corner of Woodward and Clifford the James Vernor drug store offered pills or a draft of that delectable ginger ale. In the next block between John R.-Clifford and Grand Circus Park were more small shops. One which is still remembered was the A. Hair catering company whose ice cream made life worth living in Detroit or anywhere else it could be obtained. That shop was on the east side of Woodward and a few doors above it on the corner of Witherell was the photographic studio of J. W. Hughes to whom everyone of note went to have his picture taken. The Broderick tower stands there now. Across the street at the corner of Park was the Grand Circus building, since replaced by the David Whitney building which is almost wholly occupied by doctors and dentists.

Of course there were changes on Woodward avenue in the 1890s. Old businesses would fade away and new ones would hang out their signs from year to year. Thus the Woodward avenue scene in the early 1900s had many of the names that were familiar in the previous decade. But new ones had been added and the stroller of a few years later would have seen such stores as Bird's and E. J. Hickey, both of which prospered for a while and then closed up. One which prospered and did not close up was Himelhoch's

227

whose present store next door to the David Whitney building was opened in 1913.

Beyond Grand Circus Park in 1890 was the Central Methodist Church (then called the First Methodist), where the wanderer could drop in for a moment of peace and a short prayer of supplication for the strength to get the rest of the way home. North of Grand Circus Woodward avenue was a tree-shaded street lined with the spacious homes and gardens of the well-to-do.

Just as lower Woodward was the shopping center of Detroit, most business and financial activity in 1890 was carried on along Griswold. Jefferson, long the principal business street, was now becoming a center for wholesale houses. On Griswold were the banks, the office buildings, and the rookeries where the town's leading lawyers corrected the briefs written for them by their eminently respectable young law clerks, many of whom later became equally respectable judges.

On the west side of Griswold north of Jefferson were located the railroad ticket offices and beyond, at the southeast corner of Larned, was the Newberry block. It was eventually replaced by the Norton Hotel. On the site and covering the entire block now stands the Michigan Consolidated Gas Company headquarters. Across Griswold, opposite the Newberry block was the Campau building, one of the deluxe office buildings. One can now park his car on the lot where it stood.

At the northeast corner of Griswold and Larned, opposite the post office, was the Waterman building with a bank on its first floor and offices upstairs. On the other side of Griswold at the corner of Congress was the Buhl building. This structure was replaced in 1925 by the present Buhl building. Griswold between Congress and Fort was lined on both sides by small and unimpressive structures, many of which housed banks and insurance offices. This changed, beginning in 1894 with the erection of the Union Trust building, now the site of the National Bank of Detroit. On the west side of Griswold was a small bank building at the corner of Congress, the site of the present Ford building. Next door at the southwest corner of Griswold and Fort originally stood the home of John Palmer, whose son Thomas became United States senator from Michigan and donated Palmer Park to the city. The Palmer residence gave way to the Moffatt building in 1870 and it in turn was replaced in 1902 by the first Penobscot building. In 1928 the present Penobscot building, Detroit's tallest, was erected on the site.

Continuing up Griswold, at the northwest corner of Fort was the First Baptist Church where the Dime building is now. Next door to it (or more properly directly behind it as the church faced on Fort) at the alley known as Federal court was Sharpe's, a small ramshackle restaurant and saloon famous for its corned beef hash. It was a favorite lunching place for downtown businessmen. When the Dime building was erected in 1911-12, Sharpe's moved across the street into the basement of the Hammond building. At the southwest corner of Griswold and Lafayette were the quarters of the Mechanics' Society, later replaced by the McGraw building. The site is now occupied by bank and title companies. Around the corner from the McGraw building on the south side of Lafayette where the Transportation building (the old home of the *Detroit Free Press*) now stands, were a blacksmith shop and a saloon. Before the Mechanics' Society gave way to the McGraw building, the structure on that site was used as a school or academy for boys operated by Philo Patterson. Most of Detroit's young bluebloods attended the Patterson school in the early 1870s.

Mention has been made of the Hammond building

at Fort and Griswold. Where it stood had been the home of James Abbott whom we have already met as one of the city's early postmasters. But Abbott had another slight claim to fame. His wife was Sarah Whistler, daughter of Captain John Whistler of the United States army who was stationed in Detroit during the War of 1812. Sarah Whistler Abbott was the aunt of the celebrated American artist James Abbott McNeill Whistler. Young Whistler is said to have been a frequent visitor to the Abbott home as a boy.

Some distance farther up Griswold beyond the old Capitol turned high school, at the northwest corner of Grand River was a hotel, the Griswold House famous for its dining room patronized by the theatrical and sporting crowd. It may be said to have been Detroit's first real night spot. In 1914 a group of businessmen gathered there for luncheon and organized themselves into the Kiwanis Club No. 1, thereby founding a service club which has spread all over the world.

Wandering about downtown before the turn of the century had its hazards. Even in the 1890s before the aroma of gasoline fumes perfumed the air, people complained about the traffic. Bicycle scorchers whizzed up and down the avenues, sporting types behind their high-steppers made pedestrians scurry for the sidewalks, and draymen sometimes tried to convey the impression that they owned the streets. The police department organized a bicycle squad, a detail of cops on bikes, to pursue the scorchers. It was one of those cyclized policemen who gained nameless immortality a few years later when he wrote the first violation ticket for a speeder in one of those new-fangled automobiles. Portly gendarmes with handlebar mustaches, frock coats, and coal scuttle helmets were stationed at the main intersections to help women and children to cross the street safely. It would still be a few years before traffic became so bad that young Detroit patrolman William Potts was compelled to invent the nation's first automatic electric traffic signal. It was installed in 1920 at Woodward and Michigan. Potts also is credited with inventing the first radio-equipped police car in 1921.

As the century drew to a close Detroiters began to run fevers over what was happening in Cuba. Indignation boiled over in February 1898 when news was received that the battleship *Maine* had blown up in Havana harbor. War enthusiasm was whipped up and in April the 31st Michigan Infantry (the old Light Guard) marched off to war against Spain to the beat of such lively new tunes as *The Stars and Stripes Forever*, *There'll Be a Hot Time in the Old Town Tonight*, and *Captain Jenks of the Horse Marines*. It really was not much of a war; malaria-carrying mosquitos proved much more deadly than Spaniards. The Michigan Naval Militia composed of young men of the first families had the most fun. They served aboard the cruiser *Yosemite*, and in the years that followed, being a *Yosemite* alumnus was a status symbol in Detroit.

Everything considered, Detroit came of age as a big city in the late 1880s and 1890s, and to impress the world with having attained a state of metropolitan sophistication, it staged a giant exposition. The Detroit International Fair and Exposition was opened in 1889 on seventy acres of ground on West Jefferson. The site was just west of Fort Wayne in the suburb of Delray (annexed to Detroit in 1906). Elaborate buildings dripping with the "gingerbread" so popular in that era were erected; displays, exhibits, and other attractions were put up; a good deal of red, white and blue bunting was draped around; and altogether quite a colorful show was unveiled.

It was intended that the exposition would be a permanent affair; it was to be open for ten days each year.

It lasted until 1893 when the more magnificent Columbian Exposition was opened in Chicago. Detroit learned that people preferred the abdominal gyrations of Little Egypt to more stationary attractions. In 1895 the site was sold to the Solvay Process Company, one of the big chemical concerns which in the long run has done Detroit much more good than the fair.

10

The People's City

On Stage

People always have had fun in Detroit. In the earliest times they made their own entertainment and enjoyed it. There is no record that the theater meant anything to the French; they undoubtedly had no time or interest. The British may have put on amateur shows, but there is no proof they did. It was American army officers who first brought the theater to Detroit, staging their productions in a warehouse in 1816. After that civilian thespians took over and put on performances wherever they could find a place. Ben Woodworth allowed the use of his barn in the 1830s and the City Hall was occasionally used after its construction in 1835. It may be that the City Hall rostrum was the first stage to be used by traveling or road companies. The Detroit historian George B. Catlin tells about an actor named Isaac M. Singer who was performing there in 1849 when news reached the city that Elias Howe had successfully invented a sewing machine.

"If Elias Howe can make a sewing machine, so can I," declared Singer who had been a mechanic back in Connecticut before he turned actor. Singer quit the company, went home to Bridgeport, and soon produced the first Singer sewing machine.

It would require a lot of space to list all the theaters Detroit has had in the past hundred and twenty years. They have been of all kinds and sizes, and were in many locations scattered around the town. The first real theater was opened in 1834 on the second floor of the Smart block where the City-County building is now. That same year a building originally intended to be a Methodist church was converted into a theater. It was at Gratiot and Library where Crowley's department store is today. In 1849 the Metropolitan theater on Jefferson between Randolph and Brush was built. A short time later two more playhouses appeared on the same block, the Varieties and the Comique. For many years thereafter that part of town was Detroit's theatrical district. The three theaters, which were apparently in the same or adjoining buildings, were turned into a livery stable in 1883.

Best known of the old theaters was the Detroit Opera House on Campus Martius a few steps east of Woodward. It was built in 1868, destroyed by fire in 1897, and immediately rebuilt. This was a grand house and it was there that the great performers of the late 1800s and early 1900s appeared. One of its most cherished features was the curtain painted by the Detroit artist Robert Hopkin: an idyllic scene which bore Kingsley's lines,

So fleet the works of men, back to their earth again;
Ancient and holy things fade like a dream.

It was a sad day in 1937 when the old Opera House was remodeled into a department store and the soaring verses

234

of Shakespeare were replaced by the adenoidal tones of bargain hunters. The building was torn down in 1963.

Almost equally well-known was the Lyceum on the east side of Randolph between Monroe and Lafayette. It began life as White's Grand Theater in 1880. White's was burned out in 1886 by the fire that destroyed the D. M. Ferry seed company, but it was immediately rebuilt as the Lyceum. After World War I the name was changed to the New Detroit Opera House which became permanently dark in 1928. The building is still used as a department store.

In 1875 C. J. Whitney built an opera house on Fort street where today's Federal building stands. When the post office was erected there in 1897 Whitney constructed a new house on the east side of Griswold just north of Michigan. Called the Garrick, it ran as a first-class theater until it closed in 1926. The site is now occupied by a drug store and restaurant.

Other popular legitimate theaters included the Washington on Washington boulevard near Clifford, the Shubert-Lafayette on Lafayette at Shelby, and the Cass at Lafayette and Washington. The Washington and Shubert-Lafayette were torn down, and the Cass was recently converted into a motion picture house. With their curtains lowered for the last time, downtown Detroit was left without a regular theater; in fact Detroit's only remaining professional legitimate theater is the Fisher, remodeled in 1963 from a movie palace, in the Fisher building at West Grand boulevard and Second.

Detroit had several vaudeville houses; the best known was the Temple opened in 1901 on Monroe just around the corner from Campus Martius. This was long the home of the Keith circuit and practically all the great vaudeville artists appeared there. The Temple had a regular clientele and in many respects was the city's most popular theater, but the movies dealt it a death blow. It closed in 1935 and was torn down a short time later. The site has since become part of a huge dust bowl awaiting urban redevelopment. Another popular variety house was the Miles, the home of "ten-twent'-thirt'" vaudeville. It was on the east side of Griswold north of State. Today the Griswold building is where the Miles stood.

Burlesque too was popular in Detroit and had its temples. The Avenue was a famous one; it was on lower Woodward in the block now covered by the City-County building. The Gayety on Monroe was famous, as was the Cadillac on Michigan at Washington where the Howard Johnson motor hotel was recently erected.

Closely related to the theaters as places of entertainment were the beer gardens, bath houses, and dance halls. One of the earliest was that of David C. McKinstry. In 1834 he was operating what he called a circus at the northeast corner of Gratiot and Library. This apparently housed a collection of oddities, freaks, and stuffed animals —and perhaps even some lives ones. This sort of establishment appealed to the people and down through the years there were others, the best known of which was Wonderland. It opened in the Merrill block and was a sort of combined theater and museum offering such mouth-gaping attractions as Tom Thumb, Jumbo the elephant, and other oddities, many of which were presented by Phineas T. Barnum. Later, Wonderland was operated in conjunction with the Temple Theater on Monroe street. It closed around the turn of the century.

Another McKinstry enterprise was the Michigan Gardens opened about 1837. It covered the entire block bounded by Randolph, Brush, Lafayette, and Monroe, and provided a wide range of entertainment from bear baiting and dog fights to shooting matches. It had a restaurant and bath house, and even an arboretum of sorts. Jacob Beller had a concert hall, beer garden, and bath house on the site of the Old County building on Randolph. It was described as a busy place, particularly on Saturday nights when patrons could soak off the week's grime to the accompaniment of a Strauss waltz. Toward the end of the century Beller moved out Jefferson to the Belle Isle bridge approach. The place eventually grew into a large dance hall and amusement park known as Electric Park, complete with roller coasters and a tunnel of love. The dance hall called the Pier Ballroom was one of the city's most popular places with the young people, attracted by the so-called name bands which appeared there. Another known as Riverside Park was at the west entrance to the Belle Isle bridge. These amusement parks were razed in 1928 and 1929. There were other public dance halls such as the Arcadia and the Blackstone, both on Woodward in the mid-town section.

Proper young Detroit ladies and gentlemen learned to dance in the very, very refined atmosphere of Miss Annie Ward Foster's dancing school. For several years it was on Farmer street just north of Grand River. Later, classes were conducted in Grosse Pointe. Older brothers and sisters as well as fathers and mothers attended balls and dancing parties at Max Strasburg's academy. His hall was on Temple near Woodward.

There were a few mineral bath houses, the best known being the Wayne Baths operated in conjunction with the Wayne Hotel, a gay spot on Jefferson and Third extending down to the river. It was close to the Michigan Central Depot and the boat docks. It disappeared under the wrecker's hammer in 1918.

In 1896 a group of newspapermen and a few leading citizens were invited to the Detroit Opera House to witness the first demonstration in Detroit of a novelty called the eidoloscope which was nothing more than a crude motion picture. It consisted of seven reels depicting a bull fight in Mexico and those who saw it did not think very highly of it. A short time later a better show was staged (or screened) at Wonderland. That was "The Great Train Robbery," generally acknowledged to have been the first American-made movie. It was well attended and this time the public was impressed. A new form of entertainment had come to Detroit, and it would not be long before the motion picture put vaudeville out of business and darkened many of the legitimate theaters.

The first Detroit theater devoted exclusively to showing motion pictures was opened in 1905 at Monroe and Farmer streets by John Kunsky and Arthur Caille. It was the Casino Theater, which had been a variety house, and was such a success that within a few years several new movie theaters were opened downtown. At first they were centered on Monroe between Campus Martius and Farmer street, but before long stores were being converted into movie houses, not only downtown but in the residential neighborhoods as well. The first of the neighborhood theaters was the Garden on Woodward between Selden and Alexandrine. For many years Kunsky was the local motion picture king. He entered into partnership with George W. Trendle and they built the garish movie palaces, most of which were located on the outer perimeter of Grand Circus Park. Several of these theaters are still operating, although under the impact of radio and particularly television, many of the small neighborhood theaters have disappeared.

Fun and Games

Detroit always was on the muscular side and from the earliest times its young men worked off their excess energy on the playing fields. The latter included the Detroit River where the first competitive sports were held. The French, British, and early Americans were horse racing enthusiasts; their tracks were the frozen surfaces of the Detroit River, the River Rouge, and the Grand Marais, a swampy area in Grosse Pointe. In 1825 Isadore Navarre of the River Raisin settlement (now Monroe, Michigan) issued a challenge to all of North America, offering to pit his Bas Blanc over any course from two to five miles for any wager of from fifty to ten thousand dollars. If there were any takers, the records are silent, and one wonders where Isadore could have laid his hands on ten thousand dollars. There was not that much hard money west of the Alleghenies in 1825. A track was built in 1836 or 1837 below Jefferson east of Connors and many years later there was another in Highland Park where Henry Ford built his plant. But for the most part horse fanciers raced their sulkies or light cutters on the streets. Cass avenue offered a popular stretch which was used until around 1900. When regular traffic became too heavy the sportsmen moved with their high-steppers out to Grand boulevard west of Hamilton on the stretch Ford Hospital now faces.

Boating provided one of the earliest forms of organized sport. The present Detroit Boat Club was organized in 1839. In 1873 its first clubhouse was built standing over the river at the foot of Hastings street. In 1877 it was moved to the foot of Joseph Campau and in 1891 it built quarters on Belle Isle where it has remained ever since. Many other boat clubs were organized in Detroit and the neighboring river communities about the time the Detroit Boat Club came into existence. These clubs engaged in sailing and rowing. In order to provide regular competition, they formed what was known as the Detroit River Navy. Many great crews and oarsmen developed from this competition, and Detroit Boat Club crews have regularly competed against the best the universities and private clubs in the eastern states, Canada, and Great Britain offer. The United States was frequently represented in the Olympic Games by championship crews and individual oarsmen from DBC; the sport is still carried on by the club. Other river clubs concentrated more on sailing and power boating, particularly the Detroit Yacht Club whose clubhouse was built on Belle Isle in the 1890s. DYC has frequently sponsored the Gold Cup and Harmsworth Trophy races, and was the home port of Gar Wood, one of the greatest of all the early racers.

Landsmen also were busy. Cricket had considerable vogue in the mid-1800s and was the most popular sport. In 1858 the Peninsular Cricket Club was organized. It obtained use of a large field on Woodward at Canfield, then well out in the country, and held its matches there. The Peninsulars attained considerable standing and in 1879 played an all-England team with rather disastrous results for the home town boys.

After the Civil War the popularity of baseball began to rise and as early as 1867 the game was being played at the cricket field, by that time known as Peninsular Park. Before long cricket began to be forgotten. In 1883 the Detroit

Athletic Club was organized with baseball and track as the principal sports. In 1887 the DAC built a clubhouse facing Woodward opposite Garfield. The athletic field took in most of the land between Woodward and Cass, and Canfield and Forest.

The DAC was the scene of the vigorous life. Strictly amateur, its baseball teams were of championship caliber. It obtained the services of the renowned Mike Murphy as trainer and track coach, and under his direction John Owen Jr. became the first person known to run the hundred yard dash under ten seconds. Jack Collins became the club's boxing coach and he too turned out some very fancy dans. The DAC became a social center; the clubhouse and surrounding grounds were the scene of gay parties and concerts.

Coinciding perhaps with the rise of high school athletics, the DAC began to fall on lean times. In 1912 the clubhouse was torn down and the playing field became known as Grindley Field. Its usefulness did not end, however. For several years it was the home grounds of the Central High School football teams which were either national champions or championship contenders. It was on Grindley Field that several young men learned the rudiments of mayhem which were later polished into All-American honors at the University of Michigan and other colleges. During the winter the field was turned into an ice-skating rink and in a balmier season it was the locale of the first all-city Boy Scout jamboree. In 1916 a huge rough wooden tabernacle was erected, covering most of Grindley Field, and there Billy Sunday held his revival meeting, exhorting sinners to "hit the sawdust trail" to repentance and salvation. In 1922 the present Convention Hall was built there. It was used for all kinds of exhibitions from automobile to flower shows. Convention Hall is now occupied by a number of small businesses as well as some that are not so small, such as the Vernor Ginger Ale Company.

Some of the diehard members of the old Detroit Athletic Club resolved that it should have a new birth and organized the present club where to a large extent martinis have replaced Indian clubs. The clubhouse on Madison, the center of much of the city's social life, was opened in 1915.

Baseball was Detroit's first major professional sport. A team called the Detroits was formed in 1881, and obtaining a franchise previously held by Cincinnati, became a member of the National League. The home grounds of the Detroits were at Recreation Park at Brush and Brady streets. The site is almost directly opposite the main building of Harper Hospital. When the Detroits were playing, hospital patients and attendants used the roof and upper windows as excellent vantage points from which to watch the games. This, it was claimed, had splendid therapeutic values. In 1887 Detroit beat St. Louis for the world's championship and the following year club-owner drug-manufacturer Frederick Stearns sold off most of the players. The club lost its National League franchise and became a member of the newly-formed International League. A move was made away from Recreation Park about 1893 and a new location was found at East Lafayette and Helen. In 1893 the Western League was organized and Detroit joined it.

With professional baseball drawing ever larger crowds, a bigger and more accessible field was needed and the club owners acquired a new lot at Michigan and Trumbull in 1896. Part of the William Woodbridge farm, this location had long been known as the Woodbridge Grove, a popular picnic ground and the site of Detroit's first zoo. That came about when a traveling menagerie was stranded here and local people bought the animals for public display.

That first zoo was not an overwhelming success and soon passed out of existence. What happened to the animals is not recorded. After they disappeared Woodbridge Grove served the city for many years as the hay market. Then the baseball club got it, erected a grandstand, and named it Bennett Field after the club's star catcher Charley Bennett. It was then the Detroits, but the team shortly was renamed the Tigers when the players appeared in black and orange striped stockings.

In 1901 the Western League became the American League and Detroit has played in it ever since. Ownership of the club was acquired by Frank Navin and in 1912 the field's name was changed to Navin Field. Later, when millionaire auto body manufacturer Walter O. Briggs bought the ball club, it became Briggs Stadium. When ownership passed to his successors the name was again changed to its present Tiger Stadium.

The Tigers won several league pennants in the early part of the century, but their golden era began in 1905 when a flashy young Georgian, Tyrus Raymond Cobb, joined the team and began a twenty-four year career that made him a legend. Hughie Jennings managed the Tigers in those days. Some of Cobb's famous teammates were Sam Crawford, Donie Bush, Bobbie Veach, George Moriarity, and a little later, Harry Heilman. In the 1930s a new galaxy of stars appeared on the field under the inspired leadership of manager Mickey Cochrane. They included such greats as Charlie Gehringer, Hank Greenburg, Rudy York, Goose Goslin, and Tommy Bridges. They too brought home the pennant.

Other sports became well established in Detroit. Although there had been some professional football as early as World War I, the city joined the big league in 1934 when a franchise was purchased from Portsmouth, Ohio, and the

Detroit Lions entered the local arena. In 1926 the Detroit Hockey Club was organized and purchased the Cougars of Victoria, British Columbia. In 1930 the team was renamed the Falcons and a short time later the Red Wings. Their home rink Olympia was built in 1927 on Grand River at McGraw. Professional basketball came in 1957 when the present Pistons were brought to Detroit from Fort Wayne, Indiana. Soccer was introduced in 1967 when a team was imported from Belfast, Ireland, to represent Detroit as the Cougars in a newly organized league.

Detroit had its share of pugilistic greats, including one of the greatest of them all, Joe Louis. He grew up on the east side, became a Golden Gloves winner, and then proceeded to rule the ring as the world's heavyweight champion. Golf—today the most widely engaged in of all sports —really got underway in Detroit in 1900 when the Detroit Golf Club was organized and acquired land for its course on Pontchartrain drive between Six and Seven Mile roads.

City of Many Tongues

While all these accessories of civilization helped make "life worth living," it was the people themselves who created the modern city. The pre-Civil War industrial development and that which followed required many "hewers of wood and carriers of water." While many who found jobs in the shops, factories, and stores were native Americans, there was a great increase in immigration. Between 1870 and 1930 Detroit became truly cosmopolitan—a city of many tongues. Immigrants from almost every corner of the world showed up, with the result that ethnic groups from Albanians to Ukranians were firmly planted here. So numerous were these people that in 1900 twelve per cent of the city's population spoke no English. No other major American city could make that claim.

The first national groups, the Germans and the Irish, began moving into Detroit in the 1830s and were solidly established when the big inrush, which included more Germans and Irish, began thirty or forty years later. Any consideration of national groups should include the English, Scots, and Canadians. The migration from their countries began early, almost immediately after the American occupation in 1796, and continued steadily thereafter; it continues today. Figures are not easily available of the number of British and Canadians in Detroit at any one time. Having no language problems, they assimilated immediately and did not establish colonies or neighborhoods of their own. Yet they were so numerous, especially Canadians of both English and French origin, that today it would be almost impossible to find a second or third generation Detroiter who does not have family ties with Canada. Needless to say, these English, Scots, and Canadians had a tremendous influence upon the business and social life of the city. There was a heavy influx of Englishmen between 1910 and 1930. Included among the British immigrants of that period were many Maltese who have a sizable colony in Detroit on the lower near west side in the area still known as Corktown, but which has largely been abandoned by the Irish.

The first major non-British immigration began about 1832, consisting of German refugees escaping political ferment in their homeland. They continued to come in increasing numbers. Many of these newcomers were not of peasant stock; frequently they were well-educated and there were professional people among them. These Germans included the earliest Jews to come to Detroit and it has been noted above how they formed their first congregations. The Germans settled on the near east side of Detroit around Gratiot in what was then the second and third wards, roughly the area north of Lafayette to Monroe. The German section gradually expanded, moving out Gratiot and eventually into the Grosse Pointes. For a great many years much of the east side had a distinctly Teutonic flavor.

Partly because of their language the Germans were inclined toward clannishness and preserved much of their homeland culture. They laid great stress on education and loved art, music, and the theater. In 1849 they organized the Harmonie Society for choral and concert activities, and for the observance of their festivals. The first Harmonie Hall was built in 1875 at Lafayette and Beaubien; the present clubhouse at East Grand River and Center was built in 1894. Another early German gathering place, Arbeiter Hall was built in 1868 at Catherine and Russell. The Turnverein, founded locally in 1852, had several buildings, the first on Sherman between Russell and Riopelle streets, built in 1860, and the latest on East Jefferson at Fischer, abandoned because of financial difficulties in 1947.

Being strong for social gatherings, the Germans had many other organizations, including dramatic clubs, workers' halls, and drinking and eating places. One of the most recent of the latter was the Deutsches Haus at Mack and Maxwell. There during the bleak days of prohibition one could find *gemütlichkeit*, good beer, bowling, and voices raised in song. The outbreak of World War II marked its end.

The German community greatly enriched Detroit. Many of the original immigrants brought some small capital with them and established their own shops and businesses.

Many were skilled tradesmen and found a ready market for their crafts. Others were teachers and musicians. The children of this first generation entered the professions and a large number became physicians, attorneys, and educators. The German language continued to be spoken in the homes, churches and parochial schools, and was taught in the public high schools until World War I when it became less popular. Several German language newspapers flourished and the *Abend Post* founded in 1868 is still being published. The Germans also became a potent political group in both the city and county governments. At least five held the office of mayor between 1860 and 1917.

The Irish came close on the heels of the Germans. Forced to flee their native island because of famine and political troubles, they began to arrive in Detroit in considerable numbers in 1833. Their migration, like that of the Germans, continued to be heavy up to the time of the Civil War, but was particularly so in the 1840s. Unlike the Germans, the Irish lacked professional skills and became laborers in their new home. They worked on public projects such as road and rail construction, and found jobs in the factories. Many of the young women became domestics and the men who had a way with horses manned the livery stables or became coachmen for the affluent. Most of the streetcar motormen and conductors were Irish. Being gregarious, they found saloonkeeping to their liking and soon were as much in evidence in the City Hall as their German neighbors.

While the Germans settled on the east side, the Irish took over the lower west side and Corktown, which centered mostly around Most Holy Trinity Church, became a colorful and occasionally uproarious enclave. Corktown existed almost as much in sentiment as in geography and its borders are rather vaguely defined. Some place it between Lafayette and Myrtle with its eastern boundary at First street and its western limit at Brooklyn or even beyond. But many an Irish-Detroiter born outside these boundaries claimed Corktown as his native hearth—and there were few to dispute him. Even today to have sprung from Corktown is a badge of honor and a distinct political asset, although Corktown became pretty well depopulated of Irish by 1920. Maltese, Mexicans, and Negroes live there now, and Mrs. Murphy would hardly recognize the old place.

The largest national group to adopt Detroit as its home town was the Poles. A few Poles were here at a relatively early date, but the big influx began in the mid-1870s. Unlike the Germans and Irish, the Poles were actively recruited through immigration offices or bureaus which the state of Michigan maintained from 1869 to 1885. Agents of the commission also met the immigrant ships at eastern seaports and channeled the new arrivals to the city.

They were greatly needed at the time as common labor in the railroad shops and stove works, although some among the first arrivals were employed in the fields of the D. M. Ferry seed farms. The Poles settled first in communities on the east side north of Gratiot between Orleans and Dubois streets, an enclave which spread in all directions and which still retains predominantly Polish neighborhoods. Others made their homes in Hamtramck close to the automobile plants; until recent years that suburb with as many as seventy thousand people was more a Polish than an American city.

There was an almost constant stream of Polish immigration which continued until World War I and was then resumed for a few years immediately following. The later arrivals found work in the automobile factories and settled in other sections of Detroit, particularly the Michigan-

Junction avenue area on the west side, as well as in Dearborn and the downriver towns.

The Poles were good citizens, although at first they created serious social problems. Because of their language and customs, much different from what Americans knew and understood, they did not assimilate easily. They had a tendency to withdraw into their own social environment, and their life was centered around their churches and their Dom Polskis or social halls. Nevertheless, they were community conscious; they became home owners and their leaders showed them how to become a vocal element in the body politic. As a result the second and third generation Poles broke out of the boundaries of their original neighborhoods, and while there remain large Polish districts where the language is still heard and the old ways adhered to, the present population of Polish descent is scattered everywhere through the city. The Poles added much color to the local scene with their singing and dancing societies and their veterans' organizations. Traditionally opposed to the Russians, they comprise a staunch anti-Communist bloc. Polish language newspapers had and still have a large circulation. Several local radio stations regularly broadcast programs in Polish. In 1930 there were an estimated 350,-000 Poles in the Detroit metropolitan area.

Other national groups in small numbers were in Detroit almost from the time of its founding. But for most of them, other than those already mentioned, the big influx of immigration occurred generally between 1900 and 1919, and it was the spectacular growth of the automobile industry in most cases that swelled the city's foreign-born population. Among the larger groups that appeared during this period were Armenians, Syrians, and Lebanese, about 65,000 each. Many Armenians located in Highland Park and adjoining sections of Detroit.

The Belgians began to arrive about 1890. Many came to Detroit after first settling in Buffalo, New York, and the term Buffalos, now seldom heard, was applied to them. They found homes in the northeast part of the city, and while less numerous than several other national groups —there were about 12,000—they exert a strong civic influence through their clubs and other organizations.

About 35,000 Greeks settled in Detroit, making their first appearance in 1886. They are scattered throughout the city now, although there is a thriving and colorful Greek Town where their restaurants and coffee houses are located around Monroe and Beaubien streets.

Immigrants from Hungary came in sizable numbers beginning in the late 1890s. A large Hungarian colony grew up in the southwest part of Detroit in the section once known as Delray. An estimated 55,000 found homes in the city where the men were employed by the railroads and in the Solvay Process Company plants.

The Italians can claim to have been among the city's founders. Alphonse Tonty, Cadillac's lieutenant, is believed to have been a native of Italy. Ultimately some 150,000 Italians found their way to the city, the first contingent arriving in 1880. They were Lombards from a town near Milan. The later and heavier influx largely came from southern Italy and Sicily. The first Italian colony in Detroit was north of Fort street and south of Gratiot in the neighborhood of Mullett, St. Antoine, and Orleans streets. Today's descendants of those immigrants are inclined to remain east-siders and their homes extend all the way into the Grosse Pointe communities. Italians still maintain close nationalist ties through their churches, social organizations, and like many other groups, a native-language newspaper. Until recently there were regular radio programs in Italian.

The Russians began to arrive in substantial numbers

about 1900. Many were Jews fleeing the pogroms and persecutions of their Czarist homeland. They first established themselves in Detroit on the lower east side along Hastings and adjoining streets. As their numbers increased the colony pushed north along Oakland avenue and then expanded again into the near northwest section. Progressive and industrious, the Jews firmly established themselves as an important influence on the city's business and professional life.

Another large group are the Ukranians of whom about 100,000 settled in and around Detroit. Many came to work in the automobile plants. They had no clearly defined neighborhood of their own, but mingled with the Poles and other eastern European groups in the upper east side and Hamtramck areas. Other nationalities strongly represented in Detroit include Slovaks (60,000), Rumanians (45,000), Swedes (25,000), Finns (20,000), and Bulgarians, Croatians, Lithuanians, Mexicans, Norwegians, and Serbs (about 10,000 each). The result of this immigration, particularly between 1900 and 1930, as revealed by the census of the latter year, was that thirty per cent of Detroit's population was foreign born.

It is a sad fact that while most of the white foreign born and their descendants were quickly and easily absorbed into the pattern of life in Detroit, one group of native born Americans was not accepted and was the object of shameful discrimination both socially and economically. These, of course, are the Negroes. Ironically, a good deal of this discrimination came from the non-native element, from people who spoke the English language imperfectly. Negro experience in Detroit, at least in the 20th century, was not much different from that in most other urban centers in the United States.

There have been Negroes in Detroit for almost as long as there have been white men. Those who came first came as slaves, many having been taken prisoner by the Indians in raids against Kentucky and border areas during and before the Revolution. In the mid-1800s many Negroes who escaped from the South were encouraged to find refuge here and were welcomed. From the time of the Civil War, Detroit had a sizable Negro community which increased slowly but steadily. The Negroes of that period were employed as household domestics, waiters, barbers, caterers, and house painters. Many were self-employed. Their homes were congregated on the lower east side along Congress and Larned from Randolph street east. As their numbers increased they began to fill a corridor between Beaubien and Dequindre which ran north to East Grand boulevard and beyond. There were other settlements which sprang up on the west side.

During and soon after World War I, Detroit faced a manpower shortage and major local industries sent recruiters into the South to enroll Negro workers. Thousands flocked to Detroit as they did to many other northern cities, enticed by promises of high wages and the prospect of a better life than they had known on their small southern farms. They were employed in foundries and other heavy industries which had little attraction for white workers. They were at the bottom of the economic scale, and when the war bubble burst, and again when the depression of the 1930s struck, they were the first to be laid off. Few had had time to establish themselves firmly, they were forced to live in deplorable slums, and many could not have existed at all except for public relief. In 1930 Detroit's Negro population was about 120,000 or between ten and fifteen per cent of the total number of inhabitants.

At the outbreak of World War II the industrial recruiting was begun again, only this time on a larger scale and with a new and socially dangerous element added. Not only were the southern Negroes encouraged to come to Detroit and work in the war industries, but thousands of whites from West Virginia, Kentucky, and Tennessee—the so-called hill billies—were also recruited. The two racial strains mixed no better than oil and water. The result, along with other contributing factors, was serious racial unrest which will be considered in more detail later. But the tremendous upswing in the Negro population brings it very close to becoming the predominant group. In 1940 there were more than 200,000 Negroes in Detroit; in 1967 the number was estimated to be in the neighborhood of 650,000 or close to forty per cent of the total population. Public school enrollment in 1967 was about fifty-five per cent Negro.

Naturally their former enclaves could not hold this swelling Negro community. There was a postwar flight of middle class whites to the suburbs and Negroes moved into the homes they vacated. Today the so-called inner city, the section within encircling Grand boulevard, is almost totally Negro occupied, as are wide corridors stretching out all along the main thoroughfares. There are in fact very few all-white neighborhoods remaining in Detroit, and with the backing of civil rights legislation and the gradually improving economic status of the Negro, even those are being rapidly integrated.

11

A Whiff of Gasoline

'The Darn Thing Ran'

There was a last minute bustle of activity in John Lauer's machine shop on the east side of St. Antoine street just south of Jefferson avenue. The time was about 11 p.m., March 6, 1896. It was cold and a few flurries of snow flicked the buildings and the streets. Then everything was ready. A couple of husky men opened the barn-like doors and helped roll a strange contraption into the street. It looked something like a buggy, but it was not a buggy. It had no shafts for a horse. It had high lightweight carriage wheels, but it was not a carriage.

Charles Brady King, a young man wrapped up in a short coat for protection against the cold, a muffler around his throat, and a hard hat perched on his head, climbed into the vehicle and grasped the steering tiller. Somebody spun a crank, an engine snorted and popped, King threw in a clutch, and the first automobile to appear on the streets of Detroit moved uncertainly up St. Antoine toward Jefferson.

To the sputter of the engine and out of a cloud of blue gasoline fumes turned white by the frosty air, a new era emerged. It concerned most of the world, but it concerned Detroit most of all. Then and there the automobile age dawned.

King was thirty-two years old. Born in California, he had been in Detroit for three years, employed as a mechanic in one of the railroad car shops. On his travels he had seen horseless carriages in Chicago, and fascinated by them, had resolved to build one for himself. He obtained space in Lauer's shop and worked nights until his automobile was completed. This was its test run.

At Jefferson, King steered west and went to Woodward where he turned north and chugged up to the Russell House at Cadillac Square. Then the motor died and there is no account of how King got his machine back to Lauer's. Epochal as that short drive was, it stirred only casual public interest. A local newspaper dutifully reported: "The first horseless carriage seen in this city was out on the streets last night. . . . The apparatus seemed to work all right, and it went at the rate of five or six miles an hour at an even rate of speed."

King was not the only Detroiter tinkering with a horseless carriage in 1896. On the north side of Bagley avenue between Grand River and Clifford lived the night shift engineer of the Edison Illuminating Company. Although he had a steady job at $125 a month, he gave no promise of setting the world on fire. He had been a farmer, machinist, watch repairman, and not a notable success at any of those trades. His name was Henry Ford. There was a small brick shed at the rear of his Bagley avenue house and in his spare time Ford worked out there putting together a machine much like King's in appearance. He finally got it assembled on June 4, just three months after

King's motor debut. To get it on the street Ford had to knock out part of the shed's wall. The building was removed from its original site many years later and is now at Greenfield Village. So is the machine.

Ford cranked up his quadricycle, as he called it, and nobody was more surprised than he was when it started. "The darned thing ran!" exclaimed Henry Ford.

At the time neither Ford nor King had any idea they were launching a great industry. King became more interested in art and music and did not contribute much after his first machine to the automobile industry in Detroit. Ford was merely playing with a mechanical toy. If he had any ideas of developing or improving his machine it was to increase its speed and stamina and perhaps race it against a horse or another automobile. It would be almost five years before he awoke to the commercial possibilities.

It was Ransom E. Olds of Lansing who first started manufacturing automobiles in Detroit. Olds began his experiments in Lansing prior to 1895, working with a friend Frank Clark. Olds's father made stationary engines and Clark's father made carriages. The two young men joined forces and their fathers' facilities (and money), and built a car which they called the Oldsmobile. Their fathers were not happy about what they considered a waste of their off-springs' time, but the boys persevered. They organized the Olds Motor Works in Lansing in 1897 and then had a difference of opinion. Olds bought out Clark, sought financial backing, and found it in Detroit. His angel was Samuel L. Smith who had made a fortune in copper and lumber. He gambled $199,600 on the venture with the proviso that the manufacturing would be done in Detroit and his two sons would be given jobs in the company. As a result the Olds Motor Works opened for business in 1899 in a small factory on East Jefferson near the Belle Isle bridge where the Uniroyal tire plant stands now. The first hand-made Oldses were pretty good machines. They ran well on paved streets and the company sold all it could make, which was not many. The Olds cost $2,382 which only the wealthy could afford.

Then Olds had a lucky break which he probably did not appreciate at the time. On March 9, 1901, fire completely destroyed the plant. All the plans and machinery for producing the Oldsmobile were lost. The only thing saved was a small experimental model with a curved dash. Shortly thereafter the company's operations were moved back to Lansing and of necessity were concentrated on making this smaller car. But the ties with Detroit were not broken. Olds was no longer able to machine parts in his own factory. The manufacture of his cars became essentially an assembly process. Work was farmed out to a dozen or more suppliers, most of them Detroit shops. The Leland-Faulconer machine shop on Trombley at Dequindre, headed by Henry M. Leland, built the motors; John and Horace Dodge, who had recently been making bicycles in Windsor, supplied transmissions; the Briscoe Manufacturing Company produced radiators; and Byron F. (Barney) Everitt went to Norwalk, Ohio, and hired a young fellow named Fisher, one of seven brothers, to help make the bodies. Consequently the Olds was produced more economically. The price of the curved-dash smaller car was drastically reduced to $625. Within a year the company was turning out the first popular low-priced car and making about twenty-five per cent of all the autos built in the United States. Ransom Olds became America's first automobile millionaire.

Meanwhile Henry Ford continued to improve his model, obtained financial backing, and organized the Detroit Automobile Company in 1898. As far as Ford was

257

concerned, the venture was not a success. Always a loner, he was unable to get along with his associates. So he pulled out and in 1901 formed the Henry Ford Automobile Company in a shop on Park place.

Ford's second venture was no more successful than his first. He kept working, however, making improvements and winning recognition for himself and his car by racing. He hired Barney Oldfield to drive for him and in 1901 Oldfield set a record of sixty miles an hour on the Grosse Pointe track. This not only helped make Ford's reputation, but it also made Oldfield's as the foremost race driver in the country. Years later when Ford had become the acknowledged king of the automobile industry, he remarked to Oldfield, "You made me, and I made you." "Yes," replied Oldfield, "but I did a better job than you did." Ford personally drove a race on the ice of Lake St. Clair in 1904 which set a new world speed record of ninety-three miles per hour.

With the publicity he received Ford was ready for a fresh start, this time as a bona fide producer for a market that was rapidly opening up. He found new financial backing and on June 16, 1903, the Ford Motor Company was incorporated and commenced operations in a factory on Mack avenue at Bellevue. Among those who furnished the money—actually only $28,000 in working capital was paid in—were Alexander Y. Malcomson, a coal dealer, John S. Gray, a banker, and Horace H. Rackham, an attorney. John and Horace Dodge, who contracted to make parts for Ford in their shop on Beaubien at Fort and later in larger quarters on Monroe at Hastings, were given shares in payment. Malcomson sent his bookkeeper James Couzens around to keep an eye on the business end of the enterprise. Couzens scraped together $2,000 of his own to invest. In 1919 Ford bought him out for $29,308,857, a substantial part of which Couzens returned to the community as a philanthropist.

The new Ford idea was to build a car that would provide basic transportation not only for city dwellers, but for farmers and small town residents as well. The latter needed a machine that would get them up hills and through spring quagmires. Ford envisioned a mass-produced low-priced job so simple in construction that the farmer's hired man could repair it. Let the sports buy their Wintons and other fancy machines; the Ford would be the work horse for the common people. The concept paid off handsomely right from the start. In the first year of operation 1,708 cars were sold. It quickly became evident that the one-story Mack avenue plant would not suffice and in 1906 Ford moved to larger quarters on Piquette avenue at Beaubien. There in 1908 he began production of that automotive wonder of all time, the Model T—the Tin Lizzie. Ford soon was unable to meet demand and within two years the company was six months behind on deliveries. So another move was made. Famed Detroit architect Albert Kahn was called upon to design a radically new plant, the site for which was far out Woodward in Highland Park. Kahn pioneered in industrial architecture for Ford, utilizing reinforced concrete and glass as structural elements, and providing facilities which brought the work to the man instead of sending the man to the work. Ground was broken in 1909 and by January 1, 1910, the Highland Park factory was in partial operation. For the time being the Piquette factory was retained.

Ford's success can be attributed to many factors. Price was important. A Model T roadster could be bought for as little as $275 and there were no added extras or excise taxes. A nation-wide dealer and service system was set up, and Ford insisted that a complete stock of parts be carried in each one. No waiting was required while a new spring or axle was shipped from the home plant or nearest parts depot. The smallest cross-roads country village was able to take care of the cars of the farmers in the vicinity or the traveler in distress.

In 1913 something new was developed at the Highland Park plant—the first automotive assembly line was put in operation. Standardization of parts had already been perfected. Now Ford made these parts flow in a continuous stream to the moving line, reaching it just as they were needed by a worker who performed only a single operation. He did his job of attaching a part swiftly as the car moved past him to the next man and the next operation, and so on to completion. At the end the body was skidded down an incline just in time to land on the assembled chassis. It was bolted into place and driven away under its own power. By this system production was made more economical, more efficient, and given an almost unlimited quantity potential.

The next thing Henry Ford pulled out of his bag of tricks made the competition and the entire industrial world reel, and had almost as much impact upon Detroit as did Antoine Cadillac's running aground at the foot of Shelby street in 1701. On January 12, 1914, Ford announced that henceforth each production worker in his plant would be paid five dollars for an eight-hour shift. To workers for whom $2.75 a day or less was standard pay for unskilled or semi-skilled labor, this sounded like a new gold strike. Men left the farms in Michigan and other states, and even in Europe the word got around. Job-seekers packed their scanty belongings and headed for Detroit. Other employers screamed foul and socialism as their employees quit and lined up at the Ford hiring gates. So dense was the throng of job applicants that it was necessary on one occasion to use fire hoses to disperse them.

There were strings attached to the five-dollars-a-day, but most applicants did not bother to read the fine print. In order to earn that rate a man had to be on the payroll for six months and to be of good moral character. Ford ran a paternalistic shop, and to be sure his men lived up to the moral standards he prescribed, set up a social service department which in effect told the workers how to live and how to spend their money. Investigators stopped by the employee's home to see what he was doing with his new-found wealth. If he was extravagant, if he spent money on cigarettes or a bottle of liquor, he was as likely as not to be fired. But that did not discourage the job hunters who poured into Detroit and accounted in large part for the sudden growth of the city and the development of many new residential areas. In 1900, about the time the automobile industry was born, Detroit's population was 285,-704. By 1910 it had increased to 465,766, and in 1920 it had almost doubled to 993,678. In addition Highland Park boomed to about 45,000 and adjoining Hamtramck counted nearly 50,000 residents. Not all of this growth can be attributed to Henry Ford, of course, but he did his share.

Parade of the Giants

The Detroit Automobile Company got along very well without Ford. After his departure Henry M. Leland was called in to take charge, and soon thereafter his Leland & Faulconer Manufacturing Company was merged with the auto concern. It took a little while to get going but in

1903, the same year Ford launched his new enterprise, Leland and his associates put their first car on the market under the name of Cadillac. Very shortly the name of the company was changed to the Cadillac Motor Car Company, operations being conducted in a plant at Cass and Amsterdam just behind the streetcar yards which then and for several years longer were at Woodward and Amsterdam. Thus by 1903 two components of the future General Motors Corporation—the Olds and Cadillac—were thriving, and with Ford the foundations for two of the Big Three had been laid.

Others were watching Olds, Ford, and Leland with interest, and more than one week-end mechanic was at work in his own barn or in rented quarters in a shop somewhere in Detroit. In time some of their efforts blossomed into major motor companies; others of course withered on the vine, either because of mechanical shortcomings or lack of financing. Some cars were a success in spite of their inventors. A case in point was David D. Buick, a capable engineer in the plumbing supply business. He was successful in inventing a method of applying porcelain to bathtubs, toilets, and wash basins. The automobile bug bit him, however, and in 1903—a significant year for Detroit in regards to the automotive industry—he built a car which he named for himself. But he used up his resources in doing so and was forced to sell out. The company wound up in the hands of Flint wagon-maker William Crapo Durant. Operations were moved to Flint, and after two or three years of extremely hard going, Buick Motors experienced a turn in fortune and began to prosper. Durant was a soft-spoken man who more resembled a Y.M.C.A. secretary than one of the two-fisted hell-roaring grease monkeys who were beginning to make the wheels of the new industry spin. He had a keen head for figures, and there was a streak of the gambler in him, but above all he foresaw the future with clarity. He realized that there were too many individual companies entering the field, that competition would stifle many of them, and that the industry's salvation and progress depended upon the centralization of resources, production, and marketing. A combine which would offer the individual a range of cars to choose from according to his needs and his pocketbook was Durant's great idea.

With that in mind he formed the General Motors Company in 1908 with Buick as the cornerstone. (General Motors Corporation was formed in 1919.) He offered to buy out Henry Ford and almost had a willing seller, but at the last minute the deal fell through. Two years later Cadillac was acquired, then Oakland (manufactured in Pontiac and the parent of the Pontiac car). Olds became part of the new family, and then General Motors bought Chevrolet, at that time produced in Detroit, and moved it to Flint. With Chevrolet, Durant now had a low-priced car in his stable, something that would compete with the Ford Model T. Other companies, particularly parts and accessories firms, including the Fisher brothers' body works, were added from time to time. With its head office in Detroit and its manufacturing activities widely scattered, General Motors was on its way to becoming the giant of all American industrial enterprises.

The year 1903 saw yet another famous Detroit car launched. That was the Packard, originally built at Warren, Ohio. On a trip to New York, Henry B. Joy and his brother-in-law Truman H. Newberry, both scions of lumber and railroad wealth, saw the Packard for the first time and were impressed by the ease with which it could be started. They shortly acquired the company, moved it to Detroit, and began production in a plant of advanced design—one of Albert Kahn's masterpieces—on East Grand boulevard near Mt. Elliott. There it flourished, building a quality passenger car and a sturdy truck.

There were others as well. In 1904 Jonathan Maxwell, who had been Olds's factory manager, persuaded Benjamin Briscoe to back him in building a new car. Briscoe had a plant which turned out stampings for several of the early motor companies and for a year had controlled Buick. He found the money and soon the famed Maxwell was on the streets, rolling out of the factory at East Jefferson near Connors. From time to time during the next dozen years Maxwell either bought or merged with such pioneer companies as Chalmers, Metzger, Brush (the favorite light runabout of doctors), Columbia, and Flanders. The Maxwell was the genesis of the third of the Big Three. After World War I the company ran into trouble and one-time railroad master mechanic Walter P. Chrysler was called in to put it on its feet. Chrysler moved to Maxwell's front office from the Buick plant where he had been general superintendent. He surrounded himself with some superb talent in the persons of K. T. Keller and James M. Zeder. In 1922 he bought the company and the Chrysler Corporation was born.

The years before 1910 saw many others enter the field—Hupp and Paige in 1908 and Hudson in 1909. Hudson was organized by Roy D. Chapin, an Olds alumnus, with the financial backing of department store king J. L. Hudson, which accounts for the company's name. Still others such as Krit, Saxon, Liberty, and Rickenbacker appeared on the scene. In 1914 the Dodge brothers broke with Ford in whose company they were substantial stockholders and for whom they were major parts suppliers. Ford bought them out and the Dodges, two of the most engaging roughnecks the automobile or any other industry ever knew, cast about for something to do with their millions. They established the Dodge Brothers company, producing the Dodge car in a new plant in Hamtramck. They prospered exceedingly with a fine line of well-built moderately-priced cars and sturdy trucks. But with the death of both brothers in 1920, the company faltered and Walter Chrysler, seeking to emulate General Motors by rounding out his line, bought the Dodge company in 1928 for one of the largest cash deals in history. It became the Dodge division of the Chrysler Corporation, and so it remains to this day.

Along with the automobile manufacturers, the first decade of the century witnessed the mushrooming of the great parts and accessories companies. Many started as small shops, but by obtaining contracts from the motor manufacturers, they grew and prospered along parallel lines. Among some of the more important, especially from the standpoint of Detroit's economy, were Murray Manufacturing Co., McCord Manufacturing Co., Briggs Manufacturing Co., and Kelsey Wheel Co., present-day Kelsey-Hayes Corporation.

Why Detroit?

What was peculiar about Detroit that it so quickly became the heart and nerve center of the automobile industry? The horseless carriage was not invented here. It appeared on the streets of other cities months and even years before Charles King took his first ride. Companies were already manufacturing autos in other cities and states before Detroit got into the business. In fact, the first automobile show was held in New York in 1900 before any

Detroit company was in actual production. The answer to the question lies in Detroit's background, its economic climate, and its tradition.

More than most other cities, Detroit possessed the ingredients for making the automotive pudding. First of all, it had been for several years the center of the marine gasoline engine industry, building the power units for the launches and motor boats on the Great Lakes and other waters. The shops were here, the know-how was here, the supply of skilled labor was here. Second, Detroit was the center of the malleable iron manufacturing industry; it had plants which could turn out castings, and it had others which were turning out springs, copper and brass parts and fittings, and paints and varnishes. There were no large companies engaged in manufacturing wagons and carriages, but there were several small ones, so finding body makers, wheelwrights, and blacksmiths was no problem. The era of northern lumbering was passing and there was a huge supply of labor with basic or developable mechanical aptitudes. Furthermore, Detroit was sensitive to the need for effective transportation. The lakes were frozen four or five months of the year and Michigan was not located on any of the main railroad lines. There was a natural local interest in anything that would move people and goods, and while this was not a major consideration in automotive development, it had some influence.

There was another very important factor. Detroit had capital and lots of it. In the second half of the 19th century fortunes had been made in lumber, mining, and shipping. It is hardly an exaggeration to say that there were many Detroiters who had more money than they knew what to do with. The sons of these families, young men at the turn of the century, were inclined to be gay blades and the sporting aspects of the automobile appealed to them.

Risk capital was available for the indulgence of their hobbies, but in a sounder sense, it was there to finance ventures which gave promise of being economically sound. So that was why Detroit became preeminent in the industry; capital, skilled labor, and materiel were all at hand without the necessity of going afield for essentials.

Those were exciting days in Detroit when the automobile industry's roots were taking firm hold. People thought and talked automobiles. Everyone was an expert. Groups gathered at the curb and hotly discussed the merits or faults of whatever car happened to be parked there at the moment. Arguments were clinched by kicking the tires. Millionaires, less than a decade from the lathes and grinders, with the grime of the machine shops still under their finger nails, wheeled and dealed in the Pontchartrain bar or later at the DAC. William E. Metzger set a pattern of sorts back in 1898 when he opened the first automobile showroom on the south side of Jefferson at Brush. Almost immediately dealerships sprouted like hyacinths in the spring.

The price of gasoline tumbled in 1901 when the first Texas gusher, Spindletop, came in. The cost of fuel fell from about a dollar to a few cents a gallon, cinching the future of the gas combustion engine. Most of the gas pumps then were inside barns and blacksmith shops, soon to be renamed garages. Then the pumps were moved to curbside where they were an infernal nuisance. But an enterprising dealer moved his back from the street, cut the curbs, and made the nation's first drive-in gas station at the northeast corner of Fort and First, a station which is, incidentally, still in business. Residential streets, particularly in the new north end, were made hideous by a steady parade of chassis with the driver perched on a box, stirring up the dust of the unpaved avenues, for in those days almost all machines were road tested before the bodies were attached and the customers took delivery.

Traffic became increasingly a problem. George W. Bissell, a well-to-do lumberman, gained some sort of distinction on September 2, 1902, when he became the city's first automobile accident fatality. This occurred when his carriage was hit by a car at Brooklyn and Lysander. Motorists were beginning to tire of being restricted to city driving because the rural roads were so bad. Their complaints were answered by the Wayne County Road Commission which laid the world's first concrete highway in 1909, thus beginning the era of good roads. This concrete ribbon consisted of a one-mile stretch on Woodward between Six and Seven Mile roads. In 1911 County Road Commissioner Edward N. Hines had the world's first white center line painted on the River road near Trenton. Detroit's first Stop street signs went up in 1923, installed by the Detroit Automobile Club, forerunner of the Automobile Club of Michigan, founded in 1916.

Even the local people sometimes thought of Detroit as a one-industry town. That was a gross misconception. The automobile was uppermost in most minds; it was creating new wealth and bringing in hordes of new workers. True, the stove and railroad manufacturing industries were petering out, but there still were pharmaceuticals, marine equipment, and shipbuilding. Attracted by a skilled labor supply, other new industries came to Detroit. In 1904, for example, the Arithmometer Company of St. Louis, which was making adding machines, moved to Detroit and occupied a building at Second and Amsterdam. The following year it was incorporated as the Burroughs Adding Machine Company, later changed to the Burroughs Corporation. Its headquarters continue to be at the site of the original plant, although its operations are now virtually worldwide. Salt mining and chemicals accounted for a lot of new employment. To coordinate and stimulate business activity the Detroit Board of Commerce was organized in 1903. Detroit was in high gear.

12

The Twentieth Century City

World War I

In 1917 a different kind of excitement shook Detroit. On April 6 war was declared against Germany. It has been said that the United States was unprepared for war, which was true, and that it came as a surprise, which was not true. People were being conditioned for a state of war long before the declaration. Detroit particularly was aware of what was going on. Canada had been involved since 1914; Windsor troops, notably its Scottish militia regiment, were early in the fray, and many Detroiters crossed the river and entered the Canadian army and air force. In 1916 former President Theodore Roosevelt, preaching preparedness, visited the city and delivered his famous "Damn the mollycoddles, give us men!" speech in the Detroit Opera House. On that occasion he became the first distinguished guest to be put up at the new Detroit Athletic Club.

About the same time Mexican bandit Pancho Villa was terrorizing the Texas and New Mexico border, and the hell he raised led to a punitive force's being sent into Mexico after him. The United States and Mexico came perilously close to war and national guard units were mobilized. Detroit's old Light Guard, now the 31st Infantry, was sent to Waco, Texas, for training. It was sort of the overture before the curtain was raised on the main performance.

In Detroit tensions mounted after 1914. On the one hand, there was a large population of Canadian and British extraction, and on the other, a large German community and the more recent immigrants from central and southern Europe. In all probability neither group clearly understood the issues involved and they merely followed their national sympathies. Henry Ford, in one of his more esoteric moments, tried to settle the whole European conflict in 1915 by chartering a ship and carrying a load of assorted characters across the ocean for the purpose of "getting the boys out of the trenches by Christmas." The expedition was a dismal failure.

With the declaration of war there was immediate mobilization. Once again the national guard was called into service and the Michigan units, only recently returned from Texas, were joined to those of Wisconsin to form the 32nd Division. The Detroit contingent, the 31st Infantry, and the 32nd Infantry, largely from outstate, became the 63rd Brigade. The regiments then became the 125th and 126th. Joining them were a medical detachment, a headquarters unit, the 119th Field Artillery, a machine gun company, and part of a cavalry squadron. When at home the latter was based at an armory on Collingwood avenue just west of Hamilton. Many thousands more volunteered and went into the regular army, the navy, and the marine corps. Two base hospitals were organized; No. 17 was made up of doctors and nurses from Harper Hospital, and No. 36 represented the Detroit College of Medicine.

After about a year of training the 32nd Division arrived in France on February 8, 1918, and by mid-May the troops were committed to combat. Later they participated in the Oise-Aisne and Meuse-Argonne offensives. For their part in helping crack the Hindenburg line they were nicknamed the Red Arrow Division and were given the shoulder insigna of a red arrow piercing a line. Recognized as one of the best United States combat divisions, its casualties totalled 2,898 killed and 10,986 wounded. Following the armistice these Detroiters and their Michigan and Wisconsin comrades served at Koblenz on the Rhine as part of the army of occupation until April 1919. Upon their return they staged a thrilling triumphal parade up Woodward avenue.

Guardsmen and volunteers did not provide the total manpower needed and the draft was resorted to. On June 5, 1917, all Detroit men between the ages of twenty-one and thirty flocked to voting booths, schools, and other public places to register. Two later registrations were necessary before the war ended. Many of the men drafted from Detroit and Michigan trained at Camp Custer near Battle Creek and became part of the 85th Division. Eventually they went overseas, but were used as replacements in other outfits.

One regiment of the 85th, however, had a strange adventure. The 339th Infantry, with a substantial representation of Detroiters, was sent to Archangel in northern Russia in 1918 to fight the Bolsheviks and provide what it was hoped would be a rallying point for non-Communist Russians. Badly armed and equipped, the regiment along with other army units experienced extreme hardship. Finally brought home in July 1919, they were given the name of the Polar Bears. Altogether Detroit furnished about 65,000 men and women to the armed forces in World War I.

On the home front the civilian population also was mobilized to support the war effort. With the departure of the National Guard, a home guard force was organized. Known as the Michigan State Troops, two regiments, the 551st and 552nd, were raised in Detroit and the surrounding area. In addition a more muscular force serving on a full-time basis was created. This was the Michigan State Constabulary patterned after the Royal Canadian Mounted Police. After the war the constabulary became the Michigan State Police. In Detroit they were kept busy guarding railroad yards, the water front, and other strategic places. A careful watch was kept on the Michigan Central railroad tunnel connecting Detroit and Windsor. Federal authorities professed knowledge of an enemy spy and sabotage ring operating in Detroit and Canada. The Detroit ring was directed by Karl Kalschmidt. He and several others were arrested and convicted. Some prominent German-American Detroiters were interned on farms in the Oscoda region. These activities, plus the nationalistic tensions which existed, led to the persecution of several loyal German-American families. Yellow paint was splashed on their homes, and they were threatened with physical violence and ostracized by their neighbors. A volunteer counter-espionage organization, the American Protective League, was formed. The duty of its members was to report any suspicious actions or utterances of those with whom they came in contact. Even school children were enlisted in this enterprise which was, to say the least, not very edifying, but it was excused as a wartime necessity.

Liberty bond drives were organized and well subscribed to. Detroiters served in the Red Cross, Y.M.C.A., Knights of Columbus, and Salvation Army, all of which provided aid and comfort to servicemen with their canteens and other helpful efforts at home as well as overseas. Food and fuel caused grave concern and serious shortages were felt. High school students and women were recruited in Detroit and sent out to work on farms in the state, particularly at harvest time. Breadless and meatless days were proclaimed, unessential businesses were encouraged to close on Mondays to save coal, and early in January 1918 the fuel shortage became so acute during a prolonged spell of bitterly cold weather that all businesses except hotels, restaurants, and drug stores were required to shut down for five days. During February the public schools were closed.

The harsh winter, the lack of fuel, and the crowding of workers contributed to the outbreak of an influenza epidemic in 1917. It was particularly virulent during 1918. The epidemic was worldwide and took millions of lives, both civilian and military. Detroit suffered severely; nearly everyone was stricken to some degree by the Spanish flu, as it was called, and hundreds died. For weeks many Detroiters went about wearing gauze masks in the fond belief that such devices would give protection. Unfortunately they did not.

In the late summer of 1918 the German armies began to collapse and on November 11 an armistice was signed. A few days before the 11th a premature announcement of peace resulted in general rejoicing followed by disappointment. But the word that flashed on November 11 was official and authentic, and Detroiters laid down their tools, quit their offices, homes and classrooms, and poured into the downtown streets to blow off steam. It was the wildest celebration the town had ever witnessed. The mass of humanity packed into Woodward avenue in front of the City Hall is said to have been the largest crowd ever assembled in Detroit up to that time, and it has been surpassed only once. (When campaigning for a second presidential term in 1936 Franklin D. Roosevelt was greeted by a larger throng in Woodward avenue, Campus Martius, and Cadillac Square.) The state troops, called out to help police handle the crowd, gave up, checked their rifles in nearby stores, and joyfully joined the celebration.

The next task was to return to normal as quickly as possible. Gradually the troops returned; they were briefly feted at the railroad stations by welcoming committees and given silver remembrance rings by the city. Then they started looking for their old jobs in the stores, offices, and factories.

The automobile industry too went to war in 1917 and for the first time in history it became a major factor in the production of munitions and other tools of war. It was partly the industry's productive resources which helped shorten the period of hostilities and assured the Allied victory. Even before the United States entered the war some auto plants held contracts from the Allies, so the conversion was not an immediate thing. Nor was it ever a complete one. Unlike in World War II, production of cars for the domestic civilian market was not halted, although it was slowed down.

Nearly every conceivable type of military equipment was turned out by the automotive and allied industries. Guns, ammunition, even the tin hats of the doughboys were produced in huge quantities. World War I was history's first motorized war and the trucks, ambulances, and staff cars that came from Detroit probably ended for all time the need and usefulness of cavalry and horse artillery. Old Dobbin was really retired to peaceful pastures. The first major automobile order from the government came six weeks after the declaration of war. It was for three thousand Ford ambulances. So much rolling stock and materiel began pouring out of Detroit that the already overburdened railroads could not handle it. So the state of

Michigan built a new concrete highway between Detroit and Toledo to facilitate motor hauling. It is the present-day Dixie highway.

One notable Detroit product was the famous Liberty engine for Allied aircraft. Designed by Packard's chief engineer Colonel Jesse G. Vincent, it was built by Packard, Ford, Cadillac, and a new concern, the Lincoln Motor Company organized in 1917 by Henry M. Leland and his son Wilfred. Lincoln was the principal builder of Liberty engines. A plant was constructed at Warren and Livernois, and the area around it was made hideous day and night by the deafening roar of hundreds of engines being block tested in open fields surrounding the factory. After the war the Lelands brought out the luxury Lincoln automobile. In 1922 the Lincoln company was purchased by Ford for $8,000,000 and the Lincoln division, to which was added the Mercury line, became part of the Ford Motor Company.

The Ford Rouge plant, under construction when the war broke out, was used for the production of Eagle boats, small but fast vessels designed for patrol and anti-submarine warfare. Out at the Highland Park plant as a portent of things to come, the company built small armored tread-operated vehicles looking something like over-grown bugs. Operated by one or two men and armed with machine guns, they were called Whippet tanks. To test them Ford built some artificial hills on the grounds just north of the plant on Woodward avenue, now used as a public playfield. Security was not as tight as it was in the war that followed and the public could watch those Whippets being tested. Home front military secrets were not really secrets at all in World War I.

The war left many marks upon Detroit, the most obvious being a bulging waistline. As thousands of new workers flocked to the local plants for war jobs, and as returning veterans sought to pick up their lives, a serious housing shortage developed. A newspaper ad of a flat for rent would frequently be answered by a line of applicants a block long. The result was a building boom and to obtain lots it was necessary to expand the city's boundaries. Small annexations had been made from time to time before the war, such as Delray in 1906 and Fairview on the east side in 1907. In 1916 a large area on either side of Woodward extending roughly from the Highland Park city limits to Eight Mile road was annexed. Then beginning in 1922 sizable sections were added in the Livernois area, in 1924 and 1925 huge parcels on the northwest and northeast perimeters were taken in, and in 1926 the last major annexation occurred when Redford became part of Detroit. With Redford, Detroit's area had grown to about one hundred and forty square miles.

Putting the House in Order

There were social as well as economic and geographical changes too. One of these was the appearance of women in factory jobs in large numbers. Woman's place no longer was in the home, the classroom or the office, but on the production line. During the first flurry of activity as industry strove for postwar normalcy, there was high employment and prosperity in Detroit. Workers bought new automobiles and reported to work in the factories sporting expensive silk shirts—perhaps a reaction to the drab uniformity of wartime garb.

Beginning in 1920 there was an economic recession, but it was of short duration, and by 1923 things were
booming again. A spiral of inflation was building up and
people were complaining about the high cost of living—
HCL as it was referred to. There was the beginning of wild
speculation in securities and real estate, and there was much
over-spending. The brakes were off and Detroit, along with
the nation and much of the world, was heading toward the
big skid climaxed by the crash of 1929.

During the years immediately before, during, and
after World War I, Detroit put its house in order and mod-
ernized its municipal government. The progressive movement, which began in 1890 when shoemaker Hazen S.
Pingree was elected mayor, started to bear fruit as reforms
were instituted. Pingree, or Ping as his fellow citizens fondly
called him, served six years. He gave Detroit one of its most
colorful administrations.

Today Ping would be called a liberal; in his time
he was known as a progressive. In fact he was in the fore-
front of that era and movement which produced such men
as Theodore Roosevelt, George Norris, and Robert LaFol-
lette. He fought the so-called vested interests to a standstill
and he beat them. He cleaned up graft-ridden municipal departments and laid the foundations for the relatively clean
nonpartisan form of municipal government later adopted.
He cleaned out the notorious red light district on the lower
east side and made the liquor interests mind their manners.
He fought the entrenched combine that controlled the street
railway franchises, forcing them to reduce fares under threat
of municipal ownership. When he felt the conservative
newspapers were not stating his position fairly, Ping refused to talk to reporters. Instead he posted his own bulletins on the door of the City Hall and the citizens flocked
downtown to read them.

When economic panic and depression struck in the 1890s, causing widespread unemployment, Pingree sought to relieve hardship by having the City Hall lawn, public parks, and other vacant land plowed up and turned into vegetable gardens on which Detroit's poor families could grow their own food. They were known as Ping's Potato Patches, and while it may be doubted that they actually saved anyone from starvation, the people loved him for them. In 1896 he was elected governor of Michigan and was reelected in 1898. He died while on a trip to London in 1901. His appreciative fellow citizens by popular subscription, much of it the pennies of school children, raised the money for a heroic seated statue of Pingree which was placed in Grand Circus Park in 1903, a perpetual monument to the man who was one of Detroit's foremost public servants.

After the turn of the century Detroit became too big and too complex a city to tolerate any longer a graft-ridden inefficient municipal government controlled by ward-heeler politicians. In 1912 the Detroit Citizens League was organized and its publication *The Civic Searchlight* became the bible of the independent voter. It threw a sharp beam of light into some dark and murky corners of the city hall. Behind the league were such men as Henry M. Leland, marking the first noticeable instance that the automobile industry was concerned with civic betterment. As a result of pressure by the Citizens League, aided by church groups, the Board of Education was reorganized in 1916. A school board of seven nonpartisan members, elected from the city at large instead of from wards as in the past, was provided for and public education was largely removed from the arena of partisan politics.

In 1918 Detroit voters adopted a new city charter which also provided for nonpartisan government. The charter established a strong mayor with power to appoint members of various commissions, most of whom served without pay. The common council was reduced in size from forty-two members (two elected from each ward) to nine members elected from the city at large. James Couzens, Henry Ford's former associate, became the first nonpartisan mayor under the new charter. In 1920 the reform movement was further advanced by the reorganization of the municipal courts. The old police courts were abolished and their jurisdiction was consolidated with that of the strengthened recorder's court. A new Recorder's Court building on St. Antoine street adjoining police headquarters had been built in 1917.

Mayor Couzens was elected on a platform of ending the streetcar monopoly, and the issue of municipal ownership became a lively and bitter one during his term of office. Couzens dramatized the question in 1918 by boarding a streetcar, refusing to pay the full fare, and having himself thrown off. In office he sought to smash the combine by using city funds to build the St. Jean line, in reality a belt line which circled the city and crossed Woodward at Clairmount avenue. This line went into operation in 1921 and private ownership was doomed. In 1922 the question of municipal ownership was placed before the people and was approved. The old Detroit United Railways, which had operated under city-awarded franchises, now became the municipal Department of Street Railways (DSR).

It took too long to lay tracks and extend lines to meet the needs of a rapidly expanding city. The DSR was no more successful in providing adequate service than the privately-owned system had been. To give more facilities the Detroit Motorbus Company was organized in 1920. Eight double-decked busses of the type then used in London and on New York's Fifth avenue were purchased in

England. At first service was given on Woodward and Jefferson from Grand Circus Park to Waterworks Park east of Belle Isle. Proving popular, additional busses were obtained and passengers could ride on Second avenue to Palmer Park. The competition hurt the DSR, however, and in 1932 the city took over the Detroit Motorbus Company and made it part of the municipal system.

For several years jitneys operated on Detroit's main streets. These were private automobiles licensed to carry passengers. Owner driven, they were much like taxicabs except they were restricted to a specified street. The fare was ten cents. These too proved to be convenient and popular, but they cut deeply into the business of the DSR. They were finally banned by city ordinance, but it took a six-year court fight before they were finally put out of business in 1928.

Eventually the DSR became completely motorized and on April 7, 1956, the last Detroit streetcar made its run on Woodward avenue. Thousands turned out to witness what to many was a nostalgic event. Detroit's streetcars were shipped to Mexico City where they are still in operation.

The Technicians

The new technology of the automobile age as well as the increased population made new educational facilities a necessity. Expanding business and all that went with it called for technical and professional skills which the universities and colleges of Michigan and other states could not easily supply. The result was the growth of institutions of higher learning to supply local needs and provide educations for stay-at-home students at a lower cost than was possible at the older established schools.

The beginning of this movement antedated the automobile industry by several decades. In 1868 a group of Detroit doctors, recognizing the need for better medical education, organized the privately-owned Detroit Medical College. Its first classrooms were in one of the army barracks on the grounds of Harper Hospital. After a brief residence there the school moved in 1883 to Farmer street between Gratiot and Monroe and changed its name to the Detroit College of Medicine. Still later it absorbed the rival Michigan College of Medicine. About 1890 new quarters were established at St. Antoine and Mullett adjacent to St. Mary's Hospital. A new medical school is now located nearby on the Chrysler expressway at Rivard.

For many years the medical college turned out practitioners of high quality, most of whom established themselves in Detroit and other Michigan communities. In 1918, finding the financial going difficult, the college was taken over by the Detroit Board of Education and in 1933 it became the medical college of Wayne University. The university, celebrating its centennial in 1968, dated its origin from the founding of its oldest college, the Wayne State College of Medicine.

Meanwhile, in 1913 a pre-med course was offered to high school students at old Central High School. This was successful and in 1915 post-graduate training was offered in other departments of Central. Proving popular, this program led to the establishment in 1917 of the Detroit Junior College offering a two-year curriculum with credits accepted at the University of Michigan and other institutions. In 1923 the junior college became the College of the City of Detroit offering regular four-year courses. By this time the college had all but completely crowded out the high school students, so a new Central High was built in 1926 at Tuxedo and Linwood. The old school at Cass and Warren then became Old Main of the new college. New schools were added, such as the College of Education which had long existed as the Detroit Normal School. Thus in 1934 City College attained university status and was named Wayne University. It remained under Board of Education control until 1956 when it was given the same status as other state-supported institutions and its name became Wayne State University.

Before Wayne State was even thought of, the Detroit College was founded in 1877 by priests of the Jesuit order. Its first campus—one of the asphalt variety—was on the south side of Jefferson between St. Antoine and Hastings. Additional facilities soon were needed and more property was acquired and buildings were erected on the north side of Jefferson adjoining SS. Peter and Paul's Church. A building on Larned street also was used.

Many of the students were employed during the day and attended evening classes. New departments were added from time to time—law, engineering, business administration, and dentistry. The college became so large and so important to the community that it was reorganized in 1911 as the University of Detroit. Expansion was restricted in the downtown location, so in 1922 a large campus of forty-two acres was obtained at West Six Mile and Livernois, and in 1927 the university moved there. The downtown campus was retained for night school and certain other activities. For several years the president of the University of Detroit was the Reverend Father John McNichols and in his honor the name of Six Mile road was changed to McNichols road. In 1927, too, the University of Detroit gained a fair neighbor when Marygrove College, a Catholic school for women, was opened at McNichols and Wyoming avenue.

There have been and are other important educational institutions in Detroit intended to fill the need for technical skills and know-how. In 1891 under the auspices of the Y.M.C.A., a technical school was opened which in time became the Detroit Institute of Technology, emphasizing engineering and science, but also offering degrees in other disciplines. In 1892 the Y.M.C.A. sponsored the Detroit College of Law which continues to thrive. With Wayne State and University of Detroit, DCL gives Detroit three excellent law schools.

In 1931 the Lawrence Institute of Technology was opened in a building which had formerly been part of the Ford Motor Company's Highland Park plant. Supported largely by local industry, Lawrence Tech with a greatly expanded curriculum has occupied modern buildings on a spacious campus at Ten Mile road and Northwestern highway since 1955. The Ford company early established the Henry Ford Trade School for the training of apprentices, and similar programs were instituted by General Motors and Chrysler. The latter have been expanded into engineering institutes which provide on-the-job education for selected employees comparable to training obtainable in most regular universities.

Another noteworthy educational institution which has attracted world-wide attention is the Merrill-Palmer Institute. It was established in 1918 by a bequest of Lizzie Merrill Palmer, daughter of the owner of the old Merrill block and wife of United States Senator Thomas W. Palmer. Originally a home-making institute, the scope of the school has greatly expanded into an advanced center for sociological and psychological training in the field of family and community services. Students are attracted from all over the world to its campus on East Ferry between Woodward and John R.

An Industry Comes of Age

In the postwar period the automobile industry may be said to have grown out of the adolescent stage and reached maturity. Actually, the process began before the war. In 1917 United States production of cars and trucks was 1,873,949 units. In 1918 war work lowered the output, but 1919 saw the cars rolling out of the plants at a rate equal to 1917. With some ups and downs, but mostly showing steady increases, domestic production rose year by year until 1929 when the five million unit mark was broken for the first time. Not until 1948 was that figure reached again.

Several factors contributed to this growth throughout the 1920 decade. It was a growth which led to the day when the production of motor vehicles and all the ramifications of a mighty enterprise made the automobile industry America's number one manufacturing activity, both from the standpoint of the value of the product and the number of people employed. This reflected an ever-expanding market, both domestic and foreign, but mainly domestic. Millions of soldiers learned to rely on the automobile during the war and became accustomed to using it. A car was one of the first things the veteran wanted when he returned to civilian life. The invention and perfection of the self-starter by Charles F. Kettering made the auto available to women by eliminating the crank and the broken wrists and sprained shoulders which went with it. Cadillac was the first to adopt the starter as standard equipment in 1912, by 1914 it was standard or optional on most models, and by 1920 it was standard equipment on virtually all cars. The ladies began to foresake their glassed-in electric machines—"show cases on wheels"—for the family gas buggy. Good roads encouraged more driving too, especially in the country, and soon the automobile was as essential a piece of farm equipment as the cow.

Out of the upsurge in sales and production emerged the Big Three as really big, and the day of the small independent was coming to a close. Some of the latter never recovered from the depression of the 1930s; others like Packard quietly gave up after World War II. But it was not all smooth competitive driving even for the giants, as Ford found out. His Model T, the famed Tin Lizzie, ruled the low-priced field until 1925 when good roads, a supply of cheap used cars, and the classier Chevrolet gave Ford trouble. By 1926 Ford sales were running a poor second to Chevrolet, and the next year the Model T was discontinued after fifteen million had been produced. The Model A appeared in 1928 and Ford was back in competition, although the Ford Motor Company never again had the field to itself as it did in the heyday of the Model T.

The entire industry in fact was becoming more sophisticated. The older generation of pioneer car builders, the inspired mechanics, began to be replaced by a new breed, the bright young engineers and sales executives out of MIT and other leading universities. The rewards for these new men were generous. Detroit was a wonderful place in which to work, but they wanted more gracious and spacious living, and the plush bedroom suburbs of

Birmingham, Bloomfield Hills, and Grosse Pointe became status symbols. The names of the old pioneers vanished one by one—Maxwell, Chalmers, Briscoe, and even Durant. They were replaced by new men. Charles F. (Boss Ket) Kettering, William S. Knudsen, Charles E. Wilson, Charles E. Sorenson, Alfred P. Sloan, K. T. Keller, Fred and James Zeder, George Mason, and B. Edwin Hutchinson were the monarchs in the automotive jungle. Some of them and others who followed never knew what it was to wear overalls.

Gradually the industry began to decentralize. It was more economical and efficient to assemble cars in plants close to the consumers. Before long Detroit proper was producing relatively few complete automobiles, although its suburbs and the metropolitan area were turning them out by the hundreds of thousands. However, the city continued to be the industry's nerve center. General Motors completed its headquarters building at West Grand boulevard and Second in 1921. At the time it was the world's largest office building. In 1928 the Fisher brothers built the monumental Fisher building across the street from the General Motors citadel. And out in Dearborn the Ford Rouge plant, in full operation by 1920, was pointed out to awe-struck visitors as the world's largest industrial complex. Ford's command post also was shifted from Highland Park to Dearborn.

Look to the Skies

Detroit got its first look at an airplane on July 14, 1910, when an intrepid barnstormer Arch Hoxey flew a biplane at the State Fairgrounds. It was less than seven years since the Wright brothers had successfully launched the first heavier-than-air machine at Kitty Hawk and flying was still something that had to be seen to be believed. Fliers like Hoxey were in the same class as circus performers and his exhibition was regarded with the same open-mouthed curiosity with which Detroiters gazed upon the first elephant displayed in the city in 1819. If the appearance of the first airplane made any impact upon Detroit, it was not apparent. Too much concerned with getting their new gas buggies to run, Detroiters were not inclined at the moment to lift their eyes from the road to the sky. But World War I changed that and Detroit suddenly became very air conscious. There was chivalry and romance in the accounts of the exploits of the gallant fliers that came back from overseas. The Royal Canadian Air Force drew adventure seekers from the United States before America entered the war, and the deeds of men like Captain Eddie Rickenbacker, a former auto racer, stirred the imagination. In 1917 Selfridge Field was established near Mount Clemens through the efforts of men like Henry B. Joy, president of Packard, and William B. Mayo, Ford's chief engineer, both aviation enthusiasts. When the auto plants began to turn out Liberty engines and other aircraft parts, Detroit awoke to the fact that the air age had dawned. When men who learned to fly in the air corps returned to civilian life, there was a ready-made pool of flying buffs, trained pilots, and a potential market of sorts for aircraft. But above all, there was now public interest in aviation.

In 1920 the first airmail was flown into Detroit, and in 1922 a seaplane service operating from a ramp just above the Belle Isle bridge began to carry passengers to Cleveland. In the same year a young genius William B. Stout, who had been a Packard engineer, designed an all-metal plane powered by a Liberty engine. Stout attracted the attention of Henry Ford who saw possibilities in the airplane and laid out the area's first real civilian airport on Oakwood just south of Michigan in Dearborn. From that field Ford operated the world's first air freight service, ferrying parts from Dearborn to his plants in Cleveland and Buffalo. In the shops adjoining the airport Stout built a trimotor metal job which was taken over by Ford in 1925. This was the famed Ford trimotor transport capable of carrying twelve passengers. It was an extremely reliable ship and as late as 1967 there were still two or three in service.

Until 1927 the Ford airport, now the company's proving ground, was the center of Detroit's aviation activity. It served a variety of purposes. Not only was it the terminal for passenger and mail service, it was also used for aircraft shows, reliability tours, air sightseeing, and other activities. At one end of the field a mooring tower was erected and in 1926 the dirigible Los Angeles tied up there. The field was something of a scientific base as well because in 1926 a Stout-Ford trimotor was built and equipped for south polar exploration by Admiral Richard E. Byrd. An earlier plane, a Fokker, was donated by Ford for north pole exploration. Named the Josephine Ford, it is on view today in the Henry Ford Museum.

In May 1927 aviation was given tremendous impetus by the successful New York to Paris nonstop flight of Charles A. Lindbergh. This was of particular interest to Detroit because Lindbergh was a native son. His birthplace was at 1120 West Forest avenue, now adjacent to the Wayne State campus. Although he lived there only a short while, his mother Evangeline Land Lindbergh, a teacher at Cass Technical High School, was a Detroit resident at the time of his famous flight. Lindbergh also was the grand-nephew of John C. Lodge, his mother's uncle, who had been mayor of the city and was long a member of the common council.

With the upsurge in aviation interest, resulting in large part from Lindbergh's feat as well as the 1927 around the world flight of two other Detroiters, Billy Brock and Ed Schlee, Detroit began to think of itself as the emerging aviation capital of the world. Enthusiasts pointed out that the same elements of skill, know-how, and material that made the city the center of automobile production were applicable to aircraft. Companies were formed, notably the Buhl Aircraft Company, the Verville Aircraft Company, and the Stinson Aircraft Corporation. Each one produced excellent ships, but with the exception of Stinson which was absorbed by the Cord Corporation, they did not survive the depression of the 1930s. Several aircraft engine and parts companies were established and some of them continue to operate. Among the better known were the Warner Aircraft Corporation and Continental Motors. The Detroit & Cleveland Navigation Company bought a pair of German-built flying boats for a Detroit-Cleveland-Buffalo passenger operation, but the project was abandoned before service actually began.

At one point a group of aviation enthusiasts began thinking in terms of a General Motors Corporation of the air. In 1929 they organized the Detroit Aircraft Corporation, a holding company which controlled or sought to control several of the most active and successful companies in the aircraft industry. Among the organizers were William B. Mayo of Ford and Charles F. Kettering of General Motors, and the company president was Edward S. Evans who had successfully developed a railroad freight car loading system for the shipment of automobiles. The nucleus of Detroit Aircraft Corporation was the Aircraft Development Corporation which had a navy contract to build a large all-metal dirigible. This company was formed in 1922 and by 1927 its airship was well on the way to completion. The parts were fabricated in a shop at West Jefferson and Clark, but the ship was put together in a huge hangar erected in 1927 adjoining a private airport on the southern tip of Grosse Ile. The dirigible was finally delivered to the navy and proved as successful as any of the lighter-than-air ships. It was in operation at Lakehurst, New Jersey, for about ten years. In addition to the dirigible, Aircraft Development Corporation held the franchise for erecting dirigible mooring towers and built one at the Ford airport.

Detroit Aircraft acquired the assets of Aircraft Development, Ryan Aircraft Corporation, builder of Lindbergh's *Spirit of St. Louis*, a tool company, an engine company, a flying service, and negotiated for the Lockheed Aircraft Company. In addition, it took over the Grosse Ile airport which eventually became a naval air station. But the scheme was too grandiose, business was not forthcoming, and although many Detroiters bought stock in Detroit Aircraft, the depression burst the bubble.

Gradually activities began to shift from the Ford airport after 1927 when the Detroit City Airport was built at Gratiot and Conner avenues. Commercial services as well as private fliers began to use this new municipal field and before long it was claimed to be the busiest commercial airport in the United States. It was still busy in 1967, largely used by private fliers and company planes. Until the end of World War II it was the area's principal passenger terminal. Both during and after the war major operations centered at Willow Run Airport, the city airport being too small to handle the big jet passenger planes. Even Willow Run soon became inadequate and the huge Metropolitan Airport was developed by Wayne County, an outgrowth of the old Wayne County Airport, long used for private flying and as a national guard air base. During World War II its facilities were improved to handle the bombers produced in the area. In 1966 the last of the commercial lines left Willow Run and all the major lines concentrated their operations at Metropolitan.

Detroit never became the aviation capital of the world; no one city did. But interest in aviation has always been great in Detroit; its money, its talents, and its products helped develop the industry and are among its major bulwarks to this day. The city may not be predominant in the field, but without Detroit the aircraft industry would be much less than it is.

51. Downtown Detroit Today

52. Downtown Detroit

53. Washington Boulevard

54. Detroit Harbor Terminals
55. S.S. Ste. Claire

56. On the Dock

57. Ford Assembly
    Line

58. General Motors Technical Center

59. Chrysler Corporation Headquarters

60. Lem Barney of the Detroit Lions, N.F.L. Rookie of the Year 1967.

61. Ecorse Marathon

62. Gordie Howe of the Detroit Red Wings Hockey Club

63. Dave Bing of the Detroit Pistons Basketball Team

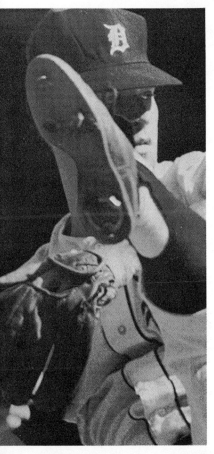

64. Mickey Lolich, Detroit Tigers' Hero of the 1968 World Series

65. Denny McLain, Winner of 31 Games for 1968 Detroit Tigers

66. Tigers Win World Championship in Baseball—City Goes Wild!

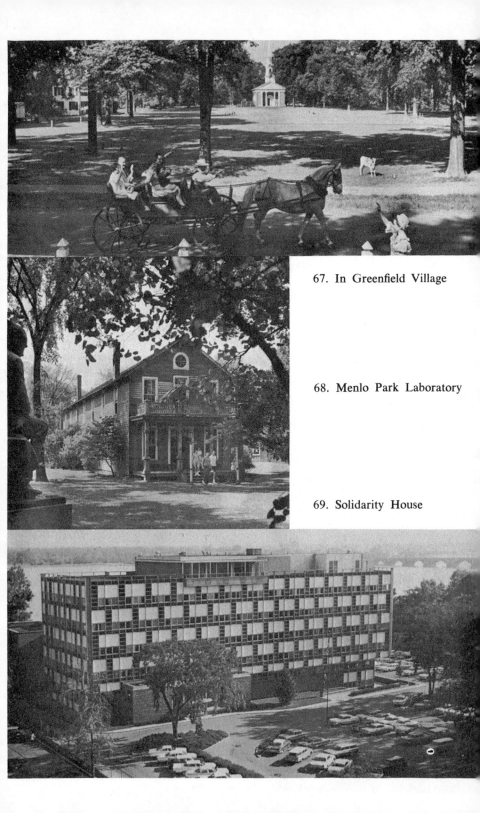

67. In Greenfield Village

68. Menlo Park Laboratory

69. Solidarity House

13

Social Upheaval

'Joe Sent Me'

"Detroit—Soused and Serene!"

That was the label hung on Detroit by a national magazine article describing the city during the prohibition years. The caption was only partly correct. Detroit may have been soused, but it certainly was not serene. Even the term soused may give the wrong impression. Beyond doubt Detroit drank its share of bootleg hooch but its chief role in prohibition was not that of consumer. The city was the distribution center, the funnel through which flowed gallon upon gallon of bootlegged booze which slaked the parched throat of much of the American Midwest. Detroit may be said to have had two major industries during most of the 1920s—the manufacture of automobiles and the distribution of Canadian liquor. Sometimes it was hard to tell which enterprise rated as number one.

It began back in 1916 in a reform-minded period when the state of Michigan amended its constitution to prohibit the manufacture and sale of intoxicating liquor. The amendment took effect May 1, 1918, amid scenes of general sorrow. On the night before the ban went into effect the mourners gathered for the obsequies in their favorite saloons and endeavored to drink up all the remaining supply. Of course they were unsuccessful but they made a valiant try. Affluent citizens bought out the wholesale and retail liquor dealers and stocked their cellars with cases, kegs, and barrels of the choicest varieties. They were prepared to last out the drouth.

On the morning of May 1 many saloonkeepers, perhaps a majority, were open for business, although not quite as usual. The shades were drawn; the doors were latched and fitted with small peepholes so that only those known to the proprietors (who had extensive circles of friends and acquaintances) could be screened for admittance. Thus was born the era of the blind pig, the speakeasy, the joint. It is worth a minor observation that many of these places never went out of business, but were still operating fourteen years later when prohibition was repealed. As the old saying went, anyone who couldn't get a drink simply wasn't trying.

For the first couple of years of prohibition Michigan was theoretically dry but Ohio was not. Traffic between Detroit and Toledo increased noticeably. A steady stream of fast cars and trucks roared up Telegraph road bringing in liquid cargoes to keep Detroit's whistle wet. These loads, carried in wholesale lots, were of great value to the rum runners. As a result hijacking became a popular sport. The caravans picked up speed and hoodlums were hired to ride shotgun, and the sound of gunfire rose to a crescendo. In this manner the prohibition era spawned organized crime and violence.

On January 16, 1920, the 18th Amendment to the United States Constitution became effective and prohibition became national. Detroiters toasted the event in their favorite speakeasies, national prohibition caused the Ohio spigot to be turned off, and the illicit liquor operators turned to Canada as the chief source of supply. Immediately rum running began across the Detroit River. This traffic soon involved others than local operators. Canada became the supplier not only for Detroit but also for Chicago and other midwestern markets. Syndicates, such as that led by Al Capone, moved in and the smuggling of beer and whiskey from the Windsor area became a well-organized big business.

No one can accurately state the value of the liquor carried across the Windsor-Detroit border in the 1920s, but hundreds of millions of dollars would be a reasonable guess. It was said that eighty-five per cent of all the liquor smuggled into the United States from Canada crossed here. At times the business amounted to 500,000 cases a month.

There was no place along the St. Clair and Detroit Rivers where smuggling was not carried on, although the heaviest activity was in the Ecorse and Wyandotte districts. Boat houses lined the shore and each night fast high-powered boats made runs to the Canadian side, picked up loads, and returned, all in a matter of minutes. Later, fast tugs were used for carrying heavier loads. It was not speed boats alone which transported the liquid treasure. After the Ambassador Bridge was built in 1929 and the Detroit-Windsor Tunnel in 1930, booze came across by the truckload. It was not unusual for rail shipments to come in under spurious bills-of-lading. Individuals brought in single bottles hidden under their coats or in the upholstery of their cars. Women, safe from search by authorities, tucked bottles inside their girdles and waddled blithely through customs. This contraband was known as girdle or panty whiskey.

Every sort of ingenious device was used to get liquor across the border and to distribute it. A bank vault in what is now St. Clair Shores was used as a storage place. It held more cases of whiskey than currency and securities. In at least two instances windlasses were rigged on the American shore and sled-like contraptions were hauled over the river bed. When customs or enforcement patrols were known to be out on the prowl, rumrunners were advised by a system of signals tooted by the locomotive engineers in the railroad yards along the river front. The Detroit-Windsor Tunnel was referred to as the Detroit-Windsor Funnel. There even was a rumor that a pipeline had been laid across the river, connecting a Canadian distillery with a Detroit bottling plant.

The average Detroiter cared little about where his liquor came from as long as he got it. There were many back alley breweries and stills in operation, their products of dubious quality bearing the counterfeit labels of well-known brands. Everyone had his favorite bootlegger, usually a furtive individual who, responding to a telephone call, would appear with a bottle or two, or lugging a case if that was ordered. Deliveries were made to homes, offices, and hotel rooms. Many a person became an amateur brewer and made his own. Beer—the home brew variety—was the most popular concoction. Equipment could be purchased at any hardware or dime store. The ingredients were easy to get. Quick consumption was necessary; otherwise rapid fermentation could be expected and the householder would be awakened by popping corks or bursting bottles in his basement. If alcohol could be obtained—and that was not difficult—gin was also easy to make. Added to the raw alcohol would be a little distilled water, a drop or two of glycerine, and a touch of juniper juice, available at any drug store. The mixture would then be shaken vigorously or the jug in which it was mixed would be rolled back and forth across the floor for ten minutes to provide proper aging; then it was ready to drink.

The most colorful part of prohibition centered around the blind pigs. It was estimated that Detroit at one time had as many as 25,000. These were the places at which "Joe sent me" was the password that provided admittance. Except when a periodic law enforcement drive was on, even that formula was superfluous. If you looked like you had the price of a drink, you were welcome. Blind pigs came in every assorted shape and size, and each tried to cultivate an atmosphere of its own. Some were garish nightclub types with entertainment, high prices, excellent cuisine, and a select clientele. Others attempted to preserve the aura of the old-time saloon with sawdust on the floor, red checkered table cloths, and a free lunch at one end of the bar. At the bottom of the scale were the out-and-out joints, back rooms or flats where anything went. In Hamtramck, where thirsts were monumental, liquor by the glass was even sold on the streets from parked automobiles. That was mostly to accommodate factory workers coming off their shifts who needed fortifying before undertaking the trip home. As a rule the police knew the whereabouts of most of the pigs but only occasionally interfered. There was a set of unwritten rules about closing them; as long as the blind pig operator kept his place quiet and orderly, as long as he paid off regularly and was willing to submit to an occasional raid for the sake of appearances, he was permitted to remain in business.

While the blind pigs generally did no great harm themselves, there developed a most unsavory sideline to the business. Gamblers took advantage of the blindfolded law and several casinos operated in and around Detroit. There was the Aniwa Club, for example, on Van Dyke just off East Jefferson, patronized by the Grosse Pointe social set. There also were such well-remembered places as Blossom Heath, Chesterfield Inn, the Club Royale, Doc Brady's, and

Lefty Clark's big dice parlor over a garage in Ecorse. Ecorse had the Green Lantern, too, where a lively blackjack game ran around the clock. With things on such a free and easy basis, prostitution also flourished. There were several notorious houses in Detroit and Hamtramck. In the 1930s when jobs were scarce, many out-of-work office girls operated out of their apartments in better-class neighborhoods, making the problem worse.

Conditions became bad and there was a great deal of corruption among officials. This was finally disclosed by the post-prohibition grand jury investigation conducted in 1940 by Circuit Judge (later United States Senator) Homer Ferguson. As a result of his cleanup campaign, the mayor of Detroit, the county sheriff, the prosecuting attorney, several other officials, and scores of top-ranking police officers, together with a number of underworld characters, were indicted and sent to jail.

By the mid-1920s the illicit liquor traffic was tightly controlled by the big city gangs. The one headed by Al Capone of Chicago was a classic example. These powerful gangs operated outside the law or, it might be said, within a legal framework of their own. Policemen, judges, revenue agents, and politicians were bought and expected to deliver in the form of protection. Territories were marked out and rival hoodlums attempting to poach on others' preserves were ruthlessly executed. Mass murder became commonplace, reaching a bloody climax in Chicago on St. Valentine's Day, 1929, when seven members of one mob were lined up in a garage and machine-gunned down. The episode went into the record as the Valentine's Day Massacre. Not to be outdone by their Chicago counterparts, a Detroit mob, the Purple Gang, staged a similar execution in 1931 in an apartment at Collingwood and Twelfth. Three men were killed in what the newspapers grandiloquently termed the Collingwood Massacre.

When the gangsters and hoodlums were not busy running liquor they turned to other forms of crime. Kidnapping became a serious menace and Detroit had several instances of persons' being held for large ransom. No one was really safe. Henry Ford was concerned for the safety of his family, which accounted in part for the rise to power of Harry Bennett whose job was to provide protection. Later, when prohibition phased out and kidnapping became a hazardous operation, underworld attention shifted to gambling, dope peddling, and prostitution.

Detroit had two major gangs in the prohibition period. One was the Purples; the other was the Licavoli gang named after one of its leaders. After the Collingwood Massacre and similar events the Purples were pretty much eliminated as a menace. Some of them went to prison for long terms; others were murdered gangland style. The Licavoli gang continued to operate and some of its members and associates, still living, are believed by some law enforcement officials to be powers in the present-day Mafia or Cosa Nostra. Both gangs had their origins in Detroit's lower east side, beginning as youthful street corner hoodlums, and each was at one time or another allied with the Capone and other national crime syndicates.

The operation of the gangs in Detroit left a bloody mark on the city. Murder became so commonplace as to make the headlines one day and be forgotten the next when some new act of violence occurred. Because the victims were usually other gangsters, the average citizen was shocked but seldom in jeopardy. Gang warfare did not directly involve noncombatants.

The worst outbreak of gang murder in Detroit took place in 1930. During the first two weeks of July ten men were killed by gangsters' guns. The month became known

as Bloody July. Then on the morning on July 22 there occurred one of the most spectacular murders in Detroit's
crime history. It was the shooting of prominent and popular
radio commentator Jerry Buckley in the lobby of the La
Salle Hotel at Woodward and Adelaide street. The La Salle,
once a hoodlum hangout, is now an eminently respectable
retirement home for the elderly known as Carmel Hall. The
Buckley murder was never satisfactorily solved; no one was
ever really sure of the motive and no one ever went to prison,
although the police believed they knew the identity of one
of the triggermen, a member of the Licavoli gang.

The Buckley killing had all the earmarks of a "who-
dunit." Jerry Buckley, a member of a good Corktown family, suddenly came into prominence in 1929 when he gained
access to a microphone in the studio of Radio Station
WMBC which was located in the La Salle where Buckley
also maintained a suite. As a commentator Buckley devoted
himself mostly to local affairs: municipal government,
crime, unemployment, and other subjects troubling the public. His talks were more emotional than factual, but he
caught the public's attention. He seemed to speak for the
bewildered and frustrated little man who felt his world was
collapsing. To such people Buckley was a messiah and a
champion, and they listened to him by the thousands with
a rapt and loyal attention.

There were others who claimed Buckley was not
the white knight whose mission was to right the world's
wrongs. There were rumors that he was not above making
deals, that he would champion a cause for a price, or lay off
for a price. Some believed he was working with the underworld and that his murder was the result of his failure to
deliver or a doublecross.

July 21 was the date for the recall election of Mayor
Charles Bowles who had been elected with Ku Klux Klan

backing. Buckley had opposed the recall and on July 20, the eve of the election, promised the Bowles crowd he would go on the air in support of the mayor. But when he delivered his talk he made a complete about face and strongly supported the recall movement. On the evening of the 21st he went to the City Hall to watch the election returns come in and broadcast bulletins reporting the trend of the vote. While at the City Hall he received a phone call and was overheard agreeing to meet someone, presumably a woman, later that night in the La Salle lobby.

Shortly after midnight Buckley made his final broadcast and returned to the hotel, taking a seat in the lobby. At one a.m. three men came in by the Adelaide street entrance, crossed the nearly empty lobby to where Buckley was sitting alone, and in true gangster fashion shot him to death. From a police standpoint the investigation of the crime was a bungled farce. Ultimately, however, three men were arrested and tried, but the jury acquitted them. The character of the prosecution witnesses and the conflicting testimony made a conviction all but impossible. Later investigation discounted any connection with the Bowles recall as a motive. Instead, it was the general opinion that Buckley had become involved with underworld characters and was the victim of a gang execution.

Whatever the reason, the death of Jerry Buckley was undoubtedly Detroit's most sensational murder. The public was shocked. Buckley's vast audience mourned him as few have been mourned in Detroit. It was estimated that 150,000 filled the streets at his funeral, and a couple of weeks later a memorial service held on Belle Isle was attended by more than five thousand of his followers.

The death of Buckley, official corruption, and the brazenness of the gangsters led to a public disillusionment with prohibition and strong repeal sentiment began to grow.

The depression helped this cause because it was widely felt that by legalizing the liquor business many new jobs would be created. In 1931 a government study of the effect and effectiveness of prohibition, known as the Wickersham Report, flatly stated that Detroit topped the nation in prohibition law violations. Prominent Detroit business and social leaders, supported by some well-known clergymen, organized a repeal movement. In 1932 Michigan repealed its state prohibition statutes, and the following year it became the first state to ratify the 21st Amendment which repealed the 18th Amendment. The legislature created a state Liquor Control Commission and authorized the sale of beer and wine beginning April 7, 1933. Detroit celebrated when the lid was removed and blind pig operators hastened to go legitimate by applying for liquor licenses. In many cases these were granted. On December 5, 1933, the 21st Amendment was ratified and what President Hoover had once referred to as the noble experiment passed into history.

'Mister, Can You Spare a Dime?'

President Herbert Hoover accompanied by Thomas A. Edison visited Detroit on October 21, 1929. For the latter it was in the nature of a homecoming. As a youth Edison had ridden the Grand Trunk between Detroit and Port Huron, where he lived, selling newspapers to passengers. During layovers in Detroit he spent some of his time in the Detroit Public Library reading scientific and mechanical magazines. The president and Edison were the guests of Henry Ford. The purpose of their visit was to dedicate Greenfield Village, an event that started that place on its way to becoming one of the nation's two leading tourist attractions, bringing in over a million visitors each year. They also took part in ceremonies in west Grand Circus Park where a fountain commemorating Edison's invention of the electric light was unveiled. It was one of the last gala occasions Detroit was to know for a decade or so.

Three days after that visit the stock market broke and continued its plunge until November 13, ushering in the worst financial panic the United States ever experienced. It also ushered out one of the zaniest periods in history, sometimes called the Roaring Twenties.

For ten years or more following the end of World War I, except for a recession in 1921-22, America lived in a dream world. Business boomed, employment was high, prohibition was a joke, moral codes began to relax, and everybody had fun. Detroit joined zestfully in this good time without giving thought to the likelihood that sooner or later the piper would demand his pay. The automobile industry hit a new peak of prosperity. The city grew in population; its borders expanded and new suburbs were laid out. People dreamed of getting rich quickly and engaged in wild speculation. There seemed to be plenty of money around and more could be obtained by speculating or borrowing. Detroiters built homes and bought lots in new subdivisions, paying a few dollars down and anticipating quick resales at fancy profits. The stock market beckoned with a golden finger; Detroiters flocked into brokers' offices and bought securities, many of doubtful value, on small margin. Everybody seemed to be buying everything. The trouble was that it was all being done on credit and paper profits were being pyramided. Speculation was wild and uncontrolled, and people blithely ran up unmanageable debts.

And then in that black October the bottom fell out.
The causes of the depression which followed did not orig-
inate in Detroit. They were world-wide, the results of the
war with its ensuing inflation and European financial and
political collapses. The stock market break was a signal for
the general economic collapse which followed almost immediately. Thousands lost their money in the market;
everything tightened up and the boom deflated. The great
reservoir of easy money and credit dried up almost over
night and the public stopped buying.

Detroit was one of the first cities to feel the effects,
due to its industrial nature and heavy reliance on the automobile industry. In 1929, 5,337,087 vehicles were produced. In 1930 production was down to 3,362,820, and in
1931 it touched bottom with an output of only 1,331,860.
That meant extensive layoffs in the factories. Suddenly
thousands of Detroit workers were out of jobs. Lacking resources, they could not pay their bills, their credit no longer
was good at the corner grocery store, and the merchants
themselves began to feel the pinch. Detroit went from silk
shirt affluence to hunger in a matter of a few short months.
At the beginning of 1931 the situation was critical and on
January 2 a crowd of unemployed demonstrated in front of
the City Hall. Not fully understanding what was happening,
officials called upon the police to break up the demonstration, and for the first time in its history Detroit witnessed the
shocking sight of hungry men and women being ridden
down by mounted policemen.

In 1930 a combination of circumstances led to a
political revolt and Mayor Charles Bowles was kicked out
of office in a recall election. He was succeeded by Frank
Murphy, a judge of recorder's court who eventually became
governor-general of the Philippines, governor of Michigan,
United States attorney general, and a justice of the U.S.

Supreme Court. A liberal and a humanitarian, it became Murphy's task as mayor to alleviate the widespread distress. It was obvious that to avert starvation and homelessness, public assistance in the form of a substantial welfare program was essential. The problem, though, was where the money was to come from. The principal source of municipal revenue at that time was the general property tax. Lacking money, people were unable to pay their taxes and city revenues dried up. All sorts of devices were tried to help the proverty stricken. Men sold apples on street corners, private and religious organizations established soup kitchens, and bread lines became familiar sights. The city converted three factories into hostels or dormitories for homeless men; evicted families were sheltered in tent colonies set up in parks. What public funds could be found—and they were wholly inadequate—were doled out, sometimes as little as two dollars a week to buy food for an entire family.

It was not the factory workers only who were distressed. Middle and upper income families saw their savings wiped out and their jobs vanish. Most businesses, to stay alive, drastically cut salaries and wages. Even municipal employees were hit when the treasury became empty and in April 1933 the city paid off in scrip to the amount of $8,000,000. But public employees were relatively fortunate. Most of them kept their jobs and few knew the necessity of applying for public relief. Early in 1931 as many as 48,000 Detroit families were receiving some form of welfare. At an average of four persons per family, that meant 192,000 individuals were being cared for. About twenty per cent of Detroit's work force was idle.

As might be expected, the general distress brought forth all kinds of local prophets with their panaceas. Detroit's most famous one was the Reverend Father Charles

E. Coughlin, a Roman Catholic priest who was pastor of
the Shrine of the Little Flower in Royal Oak. Father Coughlin attracted wide attention with a series of Sunday afternoon radio programs of a religious nature. A persuasive
and eloquent orator, he talked on social, economic, and
political problems during the 1930s. He quickly gained a
tremendous influence by his attacks on international bankers at whose doorstep he placed all the world's ills. He became the number one radio personality of his time.

Augmenting his radio programs, Father Coughlin
began to publish a magazine called *Social Justice* for which
he claimed 600,000 subscribers. At first he supported the
presidential candidacy of Franklin D. Roosevelt, but later
broke with him, and at one point attempted to form a third
national party. Apparently carried away by his own elo-
quence and power, Father Coughlin's speeches began to
deteriorate into bitter diatribes which became anti-Semitic,
isolationist, and in the opinion of many, almost treasonable.
He was finally silenced by his superiors in the church and
his magazine was barred from the mails early in 1942 because of its opposition to the United States war effort.

Others whose voices were raised on social subjects
included the Reverend Gerald L. K. Smith, a Protestant
evangelist who had been allied with Senator Huey Long of
Louisiana. Smith's appeal at first was to the factory worker,
and he was said to have been encouraged and subsidized by
local manufacturers because he preached against unionism.
Before long, however, he too became rabidly isolationist
and his influence waned. Father Coughlin and Reverend
Smith represented the extreme right wing. Opposed to them,
the Communist Party was active in Detroit, endeavoring to
make converts among the unemployed and the welfare
recipients.

The most dangerously explosive event of the depression occurred on March 7, 1932. It has become known as the Ford Hunger March, a Communist-inspired demonstration. For a few days prior to March 7 top American Communist leaders had been in Detroit, making speeches and working upon the emotions of their followers and the non-Communist unemployed.

About 3,000 persons participated in the march which began peaceably enough. The demonstrators assembled in downtown Detroit where they had a permit to parade. They intended to go to Dearborn, force an audience with Henry Ford, and present him with a list of demands which included union recognition, fuller employment, and better working conditions.

The crowd boarded streetcars which took them to the Dearborn city limits where they formed the parade. As they attempted to enter Dearborn they were stopped by forty members of that city's police department on the grounds that they had no Dearborn parade permit. The leaders urged their followers on anyway. They were met by a barrage of tear gas and a melee followed. The Dearborn police were attacked and shots were fired by both sides. Four were killed and a hundred were wounded or injured. Among the latter was Ford's service chief Harry Bennett who came to the scene carrying a white flag and bearing the assurance that the company would start rehiring for new model production within a few days. The mob was finally broken up when Detroit police went to the aid of the Dearborn officers. The march never reached the Ford plant.

During the next few days there was a series of Communist demonstrations. An estimated 15,000 persons turned out for the funeral of one of the dead marchers. Observers said later that the affair had all the ingredients for the start of a Communist revolution. That it did not come off may be attributed to the fact that most of Detroit's workers refused to follow the red banner. But as one writer said in retrospect, "It was the best chance the Communists ever had in the United States."

The most dramatic incident of the depression occurred early in 1933 when the banks of Michigan were closed by the decree of Governor William A. Comstock. Although the necessity for such a drastic act is still being debated, it had the long-range effect of clearing the air, eliminating much deadwood from the local financial structure, and helping to restore confidence and prosperity.

At the beginning of 1933 Detroit had two major banking organizations, the Guardian Detroit Group organized in 1929 and the Detroit Bankers Company created in 1930. These were holding companies, each built around a major Detroit bank, with trust companies and other financial institutions acquired by purchase or merger. The two nucleus banks were the Guardian National and the First National. The groups were formed partly from ambition— the surge toward bigness. Another factor was the necessity for the absorption of smaller correspondent banks which were in trouble. By 1933 the two groups were in an extremely shaky situation, a fact not then generally known by the public. Their conditions were a reflection of what had been going on in the speculative hectic 1920s and the early depression aftermath. The banks held mortgages on which jobless borrowers could not keep up their payments. Moreover, these mortgages were on property appraised at boomtime prices. Now the bottom was out and the banks could not hope to recover through foreclosure of mortgages which were themselves inflated. The banks also had granted large loans and now found the collateral they had accepted, most of it in securities, had shrunk to a fraction of its original value as the result of the stockmarket collapse and the generally deflated state of business.

In addition to the two big banks, Detroit had four independent banks. These were smaller, more conservatively managed, and in relatively good shape. It was feared that if the two large banks collapsed, sound banks in Detroit and outstate might be pulled down too. Efforts were made to bolster the Guardian with a large government loan, which proved to be insufficient, and a still larger one was sought. The government, unable to find security for such a loan, made a counter offer. It proposed putting up part of the needed money if the large depositors such as the Ford Motor Company, General Motors Corporation, and Chrysler Corporation would guarantee the balance. General Motors and Chrysler agreed, but Henry Ford, who had long carried on a running feud with the banks, refused to participate. Senator James Couzens declared that if a loan was made without adequate security he would "scream from the housetops."

The outlook was bleak and on Sunday, February 12, New York and Chicago bankers hastened to Detroit to meet with Detroit bank officials, industrialists, and government representatives to see if the situation could be salvaged. After a two-day conference it was agreed that the condition of the Guardian and First National appeared hopeless and they should not be permitted to open on February 14, the 13th being a legal holiday, the postponement of Lincoln's birthday.

Fearing that the failure of the two big banks to open would cause a run on the smaller banks, drastic measures were advocated. Governor Comstock was called in and asked to issue a bank holiday proclamation, closing all banks in the state effective February 14. He agreed and the proclamation was written out at the Detroit Club during the night of the 13th. Shortly before midnight Comstock and his press secretary walked around the corner to the *Detroit Free Press* and made the announcement.

Detroit was in a state of shock and disbelief on February 14. People who did business by check found they had no funds available. Employers were unable to meet their payrolls and merchants could not pay their bills. Business at every level was suddenly paralyzed. The only cash was what people had in their pockets or cash registers, or in safety deposit boxes where, admittedly, a lot was being hoarded. Large business concerns with banking connections in other cities had currency shipped to them, but even that source dried up on March 6 when President Roosevelt made the bank holiday a national one.

By March 21 solvent state banks were permitted to open under tight restrictions and limited withdrawals were allowed. But the two large Detroit banks with more than 800,000 depositors were put through a process of liquidation. Big depositors waived their claims in order that the smaller ones could be paid off; good assets were sold to two new banks, the Manufacturers National and the National Bank of Detroit. New state and federal legislation was enacted to improve banking practices, and a system of federal insurance of deposits up to $5,000 (later increased to $10,000, then again to $15,000) was put into effect. By 1934 sufficient recovery had been made so that the Detroit banking community was on a sound footing.

Just as the causes of the depression were at work before the people became aware of them, so was the process of recovery. But it was slow and painful. The problem was to keep body and soul together until things got back to normal. Following his inauguration in 1933 President Franklin D. Roosevelt presented Congress with a program of relief measures in which the resources of the federal government were used to accomplish what the states and local governments could not do for lack of funds. Among the first of these measures was the establishment of Civilian Conservation Corps (CCC) camps. These recruited jobless young men, most of whose families were on welfare. They were sent out to work on conservation projects such as planting forests, cleaning streams, rehabilitating public parks, and building rural roads. They were under the supervision of reserve army officers, many of whom were jobless themselves. Part of the youths' pay was sent home to their families.

Other public works programs followed. The Civil Works Administration was set up under the supervision of the various states, and in Michigan about 170,000 workers were employed in various activities. In 1935 the Works Progress Administration (WPA) came into existence and thousands of Detroiters were given jobs at what amounted to subsistence pay. Locally, as elsewhere, projects were created wherever anything of a public nature could be found to do. Gangs of men raked leaves in public parks; others cleaned sewers and ditches, trimmed trees, repaired streetcar tracks, rebound books for schools and libraries. Even jobless white collar and professional people were looked after. Artists were given the job of restoring paintings or decorating the interiors of public buildings; writers' and actors' projects were developed, and symphony orchestras were organized. Under another program, the Public Works Administration (PWA), federal grants were made to local communities for such undertakings as street paving and the construction of schools, libraries, bath houses, and other public buildings. Some of the projects were designed to serve no other useful purpose than to provide jobs. As a result there was some waste and much criticism from the local press and other sources. But what was overlooked by the critics was the fact that able-bodied men and women had their hope, dignity, and self-confidence restored, and their morale improved by being given a wage for productive work. Equally important, the millions of dollars spent on these projects were transformed into purchasing power which rippled the stagnant economic waters.

There were other measures of relief besides those which provided work and home welfare. A federal agency was created which enabled distressed homeowners to refinance their mortgages, thus avoiding foreclosure of their homes. Detroit City Treasurer Albert E. Cobo produced a plan which enabled property owners to extend payments of delinquent taxes over a seven-year period. This freed them from the fear of losing their homes through tax foreclosure sales. Known as the Seven Year Plan, this arrangement won Cobo such public favor that in 1949 he was elected mayor and became one of the city's most progressive chief executives. Radical changes were made in the tax system; the state property tax was abolished and a three per cent sales tax (later increased to four per cent) was adopted, part of the revenue being rebated to local communities. A 15-mill ceiling also was placed on the amount of taxes local units of government could levy.

Thus gradually a better financial base was built and purchasing power was restored. People's confidence returned and with it came signs of prosperity. Just as Detroit was one of the first cities to feel the depression, so was it one of the first to find the recovery road. A car-hungry nation began again to buy automobiles and in 1936 the auto industry produced nearly 4,500,000 cars and trucks. Many observers claim Detroit's chief industry led the nation out of the wilderness of depression and set it on the road to normalcy. The local skies brightened perceptibly in 1934 when the Detroit Tigers won the American League pennant, and again in 1935 when the team won the World Series. The Detroit Lions won the National Football League championship in 1935 and the Red Wings captured the Stanley Cup. Joe Louis was knocking over everything that stood in his way to the world's heavyweight boxing championship (1937). Its morale rising with each triumph, Detroit threw out its chest and proclaimed itself the City of Champions.

Full recovery did not come smoothly or all at once. The economic chart had its ups and downs. When it appeared in 1937 that all was well again, there was a recession. Meanwhile, relief and public works programs remained in effect, the latter until 1942. Despite better general conditions unemployment continued to be high.

But Adolf Hitler and Emperor Hirohito were unwittingly and unintentionally providing the cure for America's economic ills. The war they brought on marked the real end of the Great American Depression.

A Man is Worthy of his Hire

Out of the depression and its turbulent years grew a strong labor movement which became one of the dominant forces in the life of Detroit within a decade. The phenomenon was not limited to this city; all the major industrial centers experienced it because it was part of a national social revolution. But because of Detroit's great industrial concentration, Detroit became a sort of laboratory for the testing of those forces which contributed to the large-scale organization of labor, which emerged as a major social, economic, and political power.

Labor organization, the union movement, was not unknown to Detroit before this period of yeasty ferment. There are those who like to trace it back to 1818 when a group of men organized the Detroit Mechanics' Society. The original members, as well as those who joined in later years, were representative citizens—tavernkeepers, shopkeepers, merchants—in fact almost anyone who owned property or displayed skill in his vocation. The membership may be said to have belonged to the middle class. Their purpose in organizing was to provide themselves with a forum. It was in part educational, inasmuch as they established a library, and in part social and recreational. It was also a sort of mutual benefit society; small dues went into a fund upon which members could draw in case of need such as sickness or injury. But to call the Mechanics' Society a labor union is stretching a point. With equal justification it could be called an employers' association or a board of commerce. As a matter of fact it was none of these things and the term mechanics is somewhat misleading, although mechanics or skilled workmen certainly were eligible for membership.

Detroit's first real labor organization in the strict sense of the term was formed by the city's printers in the 1830s or before, although again this was more an association of fellow craftsmen than a regular union. In any case, the printers staged the city's first known strike in 1839. How effective it was is questionable because as far as is known none of the affected businesses were forced to close. Those early strikers, however, left a memento for the lexicon of labor. That was the term rat, applied to those who continued to work. The epithet was generally employed for thirty years or more before giving way to the equally opprobrious scab. At any rate, the printers seem to have the longest history in Detroit's organized labor movement. The

Detroit Typographical Union, claiming to be the city's oldest, was formed in 1848 and has functioned ever since.

Other union organizations came slowly and largely through an evolutionary process. In 1851 the city's clerks banded together and presented demands—suggestions might be a better term—for shorter hours. Demand or suggestion, they were heeded and were permitted to go home earlier. This was not the result of union action; the clerks' position was that of a temporary committee which ceased to exist after their point had been won.

The real union movement in Detroit became evident between 1850 and the Civil War. It was during this period of about ten years that a small handful of local unions first became affiliated with national labor organizations. For example, the printers in 1852 became Local 18 of the International Typographical Union. This is not to suggest that all members of the printing trades or other crafts were completely organized. Far from it; there were no closed shops and probably the majority of workers, such as the printers, were not members. One apparent reason for the interest in unionization at this time was due to the German immigration. Many skilled German workers were union or guild oriented and many were Socialists who brought their ideas of craft organization to this country.

The Civil War provided further impetus for unionization because of the demand for labor, and a few organizations such as those of the machinists, blacksmiths, and carpenters grew strong. In 1863 Michigan Central Railroad workers went on strike after the locomotive engineers, meeting first in Marshall and again in Detroit, organized what became the first of the railroad brotherhoods. In 1865 dock workers at Buffalo went on strike and were joined by their Detroit comrades. By the end of the war the labor movement was large enough to form a separate division in the city's 1865 Fourth of July parade.

The first important local labor leader came to the fore in the Civil War period. He was Richard F. Trevellick, a Detroit ship's carpenter with a flair for organization. In 1864 he effected a coalition of several unions with a total membership of about five thousand into the Detroit Trades Assembly. Trevellick became a national figure and helped organize the National Labor Union as well as one of its components, the Michigan Labor Union.

A depression in 1873 set the labor movement back and marked the end of the Detroit Trades Assembly. The vacuum created by its demise was partially filled by the Knights of Labor, a national organization formed in 1869. While skilled tradesmen became members, they did so with no great enthusiasm because the Knights more closely resembled an industrial union. Locally their strength came from the miners, lumberjacks, and farmers with whom the craftsmen felt they had little in common. After a dozen years the Knights began to lose members. They were pretty much replaced in 1880 when nine trade unions formed the Detroit Council of Trades which ultimately became the Detroit Federation of Labor after the founding of the American Federation of Labor in 1886. The Knights of Labor passed out of the picture completely in 1888. One of the early local leaders of the Knights was Joseph Labadie, a printer who was also a poet. He transferred his allegiance to the Federation of Labor and stands with Trevellick as one of the early sponsors of the labor movement in Detroit and Michigan.

By 1892 the Detroit Council of Trades and Labor Unions (changed to Detroit Federation of Labor in 1906) was made up of thirty-seven local unions, many of which still thrive. Others, however, have been lost in the parade of progress, and their names and functions today have a quaint sound, like the Horse-Collar Makers Union, the Cigar Packers Union, the Broommakers, and the Stove Mounters. Another which flourished at the time was the Florence Nightingale Union whose membership was composed of women, most of whom were employed in the local shoe factories.

The American Federation of Labor (AFL) unions regarded themselves as the aristocracy of the labor movement and gave little attention to the great mass of unorganized industrial workers in the early automobile and allied industries. From the beginning of the automotive industry (about 1900) more than thirty years were to pass before the plant workers found a union home. Understandably, the auto companies did not favor unionization of their industry. Auto workers were essentially unskilled; it was said that a green hand could be taught his job on the assembly line in two or three days. This made him highly replaceable. The industrial worker was undoubtedly the most expendable tool in the auto plant. While wages generally were above those paid most unskilled labor, working conditions were not good. The work itself was grindingly monotonous, seasonal layoffs were a part of industrial life, the speed-up was commonplace, and employees were at the mercy of foremen who were sometimes corrupt and levied tribute as the price for holding a job. Because there was no union organization within the factories—and none was tolerated—Detroit proudly boasted as an attraction for new industry that it was a non-union open-shop town with an adequate and fluid low-scale labor supply.

There were early attempts to plant unions in the auto factories; one in 1903, another in 1910, and again in 1916, but they did not take root. Around the time of World War I the International Workers of the World (IWW) showed some activity, and after the war and during the early depression years the Communist Party was in evidence. Actually, while recognizing the need for organization, the workers themselves could see little advantage in the craft union type represented by the AFL and there was no industrial union to receive them. Moreover, with the vast untapped pool of cheap southern labor, both Negro and white, which could easily be recruited, the average auto worker was in no competitive position openly to demonstrate an interest in an organizational movement.

The 1932 election of Franklin Delano Roosevelt as president of the United States and the inauguration of the New Deal changed matters completely in the labor field. One of the earliest pieces of New Deal legislation was the National Industrial Recovery Act which not only gave workers the right to organize, but even encouraged them to do so. It required employers to bargain collectively with them. The constitutionality of the act was challenged and for a couple of years some major segments of industry chose to ignore the law, but in the end the organizing and bargaining features were validated and implemented.

Now the industrial workers had a green light and could no longer be either intimidated or ignored. There was a considerable amount of automotive union organization in 1933, 1934 and 1935, but it was mostly on a plant basis. But in August 1935 the AFL reluctantly permitted the organization of a consolidated auto union and that was the real beginning of the United Automobile Workers (UAW). At the outset it was neither strong nor effective and lacked autonomy. It was headed by a young Kansas City preacher, Homer Martin, who was described as an able agitator but a poor administrator. Seeking stronger leadership, the UAW turned for guidance to John L. Lewis, an AFL vice president and head of the United Mine Workers' Union. Lewis provided the auto workers with professional organizers, but more important, he walked out of the AFL taking the UAW with him. He formed the Committee for Industrial Organizations which in 1938 became the Congress of Industrial Organizations (CIO).

Despite the efforts of professional organizers, some of whom in the early days were Communists, the real drive within the auto plants came from a dedicated group of men who were workers themselves—shop stewards, committeemen, and local officers. One, destined for greatness in the labor movement, was Walter Reuther, employed in a west side Detroit General Motors plant.

Progress came slowly until 1936. In December of that year Chevrolet and Fisher Body employees in Flint staged the auto industry's first major sit-down strike, a technique the auto workers borrowed from the Akron rubber workers who in turn had borrowed it from European syndicalists. The Flint workers remained in control of the factories until February 1937 despite every effort to get them out. Under the terms of the settlement finally reached, General Motors agreed to recognize the UAW-CIO as sole bargaining agent. This was the first big breakthrough. It was soon followed by an equally successful Chrysler sit-down. Other unorganized workers took the cue and for the next several months Detroit business was in a chaotic condition. Almost every plant, large and small, had its sit-down, some being violent and destructive. Many were staged for the sheer hell of it. The sit-down device even extended to retail establishments such as five-and-ten-cent stores where clerks locked themselves in until their demands, often vague and spurious, were met. It became almost a matter of worker prestige to shut down an establishment even if nothing was to be gained by it. Ultimately the sit-down was ruled illegal by the courts, but by that time the unions were solidly established in Detroit which ceased to be one of the largest open-shop towns.

The story of labor in Detroit since 1936 is practically the story of the UAW, although other unions such as the Teamsters and the United Steel Workers have been strong, militant, and effective.

General Motors, Chrysler, and most of the then-remaining independents were organized and had contracts with the UAW, but the union still had its toughest customer. That was Ford. Henry Ford had announced that despite hell, high water or the law, he would never recognize the union as a sole bargaining agent, and Harry Bennett with his private army of service department men turned the Rouge plant into a virtual armed fortress. A great portion of public opinion was solidly with Ford and hoped he would win. Many people were uneasy at the UAW's militancy and its Communist influence, and saw a grave threat to property rights in the sit-down strikes. But the UAW realized it could never hope to present a united front and be truly strong as long as one of the Big Three remained unorganized. All its resources were directed toward breaching the Ford ramparts.

That the union was successful can largely be attributed to a stupid blunder by Bennett. On May 26, 1937, a group of UAW people went to the Ford gates in Dearborn to distribute union leaflets. Among them were Walter Reuther and Richard Frankensteen. They were met at the Miller road overpass to the Rouge plant by a gang of Bennett's thugs who gave the unionists an unmerciful beating. At least one was severely injured; the others, bloody and with their clothes half torn off, were turned back, but not before press photographers recorded the whole disgraceful affair. From that moment public opinion began to shift away from Ford and the company was on the defensive.

Organizing efforts continued after the famous Battle of the Overpass, and Ford continued to resist them, but the company was waging a losing fight. In 1940 a court decision forced Ford to cease interfering with organizing efforts and by April 1941 the union was strong enough to strike the Rouge and other plants. On April 10 the strike ended when Ford agreed to a National Labor Relations Board election. It was held in May and the UAW-CIO won handily as the sole bargaining agent. Ford capitulated completely and signed what was up to that time the best contract the UAW had. It provided among other things for a union shop and dues check-off. Since then the UAW has remained the unchallenged voice of labor in the automotive industry.

The story of the UAW since 1941 has been marked by internal political struggles. In 1939 ineffective Homer Martin was voted out of office and replaced by R. J. Thomas. Martin found an executive job with the Ford Motor Company provided by Harry Bennett. Thomas guided the union through World War II, a troublesome period for the UAW which had difficulty holding its members in line and observing the wartime no strike pledge.

In 1946 the UAW staged a bitter strike against General Motors which lasted 113 days. But from the union standpoint it was effective because it proved the soundness of the strategy of striking only one of the Big Three at a time, thereby placing its target at a competitive disadvantage. The lesson was not lost upon the Big Three, although there have been occasions since then when the union has felt compelled to strike or use the threat of a strike to gain its ends. When other strikes have been called, they have not been as prolonged as the 1946 one against General Motors.

In 1947 Walter Reuther was elected president supplanting Thomas. Reuther purged the UAW of its Communist elements and brought to the union a strong administration. It was not accomplished easily, however, and internal union friction sometimes took a violent turn. In 1948 Reuther was critically wounded by a would-be assassin and an attempt was also made on the life of his brother Victor Reuther. The assailants were never caught, but they were believed to have been purged Communists.

In 1951 the UAW moved into its new international headquarters Solidarity House on East Jefferson at the foot of Van Dyke on the site of a former home of Edsel Ford. Prior to the building of Solidarity House, UAW headquarters were located in the old Hyatt Roller Bearing Company building on the southwest corner of Cass and Milwaukee opposite the General Motors Building.

Unlike the AFL, the UAW and its CIO affiliates have always believed that political action is necessary to achieve certain social gains. As a result the industrial unions, through an alliance with the Democratic Party, were successful in electing many of their hand-picked candidates to state and local office. Despite strong efforts, however, they were less successful in capturing the Detroit city hall and the municipal government remains, at least on the surface, nonpartisan. Nevertheless, men closely associated with the UAW and the general labor movement have accepted appointment to key positions on important civic boards and commissions, and in some instances have achieved considerable power.

14

War and Ferment

Arsenal of Democracy

It was a Sunday afternoon like most early winter Sunday afternoons in Detroit. Not much was going on. Those who had gone to church were back home. Many had had their dinners and were catching naps. The day was cloudy, the temperature was a raw thirty-six degrees, and there was a trace of rain. It was a good day to be indoors. A philharmonic program was being broadcast by one of the radio networks and the local audience was large.

Downtown the movie houses were doing a good business. At the Adams, Abbott and Costello with Martha Raye were romping through the slapstick comedy "Keep 'Em Flying." At the Broadway-Capitol, Edward G. Robinson and Marlene Dietrich were playing in "Man Power," and at the Madison, Bette Davis was starring in "Elizabeth and Essex." Yet it was not a typical Sunday afternoon in Detroit or anywhere else. It was December 7, 1941, a remarkably fateful day. It was, as President Roosevelt said, "a day that will live in infamy."

Suddenly about 3 p.m. there was a break in the radio program and an excited voice announced: "We interrupt this program to bring you a special news bulletin. The White House has announced that the Japanese have attacked Pearl Harbor. Please stay tuned to this station for further details." In the theaters the movies were interrupted as the radio bulletin was either flashed on the screen or read to the audiences.

With no more warning than that, the United States was at war.

The shock was great; the immediate reaction on the part of the average citizen was anger. Yet the shock wore off quickly because America's ultimate participation in the war was pretty much taken for granted. It had become merely a question of when. Unlike World War I, United States involvement in World War II did not catch the country totally unprepared. December 7, 1941, found the country well on the way toward mobilization.

Nazi Germany had invaded Poland on September 1, 1939, and the European phase of the war was well underway. In less than six months the United States had begun to polish its armor, even to the extent that in August 1940 the Chrysler Corporation contracted to build and operate a mammoth tank arsenal in Warren on the northern outskirts of Detroit. On October 15, 1940, the national guard was called into federal service after a summer of maneuvers. Once again, the 32nd Division was mobilized and sent to Camp Beauregard, Louisiana, for intensive training. In 1942 the 32nd embarked for Austrailia and served for the duration in the Pacific theater where it distinguished itself in the New Guinea and Philippines campaigns, and suffered heavy losses. Other units followed the 32nd, including the 210th Anti-Aircraft Artillery regiment, a reorganization of the old Michigan cavalry squadron, and the

182nd and 177th Field Artillery regiments. While the guard and reserve units were being called up, more than half a million Detroit men registered on October 16, 1940, for possible duty under the Selective Service Act. In November the first draftees were examined and inducted in the old Light Guard armory which continued to be used until it was destroyed by fire on April 17, 1945. At one time draftees were ushered into the armed services through the dingy halls of a former corset factory on West Fort street near Fourth. Fort Wayne also came to life as a Quartermaster Corps center used to a large extent for the reception and storage of military vehicles delivered from the local auto plants. From Fort Wayne they were driven by civilian volunteers to various camps and embarkation ports.

Altogether, 613,542 men and women from Michigan served in the armed forces between 1940 and 1945, with Detroit furnishing approximately one-third of the number.

The home front was quickly mobilized too. The day after the attack on Pearl Harbor army guards from Selfridge Field were posted at the entrances to the Detroit-Windsor Tunnel and the Ambassador Bridge to prevent sabotage which was a very real danger. Earlier in the year, anticipating what was to come, President Roosevelt had proclaimed an "unlimited state of national emergency," the effect of which was to put military bases and some civilian installations on a war footing. With the departure of the national guard, a new militia or home guard was organized, and Detroit had the strange experience of seeing anti-aircraft batteries installed in parks and elsewhere in defense against possible air attack. A military police battalion set up a semi-permanent camp in River Rouge. As a further precaution against air raids, a civil defense organization was created. Air raid warning sirens were mounted on public buildings and people were taught the meaning of their wailing signals. Thousands of Detroit men and women were trained as air raid wardens, special police, and firefighters. They were given first aid instruction and taught how to extinguish fire bombs. On May 3, 1942, a practice blackout was held and all lights in Detroit were extinguished for an hour. The city's air raid wardens, equipped with gas masks and wearing tin helmets, patrolled the darkened streets, enforcing the blackout regulations and requiring all unauthorized persons to stay indoors. Householders and others were required to equip their homes and business places with dark curtains or shades in the event the city had to be blacked out in a real emergency.

Soon after the declaration of war against Japan and Nazi Germany price controls and rationing went into effect. Detroiters were virtually frozen into their jobs and could not quit or transfer without War Labor Board consent. Wages also were frozen, but to offset that, ceilings and controls were placed on rents and the prices of food, clothing, and other essential items. To assure enough material for the armed forces and our hard-pressed allies, rationing of gasoline and tires was ordered, thus materially limiting automobile travel. To get back and forth to work, Detroiters were encouraged to organize car pools. Later in 1942 shortages of many commodities resulted in the rationing of meat, canned goods, shoes, clothes, and unhappily, liquor and cigarettes. Detroiters made up for the latter by learning to roll their own.

The need for additional workers in the war plants again resulted in a population influx. Much of it, both white and Negro, came from the South, creating new social problems, not the least of which was another housing shortage. Because of the scarcity of material and labor, only the most essential construction was permitted. Women were urged to join the labor force and thousands donned overalls or slacks and stood alongside their men folk at the factory machines. It was the era of Rosie the Riveter, and set a new social pattern. After the war women continued at factory jobs in unprecedented numbers and two breadwinners in one family became more commonplace than rare.

Actually, with the limitations and restrictions placed upon the public, together with the long and intensive work hours in the war plants, life was rather dreary and monotonous in Detroit during the war years. War nerves became a common malady doctors were frequently called upon to treat.

Mention has been made that the danger of sabotage was very real. While there was no such hysterical outburst directed at German-Americans as there had been in World War I, elaborate precautions were taken against espionage. An active Nazi spy ring operated in Detroit both before and during the war, but local authorities and the Federal Bureau of Investigation took prompt measures and enemy activity was kept well under control.

Several arrests were made including a German "countess" who moved in Detroit's upper social circles, and a Wayne University professor. The most sensational case, however, was that involving Max Stephan, a Nazi agent whose restaurant on East Grand boulevard at Jefferson served as an espionage center. Early in 1942 Stephan was arrested on charges of aiding a Nazi prisoner of war who had escaped from a prison camp in Canada. The fugitive was smuggled into the United States and harbored by Stephan who assisted him in an unsuccessful attempt to flee to Mexico. Stephan was tried for treason and on August 6, 1942, was convicted and sentenced to death. The case, which was heard in the United States district court in Detroit, was the first treason trial to carry the sentence of execution since the Whiskey Rebellion in 1794. Stephan, however, did not die on the scaffold. President Roosevelt commuted his sentence to life imprisonment and Stephan was transferred from the federal penitentiary at Milan, Michigan, where he was to have been hanged, to the one at Atlanta.

Behind the actual fighting front, the chief contribution to winning the war was made by American industry, and in this effort the role of Detroit's automotive industry was perhaps the most dramatic of all. During the war the Detroit area proudly claimed the title of Arsenal of Democracy and the claim was not without foundation.

The war production gears began to mesh many months before the attack on Pearl Harbor. In 1940 the United States National Defense Council was created. William S. Knudsen, president of General Motors, was made its chairman and in 1941 he resigned from his civilian job to become director of the Office of Production Management. A little later he was commissioned lieutenant general in the army so he could talk tough to the military who were not always enthusiastic about taking orders from a civilian. It was apparent by 1941 what American and allied war needs would be, and it was equally apparent to men like Knudsen that the automobile industry and its associated companies were best equipped to fill those needs. The problem was how to do it most quickly and efficiently. Parts for tanks, planes, and guns were vastly different from parts for Fords, Chevrolets and Packards, and yet the basic principles of engineering and production were much the same. It became necessary to find out which companies could most easily manufacture the new products of war— products they were then unfamiliar with.

The solution was found by Knudsen and the noted flier James Doolittle who had been assigned the job of coordinating facilities for the production of aircraft. Working with the newly created Automotive Council for War Production, they accumulated all the various parts that would be required. These were spread out in a sort of museum display in the former Graham-Paige plant on West Warren at Wyoming. Then parts manufacturers, tool makers, and everybody else with productive capacity were invited to inspect the display. Representatives of more than fifteen hundred companies walked up and down the aisles looking at the samples. "We can make this," one would say, pointing to a part. "We can turn out those," said another. And so it went. As each representative found something his plant was equipped to turn out, he was given a contract or subcontract. Having finished that task, Doolittle put on his air corps uniform and became a lieutenant general. On April 18, 1942, he lifted the hearts of the victory-hungry American people by leading a bomber raid against Tokyo.

More was needed than willingness and know-how. The machine that could stamp out an automobile fender could not forge a sheet of armor plate for a tank. Gradually the old machines and tools were moved out of the auto plants and stored for the duration in warehouses or under tarpaulins in open fields. The tool makers went to work and soon new machinery designed for war production was moved in. More plants were required also, involving capital expenditures the manufacturers were not always in a position to make. That obstacle was overcome by the government's construction of huge new arsenals and factories. These were then turned over to the auto companies to operate. Thus Chrysler ran the great tank arsenal in Warren, Hudson Motor Car Company took over the management of the navy gun arsenal in Center Line, and Ford assumed the responsibility for building B-24 Liberator bombers at Willow Run. General Motors operated a tank arsenal at

Grand Blanc, a few miles southeast of Flint. In August 1941 the production of automobiles for the civilian market began to be curtailed; after Pearl Harbor it came to a complete halt, not to be resumed until late 1945 and early 1946. All the industry's efforts were concentrated on the output of war materiel. There was no more competition within the industry. Closely guarded production secrets, skills, and even manpower were pooled and became common property. A few days after the Pearl Harbor attack, the Automotive Council for War Production issued a challenging proclamation:

> The nation will not lack for one gun, one tank, one engine, that the capacity and ingenuity of this industry's producers can add to the forces of our nation and its friends on all the fighting fronts.

A few figures show how well that pledge was kept. The Chrysler tank arsenal turned out more than 25,000 tanks—General Grants, General Shermans, General Pershings. The rate of output sometimes reached one thousand tanks a month. The first B-24 bomber came off the lines September 10, 1942, and soon the skies over Europe and southeast Asia were dark with them. The Willow Run plant produced 8,500 before the war ended. Other plants were equally productive. Packard built thousands of Rolls-Royce aircraft engines; General Motors factories in Detroit and elsewhere turned out almost every conceivable kind of war engines and type of munitions. Military vehicles were rolled out in an unending stream. At the Ford Rouge plant a new kind of light vehicle was developed and tested. It was named the Jeep. Ford built them and so did the Willys plant in Toledo. Both Ford and Willys were making jet propelled buzz bombs toward the end of the war.

During much of the war period Detroit bore the

appearance of an armed camp. Uniforms of all the allied nations, including the Russians, were seen on the streets. The Guardian building downtown was taken over by the army and turned into an ordnance center, a control point for all war production in the area and beyond. The ordnance center was commanded by Brigadier General Alfred R. Glancy, another General Motors production expert turned soldier. By 1944 the metropolitan area had been awarded war contracts totaling $12,745,525,000, and there would be more. In September 1942, when things were just beginning to get rolling, President Roosevelt made an unannounced visit to Detroit and toured some of the major war plants. He was pleased by what he saw.

Gradually the enemy was pushed back and the end drew near. On May 8, 1945, Nazi Germany, or what was left of it, surrendered. While the war effort did not slacken as long as Japan was still fighting, the reconversion of the automobile industry began. There was still a job remaining, and on August 6 the United States administered the coup-de-grace to Japanese war hopes when the first atomic bomb was exploded over Hiroshima. Detroit had a part in that world-shaking event, too. The Manhattan Project which built the bomb faced a monumental task and had to overcome difficulties that would have wearied Hercules. Chrysler Corporation and the Wolverine Tube Company were called upon to make equipment and develop alloys necessary to the bomb's manufacture. Their work was highly secret, as were all phases of the Manhattan Project, and the parts played by Chrysler and Wolverine Tube, each of a highly technical nature, have only recently come to public attention.

With the dreadful destruction caused by the A-bomb, the Japanese realized that their cause was lost. On August 14 the shattered and defeated Japanese Empire surrendered. When the news reached Detroit it was carnival time again. As they did at the end of World War I, Detroiters celebrated, only in greater numbers. It was estimated that half a million people poured into the downtown streets to stage a giant impromptu celebration. It was a case of letting off steam that had been pent up for four years.

'We Shall Overcome'

Following the race riot of 1863 which grew out of Civil War passions, Detroit knew a long period of racial peace and some progress was made in eliminating discrimination. Prior to World War I, Detroit's Negro community was not large. The real problem started when whites and Negroes flocked to the city from the South to work in the automobile plants. The Negroes were pushed into ready-made slums along the lower end of Hastings, St. Antoine, and adjoining streets. Conditions were so bad that as early as 1917 the Detroit Board of Commerce formed a committee to seek solutions to the Negro housing problem. Apparently none was found because the situation did not improve.

The southern whites—"hillbillies"—were not much better off. They brought with them their prejudices and their conviction that as whites they were members of a superior race. Their feeling of superiority to the Negro was one of the few compensations in their lives. This feeling, in part based upon economic insecurity, caused them to turn to the Ku Klux Klan which they imported and which flourished here and in neighboring industrial cities. In the immediate postwar period Klan membership in Detroit was numbered in the thousands. On June 14, 1923, a thousand neophytes were admitted to membership in a huge initiation ceremony. Most of the members were factory workers who found the Klan offered them companionship. The robes and ritual added a touch of color to otherwise drab lives. Of course demagogues and manipulators moved in. The Klan became a local political power, often an unruly one. They paraded, they swaggered, and they bullied those who got in their way. Late in 1923 they brazenly burned crosses in front of the City Hall and the Wayne County building, and on October 21, 1924, police were forced to use tear gas to break up a demonstration. National scandals involving the Klan leadership largely discredited the organization, and its membership and influence diminished. But it never wholly died out. It came back to life with the civil rights movement of the 1960s and as late as 1967 a Detroit newspaper ran a front page exposé of Klan activities in the area.

More sinister even than the Klan was the Black Legion which flourished in Detroit during the depression years. Said to have had its origin in Ohio in 1931 as an offshoot of the Klan, the Black Legion found fertile soil in Michigan where its headquarters was established. Like the Klan, it was a secret ritualistic organization standing for "white, native-born Protestant, 100 per cent Americanism." It posed as the protector of the sanctity of womanhood and was prepared to apply extra-legal methods to accomplish its aims. While it claimed a membership of 200,-000, its hard core was composed of a small group of armed bully-boys. They acted as the execution squad which killed for thrills as well as to uphold the supremacy of the white man and defend the sanctity of the home. Once a man was taken out into the fields at night and shot down in cold blood just so the triggermen could keep in practice.

Actually the Black Legion seems to have been used by its leaders as an instrument of personal vengeance. Anyone, member or not, who incurred displeasure was liable to a midnight ride to a secluded spot where he might be shot, horsewhipped or otherwise abused by a pack of vicious self-righteous imbeciles who had convinced themselves they were only meting out justice. It is believed that between 1931 and 1936 the Black Legion was responsible for at least fifty killings in the Detroit area.

The Black Legion made its fatal mistake on the night of May 12, 1936. Someone had marked out a non-member named Charles A. Poole as a candidate for their justice. Poole, it was reported, had been abusing his wife. He would hardly be the type to hold up as the example of a bad man. He made a living doing odd jobs, worked on a WPA project, played a little sandlot baseball, and never harmed anyone, including his wife, as far as can be ascertained. But the kangaroo court wanted some excitement and Charles Poole was available. He was lured to a Black Legion meeting and then driven to a secluded spot on the western edge of the city. The intention was to hang him, but plans went awry, and his bullet-ridden body was discovered the next day.

This time there was first-class police work and shortly some arrests were made. Dayton Dean, one of the participants in the slaying, sang, the evidence held up, convictions were obtained, and several of the perpetrators went to prison. Even more important, the bright light of publicity was turned on the Black Legion which could not stand the exposure. Public indignation ran high and the terroristic night-riding organization quietly disposed of its robes and slunk out of the picture.

About the beginning of World War II racial relations in Detroit began to deteriorate rapidly. This was not attributable to organizations such as the Klan and the Black Legion which were only symptomatic of resentment and fear on the part of a certain class of whites, a resentment which applied to Catholics, Jews, and the foreign-born, as well as to Negroes. Detroit's racial troubles had other roots, and if one single thing can explain what happened in the early 1940s, it would be the problem of Negro housing.

The war, as we have seen, caused a heavy migration of Negroes and southern whites to the city to staff the war plants. By 1941 housing had become intolerable. Negroes were crowded into segregated areas where they were forced to live under indescribable conditions and were victimized by rapacious landlords. Their resentment ran high and fear arose among many of their white neighbors who saw them as a menace to their own somewhat precarious way of living.

Long before World War II the intrusion of an occasional Negro family into an otherwise white neighborhood had led to outbursts of violence. One instance attracted national attention because of some of the personalities involved.

In 1925 a Negro physician, Dr. Ossian Sweet, purchased a house at Garland and Charlevoix in an area in which there had been some racial mixing. Dr. Sweet received some threats from his new neighbors before he moved in and to be safe he notified police that he intended to occupy the house on September 8. The moving van pulled up under police escort, but that night a crowd gathered, and during the next two days it became menacing. Several friends and relatives joined Dr. Sweet as the siege began. Ten policemen were assigned to keep the crowd away, but despite their presence rocks were thrown through windows. Finally, under the impression that someone was trying to break in, Dr. Sweet ran upstairs and grabbed a gun. At that point a car drove up and Dr. Sweet's brother and a friend got out. The crowd surged forward and began to manhandle them. Panic swept over those inside the house and suddenly from one of the windows there was a blast of gunfire. A white man sitting on his porch across the street was struck and instantly killed.

Dr. Sweet and nine of his companions, including his wife, were arrested and tried for murder. Their defense was handled by the famous lawyer Clarence Darrow and financed largely by the National Association for the Advancement of Colored People. The trial was lengthy and its sensational aspects, together with the presence of Darrow, attracted front-page attention across the country. The verdict was not guilty. It was really the first major breakthrough in Detroit and at the same time a warning of what might happen in the future.

In the 1940s another Detroit case helped to make law against housing discrimination. A Negro named Orsel McGhee purchased a home on Seebaldt avenue in the Grand River-Grand boulevard district. Having bought the property, McGhee was informed a restrictive clause in the deed provided that it could not be owned by anyone other than a Caucasian. Residents of the subdivision sued to have the clause enforced and the local court found it valid. On appeal the matter went to the United States Supreme Court which by unanimous decision ruled on May 3, 1948, that the restriction was a violation of the Fourteenth Amendment. Thus Detroit figured in another breakthrough which had national implications.

During the 1930 decade Detroit's first public housing was constructed, but none of the first projects were in

Negro areas or intended for Negro occupancy. Local housing officials were aware of the need for low-cost Negro housing and planned a project on the lower east side. However, federal authorities vetoed the site and selected one in a white neighborhood occupied predominantly by Poles at Nevada and Fenelon avenues. It was named the Sojourner Truth project after a one-time slave woman who had been active in the emancipation movement. Detroit officials and Negro leaders objected to the location, pointing out that to plant Negroes in that neighborhood would surely lead to trouble.

For a while thereafter bureaucratic confusion prevailed. White residents protested and word came from Washington that the project would be occupied by whites. A month later that decision was reversed and Negro occupancy was ordered. Negroes began to move in on February 28, 1942. A white mob immediately gathered, wielding knives, bricks, and clubs. Several Negroes were beaten and wound up in the hospital instead of in new subsidized homes. Detroit officials quieted the mob with assurance that policy had been changed again and no Negroes would be admitted. The incident provided grist for the Nazi propaganda mill and the story of Sojourner Truth was widely broadcast by the enemy. This caused officialdom once more to reverse its field and the project went back to the Negroes. They moved in, protected by a tight cordon of a thousand troops, three hundred state police, and four hundred and fifty Detroit police. If it was a victory over discrimination, it was also a warning of just how inept officialdom could be in handling a touchy situation. Neither the white people in the area nor the Negro communtiy was inclined to forget Sojourner Truth. A real powder train had been laid. The explosion came in 1943.

Detroit should have been prepared for what was to

come next. Storm signals were flying all over town. In the spring of 1943 several incidents involving whites and Negroes were reported on the west side. At the Packard plant 20,000 white workers went on strike when a few Negroes were promoted. The air was thick with tension; the only people who appeared unaware of it were those in the city hall.

The early summer of 1943 was hot and people sought relief on Belle Isle and in other parks. Negroes particularly flocked to Belle Isle to escape from the heat in their crowded sections of town. It was on the island that the trouble started on the night of Sunday, June 20. No one knows what incident touched it off, but after sundown there was a series of fist fights and attacks which were carried across the Belle Isle bridge to the mainland. A real free-for-all started between Negroes and two hundred sailors at the Brodhead naval armory. Before long a mob estimated at five thousand was mixing it up and the police riot squad was called.

Word of what was happening spread swiftly through the Negro districts. All kinds of rumors circulated. One was that a mob of whites had torn a Negro baby from its mother's arms and pitched it off the bridge into the river. There were reports of Negroes being attacked by whites and of whites being attacked by Negroes. In many cases the rumors were wildly improbable and without substance, but they were believed. Negroes surged out into the streets of the lower east side in an orgy of window-smashing and looting. White people, unaware of what was happening, went to work as usual on Monday, some driving through riot-torn streets. Some were attacked and beaten and at least one was killed.

As the news of what was going on spread across the city, white mobs gathered and started to counter-attack.

General fighting broke out, the worst between Vernor and Forest along Woodward and John R., the dividing lines of the embattled area. Streetcars were stopped and Negroes were taken off and beaten; automobiles carrying Negroes were tipped over and set on fire. Later in the day the white mob moved downtown and howling tee-shirted men and boys, many of the latter in their early teens, gathered around the City Hall. Negroes on their way home from work were caught in Cadillac Square as they transferred from one streetcar to another. One Negro was beaten to death on the Fort street steps of the Federal building while upstairs army officers were preparing for the deployment of troops. Strangely, there were no disturbances in any of the factories; whites and Negroes worked side by side through the day without incident, some without knowing what was happening elsewhere in the city.

Late Monday afternoon June 21 it seemed that the fighting was dying down. Then a group of fear-crazed Negroes who had barricaded themselves in a hotel on East Vernor at John R. opened fire on police. The place was immediately laid under siege and police guns poured volley after volley into the building. Several persons inside were killed and some of the policemen were wounded. Altogether thirty-four persons, twenty-three of them Negroes, were killed during the riot. Hundreds were injured, eighteen hundred arrests were made, and property damage ran into the millions of dollars.

Before the rioting had subsided alarmed civic leaders, aware that the police could not control the situation, called for federal troop intervention. Mayor Edward J. Jeffries Jr. appealed for aid to Governor Harry F. Kelly who was informed by federal authorities that no troops could be sent until a state of emergency had been declared and the city placed under martial law. The governor proclaimed a modified form of martial law, ordering bars and other public gathering places including movie theaters closed, and clamped on a curfew which virtually evacuated the downtown area. It was only then that the war department ordered the army in. The first troops, an 800-man military police battalion, came from its base in Rouge Park; another miltiary police battalion and other units were sent from Fort Custer. The force of 2,500 men began to arrive in the city about 9:30 p.m. on Monday. They brought jeeps, armored personnel carriers, and a tank. They were formed into patrols and fanned out through the troubled areas. By nightfall order was restored. For the next ten days Detroit was an armed camp. The troops remained until June 30, encamped on the lawn of the Public Library and at other strategic locations. But during that time there were no further incidents.

Detroit surveyed the wreckage and had an attack of conscience. It afflicted both whites and Negroes and aroused the responsible elements of both to the need for action which would prevent any recurrence of the events of June 20-21, 1943. Mayor Jeffries established a city interracial committee and that was followed by other commissions and committees at the federal, state, and municipal levels to establish justice, erase prejudice, and develop harmony and understanding.

Much progress was made in the ensuing years. Detroit was fortunate in having a strong Negro middle class which worked closely with enlightened and responsible white organizations. Negroes won election and appointment to office at every level of government. Many Negroes gained recognition in the fields of business, education, religion, and the professions.

Despite these advances and despite a generally more tolerant attitude througout the community as a whole during the 50s and 60s, prejudice and social injustice still existed. There were many welfare programs sponsored at the local, state, and federal levels, but poverty programs were not enough. The Negro was asking for more jobs; he was pleading for better housing; he was suggesting that something be done about police brutality; he was urging better education. All these demands were made because the Negro in the city of Detroit wanted most of all the respect all human beings want. But few whites listened to the moderate Negroes.

The Detroit Negro community was becoming impatient. Therefore on Sunday June 23, 1963, it served notice upon the city, the nation, and the world that the black-skinned American would no longer accept second-class citizenship, would no longer live in a segregated society or be satisfied with less than equal civil, social, and economic rights. Detroit's Negro community marched; 125,000 strong, they marched down Woodward from Adelaide street to Cobo Hall.

They marched twenty or more abreast, their arms linked in this Walk to Freedom, singing *We Shall Overcome* and *Battle Hymn of the Republic*. Their voices were joined by those of another 125,000 spectators, mostly Negroes. The long column which filled Woodward from curb to curb for a couple of miles was led by Dr. Martin Luther King Jr. With him, to demonstrate that the black man had support, were Mayor Jerome P. Cavanagh, former Governor John P. Swainson, Police Commissioner George Edwards, and Walter P. Reuther.

At Cobo Hall and Arena 26,000 flocked inside, all the two buildings could hold. Outside thousands more congregated to hear (through loudspeakers) Dr. King proclaim the demonstration the "largest and greatest ever held in the United States." Then he presented the Negro's declaration of freedom. "We want all of our rights," he said. "We want them here and we want them now."

During the summers of 1965 and 1966 many Negroes throughout the United States turned from marching to rioting. In the Watts district of Los Angeles, Negroes rioted in the summer of 1965. When the riot was over, thirty-four had died and property losses ran to $40 million.

City officials in Detroit were saying proudly: "That sort of thing can't happen here." It seemed a reasonable enough prediction. Fully forty per cent of the Negro family heads owned their own homes. No city had waged a more massive and comprehensive war on poverty. Under Mayor Cavanagh the city had grabbed off $42 million in federal funds for its poverty programs. "We learned our lesson in 1943," said the city fathers.

But there was an entirely new generation of young people of both races who were yet to be born when the 1943 race riot took place and had no recollections of the horrors of those days. The events of that time held no lesson for them, and therein lay a grave danger.

In May 1967 a blind pig called the United Community League for Civil Action opened for business at 9125 Twelfth street near Clairmount in a predominantly Negro area. The buildings in the neighborhood were old and many were in need of repair. At 3:45 a.m. on Sunday July 23, 1967, 10th precinct police led a raid on the league, arresting 82 Negro customers and the bartender. In the next hour, while squad cars and a paddy wagon ferried the arrested to the precinct station, a crowd of about 200 gathered and began taunting the police. Just as the police were leaving a bottle smashed a squad car window. As if this act were a signal, the crowd turned into a mob. Someone started spilling garbage into the street, someone else set it afire, a brick was thrown through a shop window, and the mob began looting the store.

At this point the police made a decision that was to be bitterly denounced by white and Negro moderates alike. The police might have pulled out of the area in the hope the crowd would disperse, or they could have moved forward in full force to nip the trouble in the bud. They did neither. Following the walk-softly strategy of Mayor Cavanagh and Police Commissioner Giradin, patrol cars fanned out into the area but made no effort to beat back the mob. When this no-shoot policy became evident the looters ran rampant, smashing windows and picking stores clean. Shops owned by Negroes had Soul Brother or Afro All the Way painted across their windows. These stores survived till dark, then many of them fell victim to the looters. However, most of the looters were taking revenge on the area's white merchants whose prices were comparatively high. The store owners argued they were forced to escalate their prices to offset losses by theft and extra-high insurance premiums.

At 6:30 a.m. a major blaze erupted in a sacked shoe store, the first of more than 1,600 fires in the days to come. Yet when the fire department arrived at the scene the rioters would not let them put out the fire. Hoping the rioters would not harass members of their own race, Fire Chief Charles Quinlan formed an all-Negro fire fighting force by drawing on fire companies across the city. But when this company entered the rioit area early Sunday afternoon, they too were forced to retreat as they were pelted with rocks, bottles, and bricks.

In an effort to calm the crowds Negro leaders entered the Twelfth street area. Democratic U.S. Representative John Conyers, one of the city's two Negro congressmen, climbed to the roof of his car with a bullhorn and was stoned into retreat. When the Reverend Nicholas Hood, the city's only Negro councilman, tried his hand, rioters theatened him and his family, and he too evacuated the combat zone.

As afternoon pushed towards evening there were reports of sporadic sniping. The police then set up riot command posts at Herman Kiefer Hospital and at police headquarters. Finally, Governor George Romney moved. He proclaimed a state of emergency, clamped on a 9 p.m. curfew, closed down all bars, and ordered in 400 state police and the first of some 7,300 national guardsmen.

The authorities were now moving swiftly, but the riot was spreading almost unchecked. The now familiar pattern exploded on Grand River, then on Livernois. A second front was opened up on the east side when Mack avenue erupted into another battleground. By Sunday night Detroit's inner city was out of control.

Late Sunday night Governor Romney and Mayor Cavanagh realized that the city and state police and national guardsmen would not be able to control the rioters. So at 3 a.m. Monday, July 24, Governor Romney placed a telephone call to U.S. Attorney General Ramsey Clark to ask for federal troops. The maneuvering which took place between the phone call and the time federal troops entered the riot area still remains a source of bitter controversy. President Johnson, Governor Romney said, "played politics" as the riot raged in Detroit. Members of the Johnson administration claimed Governor Romney wavered on whether to actually commit the federal troops.

Whatever the reason, getting the troops into the city proved agonizingly slow. The governor and the mayor made repeated calls to Washington. Congressman Charles Diggs and UAW President Walter Reuther asked for troops. There were debates between Washington and Detroit on the precise language the governor should use in calling for troops. The issue was, should he recommend or request? Finally at 11 a.m. Monday, the president ordered up 4,700 paratroopers under the command of Lieutenant General John L. Throckmorton to Selfridge Air Force Base. There they stayed, forty miles from the combat zone, while the president sent his personal emissary Cyrus Vance to the city for a firsthand look. Still the debate on whether to commit federal troops continued. Then late Monday evening, three units from the combined force of the 101st and 82nd Airborne troops made their way to the State Fairgrounds at Woodward and Eight Mile road, still some distance from the actual riot area.

At midnight the president went on national television to explain the state of emergency and the ordering of troops into Detroit. He also made no fewer than seven references to Governor Romney's inability to contain the riot with local action. At last at 3 a.m. Tuesday morning, twenty-four hours after Governor Romney had sent his first request, the airborne troops in full battle dress (riding DSR buses) moved through blacked-out streets to Southeastern High School and into the east side riot area.

During the day on Monday fires reached their peak when the fire department received a staggering 617 alarms. By then 44 other communities had volunteered men and equipment. At week's end the damage from fire as well as looting perhaps reached $50 million. Monday also marked the riot's first victim: a white man was shot dead while running from a looted store on Fourth street. He was the first of 44 killed.

Even though the national guardsmen were in the city in force on Tuesday, it became obvious that the weekend warriors were not trained to handle the problems they were facing. There were arguments between police and guardsmen when police tried to get the jumpy young riflemen to hold their fire while hunting snipers. The contrast between the guard and the paratroopers was obvious. The federal troops (many of them veterans of the war in Vietnam) showed few of the signs of nerves evident in the guard, and by Tuesday night they had brought a tense calm over the east side. However, on the west side Twelfth street was the scene of a raging gun battle. With the exception of tanks and armored personnel carriers, guardsmen and police were driven from certain areas twice during the night.

When dawn came Wednesday morning a restless truce seemed to envelop the west side. But the truce did not last long, for snipers launched a totally unexpected daylight assault on the police command post at Herman Kiefer Hospital.

Volunteer programs to assist the estimated 5,000 persons left homeless moved into gear on Wednesday. In the already hard-hit areas there were reports of price-gouging by grocery store owners. Some profiteers were charging $1.00 for a 25¢ quart of milk. This brought swift action from the city council. A special ordinance to control the profiteering was passed in a hastily called session.

Arrests Wednesday topped the 3,000 mark and the prisoners overflowed anything resembling a conventional jail. By the time the riot had subsided, 7,331 had been arrested, the prisoners being housed in Jackson State Prison, Milan Federal Penitentiary, county jails, DSR buses, the police gymnasium, and in police garages. In an effort to create a makeshift prison, the bathhouse on Belle Isle underwent a frenzied remodeling, and when prisoners were moved in on Saturday July 29 it resembled a prisoner-of-war compound.

Recorder's court judges and the Wayne County prosecutor's staff worked in shifts around the clock processing the flood of prisoners. Bonds averaging $10,000 were ordered for looters to keep them from getting back on the streets during the riot. Suspected snipers faced bonds as high as $200,000.

As the early hours of Thursday rolled in the riot appeared to be dying. The day also produced a false start on ending the stringent restrictions placed over the city. Governor Romney lifted the 9 p.m. to 5:30 a.m. curfew, but by 7 p.m. that same evening he was forced to reinstate the curfew when hundreds of carloads of sightseers jammed Twelfth street in an area still plagued with sporadic sniping. Also on Thursday, Mayor Cavanagh and Governor Romney appointed a blue-ribbon committee headed by department store president Joseph L. Hudson Jr. to plan the rebuilding of the riot areas. UAW President Walter Reuther pledged the help of his huge union in the clean-up task and Henry Ford II offered the resources of the giant Ford Motor Company. On Friday the last major fire of the week was reported.

Over the weekend a fearful city began to return to normal at last, and the people of Detroit were left to talk about what had happened. They had not endured a battle between white and black like that which had ripped the city in 1943. What they had been a part of was the new litany in rioting, a battle against authority, whatever its skin color. Like the riots in other cities in the middle sixties, Detroit's disaster followed a familiar pattern. The riot was started by a minor encounter between police and citizens, and went from looting to arson, and finally to sniping.

Detroit had endured a horrible disaster. But there was one tentative answer—a new beginning. As Father Gabriel Richard was heard murmuring one hundred and sixty-two years earlier, *Speramus meliora; resurget cineribus* —"We hope for better things; it will arise from the ashes."

15

Today and Tomorrow

The period since the end of World War II has been one of prosperity for Detroit except for an occasional slight bump on the economic chart. It has not been a period of peace, however. The Arsenal of Democracy remains in business. The battle smoke of the German and Japanese war had barely cleared before Detroit's armament industry went back to work making weapons for use in Korea and for our free world allies under massive foreign military aid programs. In the 1960s the demand continued to supply our troops in Vietnam.

The automobile industry outdid itself in the 50s and 60s. In 1965 output broke all previous records when 9,300,000 units came off the production lines. Production in 1966 almost equalled that figure, exceeding the nine-million mark. There were many major changes in the industry in a decade and a half. Nash, a Wisconsin-based company, became American Motors and absorbed the Hudson Motor Car Company in 1954. Then, both Nash and Hudson were discontinued and American Motors concentrated on Ramblers. In 1954 the venerable Packard was taken over by Indiana-based Studebaker; the Detroit Packard plant was closed in 1956 and the last Packard was built in 1958. Then in 1963 Studebaker gave up as far as United States production was concerned and built cars only in Canada. A new effort to enter the field was made in 1947 when the Kaiser-Frazer line was introduced. That company merged with Toledo's Willys in 1953 and then ceased passenger car production in 1955, limiting itself thereafter to trucks and jeeps. An attempt to establish another company with a car of radical design in 1947, the Tucker, failed before it could get into actual production. By 1967 the auto manufacturers of passenger cars were down to the Big Three and the much smaller American Motors. In 1967 General Motors turned out its one hundred millionth unit, a Chevrolet, and a few days later Ford passed the seventy million mark. A few independent truck companies also continued to operate.

An automotive-industry era came to a close on the night of April 7, 1947, when Henry Ford died at his residence Fair Lane at the age of eighty-three. For several years prior to his death Ford's personal grasp of company affairs had been slipping as old age crept up on him. His only son Edsel, whom he had made president, died in 1943. The elder Ford immediately resumed the presidency, but the company was really run by Harry Bennett, a one-time pugilist who headed the company's service department. In 1945 Mrs. Edsel Ford and other members of the family staged what amounted to a palace revolution and installed the youthful Henry Ford II, son of Edsel, as president. Bennett was thrown out and a complete overhaul was made at the executive level. A staff of able, vigorous, and enthusiastic young men—referred to in the industry as Ford's Whiz Kids—was brought in. Almost immediately the company's fortunes began to improve and the real danger that the Ford company was headed for disaster was averted.

As America moved into the atomic and space age, the Detroit area moved with it. In 1953 the University of Michigan set up its Phoenix project, a nuclear reactor devoted to research in the field of peaceful use of atomic energy. A large part of the money for this project came from the Ford Motor Company fund. The Detroit Edison Company, in association with some other utilities, built the Enrico Fermi atomic reactor near Monroe. Intended to develop electrical power for the area, the Fermi installation, although completed, was not in operation in 1967.

When the first American astronaut reaches the moon or some other celestial way-station, Detroit probably will be riding with him. In October 1952 Chrysler Corporation was given a contract for limited production of the Redstone missile. The first of these 250-mile-range ballistic missiles was successfully fired at Cape Kennedy (then Cape Canaveral) in August 1953. In 1956 Chrysler became the prime contractor for construction of the Jupiter missile. Meanwhile, work was continued on the Redstone, and in July 1961 Air Force Captain Virgil Grissom made the second sub-orbital flight atop a Mercury-Redstone. Later that year Chrysler became prime contractor for the production of the first stage of the Saturn rocket, and in 1966 a Saturn booster successfully launched an Apollo spacecraft into flight. Other local industries, by contributing components and electronics devices, have helped make the United States a strong competitor in the race to explore outer space.

Detroit experienced another wonder on March 4, 1947, when Station WWJ-TV introduced the first commercial television broadcasting in the area from its studios on West Lafayette near Second.

Detroit, particularly the downtown district, has undergone considerable face lifting in recent years. It began in 1950 when the north-south John C. Lodge freeway, a wide and deep traffic furrow, was dug. The Lodge was followed by the east-west Edsel Ford. In 1967 the heart of the city was being gouged by the construction of two more freeways, the Walter P. Chrysler and the Fisher. Another, tapping the northwest section, was on the drawing board and will be named for the late Mayor Edward J. Jeffries.

The chief renaissance has been in the heart of downtown Detroit, the business district. It reflects a long-time dream of developing the waterfront. For many years the section south of Jefferson avenue was cluttered with a conglomeration of rundown, dilapidated warehouses, lofts, and dock structures. Not only were they unsightly, but they also cut off public view of the river. To enjoy the riverfront at all, one had to go to Belle Isle or one of the smaller parks far from the heart of the city. The feeling was general that Detroit was wasting one of its finest civic assets. This began to change in the 1950s when the area between First and Randolph streets south of Jefferson was condemned and cleared for a Civic Center development. The first new structure in these park-like surroundings, the Veterans' Memorial Hall, was built in 1950. It stands at the foot of Shelby street, approximately where Antoine Cadillac landed to found his village in 1701.

The Veterans' Memorial was followed by the Henry and Edsel Ford Auditorium at the foot of Woodward (1956). This building, the home of the Detroit Symphony Orchestra, was the gift to Detroit of the Ford Motor Company and the Ford and Mercury dealers of America as a memorial to the two Fords. It has already been noted that Old Mariners' Church was moved from its original site on Woodward to a new location at the eastern end of the Civic Center. The last of the present units, Cobo Hall and Arena were erected in 1960 at the western end of the

center and have become one of the nation's leading ac-
commodations for conventions and exhibits.

Sparked by the Civic Center development, other imposing new structures began to dot the downtown streets.
Among the first was the National Bank of Detroit building
(1959) on Woodward at Fort. The big government complex, the City-County building, had preceded it (1953-55).
The example was now set and dingy old eyesores were replaced by modern architectural splendors such as those of
the Michigan Consolidated Gas Company, the Detroit Bank
and Trust Company, the First Federal Savings and Loan
Association, the Pontchartrain Hotel, and the Howard
Johnson Motor Hotel. These were the first major buildings
to be erected in downtown Detroit for about thirty years.
Several older but structurally sound stores and offices were
remodeled and refurbished inside and out, and present the
appearance of newness. The visitor to downtown, absent
from Detroit for a decade, would have difficulty recognizing the new version.

Attempts to renovate the city have not been limited
to downtown. The interior part of Detroit, the so-called
inner city, was in a sad state of deterioration. Slums were
spreading and those citizens financially able to do so fled
to the newer suburbs. With the help of federal funds, Detroit opened the attack on its blight with a large urban renewal program. Hundreds of acres of worn-out sub-stan-
dard property were razed. The basic idea of urban renewal
is that the land taken and cleared by condemnation should
be sold to new developers. It is a slow process, but some
progress has been made. On the lower near east side several
high-rise luxury apartments have been built and other housing has been constructed. The Medical Center is taking
form to the north on Woodward. Further north in the heart
of the Cultural Center, Wayne State University is also un-

dergoing a remarkable expansion, helping to transform the entire area.

This effort to give Detroit a new look has created its own problems. When thousands of homes are torn down, new places to live must be found for the former occupants. With housing already limited, this has not been easy and has led to strong opposition and protest movements. Heavy expense to the taxpayers also has been involved. On July 1, 1962, Detroit sought to replace some of the tax loss caused by the razing of entire districts by imposing an income tax of one per cent on residents and one-half of one per cent on non-residents who work in the city.

In 1959 the St. Lawrence Seaway development was completed, providing deep water transportation between the Atlantic Ocean and interior Great Lakes ports. This opened up great foreign trade potentialities for Detroit and in 1966 the Port of Detroit handled 1,423,604 tons of overseas cargo. Today the familiar ore carriers share the river with the salties, cargo vessels in the overseas trade flying the flags of a dozen nations.

Detroit has problems of great magnitude and complexity. But they are not unique. Every major city from Boston and New York to Los Angeles and San Francisco shares them. Since 1960 Detroit has been plagued by a rising crime rate, much of it vicious. Citizens complain that the streets no longer are safe. Much of this crime against the person is perpetrated by juveniles, reflecting social maladjustment. Racism is of serious concern despite notable advances which have been made. Poverty amid general affluence and prosperity exists to a distressing degree. Although spectacular and costly programs have been carried on in the fight against blight, the slums spread. Public transportation is inadequate and traffic congestion becomes more intensified almost daily. Water and air pollution have become grave menaces. All these problems await future solution.

The question is: Can they be solved? There are those who believe that all big cities are in an irreversible state of decline and are doomed. Doomed to what, however, is not made entirely clear. Meanwhile in Detroit, as elsewhere, men, women and children continue to work and play, and to seek their destinies with the resources available to them in the face of handicaps which somehow seem to endure.

On July 28, 1951, Detroit celebrated the two hundred and fiftieth anniversary of its founding by Cadillac. The generation now being born will observe the city's three hundredth birthday in a little more than a quarter of a century. What Detroit will be then, what will have been its triumphs and disappointments, must remain a matter of conjecture. History stops at this moment; the next second lies in the future.

Chronology

1669   French explorer Adrien Jolliet, first white man to see Detroit area

1670   Sulpician Priests Dollier and Galinée passed Detroit on their way to Sault Ste. Marie

1679   Aug. French explorer La Salle sailed the *Griffon* up Detroit River; first ship to traverse Detroit River

1701   July 24. Antoine de la Mothe Cadillac landed at site of present City of Detroit and erected Fort Pontchartrain

1710   Cadillac appointed governor of Louisiana, left Detroit in summer of 1711 and never returned

1712   May. Fox Indians besieged Fort Pontchartrain

1760   Nov. 29. François Picoté, Sieur de Belèstre, surrendered Fort Pontchartrain to British Major Robert Rogers

1761   Sept. 3. Major Henry Gladwin arrived in Detroit

1763   May 10. Ottawa Indian Chief Pontiac began siege of Fort Detroit

       July 31. Battle of Bloody Run

       Oct. 31. Pontiac sent peace offering to Gladwin; siege ended

1774   June 22. Quebec Act passed by Parliament

1775   Apr. 19. Battle of Lexington and Concord; Revolutionary War began

       Nov. 9. Lieutenant-Governor Henry Hamilton arrived in Detroit

1777-83   Detroit was center of Indian raids against American settlers during Revolutionary War

1778-79   Fort Lernoult built; later named Fort Shelby;
          razed 1827
1783   Sept. 13. Treaty of Paris signed, ending Revolu-
          tionary War
1783-96   British retained control of western forts, includ-
          ing Detroit
1787   July 13. Northwest Ordinance enacted
1788-96   Detroit included in Canadian District of Hesse;
          city under British law and Canadian courts
1794   Aug. 30. General Anthony Wayne defeated Indians
          in Battle of Fallen Timbers
          Nov. 19. Jay Treaty signed
1796   July 11. American troops under command of Cap-
          tain Moses Porter occupied Detroit
          Aug. 15. Wayne County organized; Detroit county
          seat
1798   June 3. Father Gabriel Richard arrived in Detroit
1802   Jan. 18. Detroit incorporated as a town
          Sept. 7. First post office in Detroit, Frederick Bates
          postmaster
1805   Jan. 11. Territory of Michigan created; Detroit seat
          of government
          June 11. Detroit destroyed by fire
1806   Sept. 19. Detroit Bank opened; first bank chartered
          in Michigan
          Judge Augustus B. Woodward and Governor Wil-
          liam Hull secured permission for governor and
          judges to lay out a new city, which resulted in
          Woodward Plan
1809   Aug. 31. Father Richard published first and prob-
          ably only issue of *Michigan Essay or Impartial
          Observer*, first newspaper in Michigan
1812   June 18. United States declared war on Great
          Britain
          July 12. Governor Hull invaded Canada
          Aug. 16. Governor Hull surrendered Detroit to
          British General Sir Isaac Brock

Chronology

1813   Jan. 23. River Raisin Massacre
       Sept. 10. Commodore Oliver Hazard Perry's squadron defeated British flotilla at Battle of Lake Erie
       Sept. 29. American troops reoccupied Detroit
       Oct. 5. General William Henry Harrison defeated British and Indians at Battle of the Thames; Shawnee Indian Chief Tecumseh killed
       Oct. 29. Lewis Cass appointed governor of Michigan Territory.
1813-14 Famine and plague struck Detroit
1814   Sept. Indians killed Ananias McMillan, last Indian massacre in Detroit
       Dec. 24. Treaty of Ghent signed, ending War of 1812
1816   June. Reverend John Monteith arrived in Detroit
1817   July 25. First issue of weekly *Detroit Gazette*
       Aug. 26. Catholepistemiad or University of Michigania established in Detroit; became University of Michigan in 1821; moved to Ann Arbor in 1837
1818   June 9. Cornerstone of new Ste. Anne's Church laid; razed in 1886
       July 6. First auction sale of public lands in Michigan, held at Council House
       Aug. 27. *S.S. Walk-in-the-Water* arrived in Detroit on maiden voyage from Buffalo; first steamboat on upper lakes
1818-20 Governor Lewis Cass led a series of exploration parties into interior of lower Michigan and to upper peninsula
1819   July 16. Michigan Territory authorized to elect a delegate to Congress
1824   Aug. 5. Municipal government reorganized; John R. Williams elected first mayor of Detroit
1825   May 24. Construction began on road connecting Detroit and Chicago

All Our Yesterdays

1825   Oct. 25. Erie Canal opened; influx of settlers from
       the East began
1827   May. Fort Shelby dismantled
1828   May 5. Capitol building occupied in Capitol Park;
       served as state capitol from 1837 to 1847; de-
       stroyed by fire in 1893
1830   Sept. 24. Stephen G. Simmons publicly hanged in
       Centre Park jail yard; last execution in Michigan
1831   May 5. First issue of *Democratic Free Press and
       Michigan Intelligencer* published; name later
       changed to *Detroit Free Press*
       Stevens T. Mason appointed territorial secretary;
       became acting governor when Lewis Cass re-
       signed
1832   July-Sept. Cholera epidemic
       Sept. 13. Father Richard died of cholera
1834   Aug.-Sept. Second cholera epidemic, over 600 died:
       one-eighth of Detroit's population
1835   Nov. 18. City Hall at Cadillac Square occupied;
       razed Nov. 22, 1872
       Michigan-Ohio boundary dispute (Toledo War)
1837   Jan. 16. Michigan admitted to the Union as twenty-
       sixth state; Stevens T. Mason first governor
1837-38   Patriot's War in Canada
1838   May 19. Detroit and Pontiac Railway completed
       12 miles of track to Royal Oak; first cars were
       horse drawn
1839   Feb. 18. Detroit Boat Club founded; moved to Belle
       Isle in 1891
       Feb. 22. City poor farm moved to Michigan and
       Merriman roads; developed into present-day
       Wayne County General Hospital
       Printers staged Detroit's first labor strike
1843   Board of Education opened its first school house in
       what is now Times Square; first public school
       opened in 1838

1845   June 9. St. Vincent's Hospital opened on grounds
        of Ste. Anne's Church; first civilian hospital in
        Detroit
1847   State capital changed from Detroit to Lansing
        Nov. 29. First telegraph in Detroit; line ran to
        Ypsilanti
1848   June 29. SS. Peter and Paul's R. C. Church conse-
        crated, oldest church building now standing in
        Detroit
        Detroit Typographical Union formed, Detroit's old-
        est labor union
1849   Mar. 5. Detroit Bank & Trust Co. founded as De-
        troit Savings Fund Institute
        Dec. 23. Mariners' P. E. Church dedicated, oldest
        stone church building now standing in Detroit
1850   Detroit & Cleveland Navigation Co. organized; reg-
        ular steamship service between Detroit and Cleve-
        land established; company incorporated in 1868
1851   Sept. 24. Detroit streets first lighted by gas
        Fort Wayne completed; now historical museum
1852   Sept. 27. Y.M.C.A. first established in Detroit
1853   Eber Brock Ward organized Eureka Iron and Steel
        Works which in 1864 produced first commercial
        steel by Bessemer process
1855   First ship canal at Sault Ste. Marie opened
1856   Scotten Brothers began producing Hiawatha brand
        chewing tobacco
1857   Sept. 28. Russell House opened, Detroit's leading
        hotel for 50 years
1860   Jan. 30. Detroit's first Federal Building (Custom
        House and Post Office) erected at Griswold and
        Larned; torn down 1964
1861   Apr. 17. President Lincoln proclaimed state of war;
        Civil War began
        July 6. Detroit House of Correction opened
1863   Mar. 6. Riot: 400 federal troops called in, 20 fires,
        35 buildings destroyed

Aug. 3. First streetcar line opened on Jefferson avenue from Third to Dequindre; cars were horse drawn

1864 Sept. 19. Confederate agents captured *S.S. Philo Parsons;* attempted to free Confederate prisoners on Johnson's Island

Oct. 12. Harper Hospital opened for care of Civil War wounded

Richard F. Trevellick formed Detroit Trades Assembly

1865 Mar. 25. School district library opened, beginning of present-day Detroit Public Library

1866 Oct. 26. Parke, Davis & Co. founded as Duffield, Parke & Co.

Hazen S. Pingree established his boot and shoe factory

James Vernor sold his first ginger ale in his drug store

1867 D. M. Ferry & Co. founded

1868 May 18. Detroit College of Medicine founded; became part of future Wayne State University in 1933

Detroiter William Davis invented railroad refrigerator car

Detroit Opera House built on Campus Martius; destroyed by fire in 1897 and rebuilt; remodeled into a department store in 1937; torn down in 1963

1869 Oct. 11. Negro children first admitted to public schools

Providence Hospital opened

Cyrenius A. Newcomb and Charles E. Endicott opened their department store; bought by J. L. Hudson Co. in 1927

1870 Christopher R. Mabley opened his first clothing store; company disbanded in 1929

1871 July 18. Second City Hall occupied; razed 1961, site now Kennedy Square
1871-93 George Pullman manufactured Pullman sleeping cars in Detroit
1872 Apr. 9. Soldiers' and Sailors' Monument unveiled
1873 Aug. 23. First issue of *Detroit News* published
1875 Fred Sanders opened his first confectionary store
1877 Jan. 22. Detroit Public Library building in Centre Park opened, razed 1929; Downtown Library opened on same site in 1932
      Sept. Detroit College founded; renamed University of Detroit in 1911
1878 Aug. 15. Telephones first supplied to private citizens
1880 Detroit Council of Trades and Labor Unions formed; became Detroit Federation of Labor in 1906
1881 Apr. 2. Joseph L. Hudson opened his first clothing store
      Peninsular Stove Co. organized by James Dwyer; Detroit recognized as nation's center for stove industry
      First professional baseball played in Detroit; Detroit Baseball Co. had been organized on Nov. 29, 1880; team was a member of National League, 1881-88
1883 Detroit Athletic Club organized
      B. Siegel Co. building on Woodward avenue opened
1884 First of 72 electric arc street-light towers built
1885 Mar. 25. Detroit Museum of Art organized; name changed to Detroit Institute of Arts in 1919
1888 Dec. 6. Grace Hospital opened
1889 Hammond Building erected, first skyscraper in Detroit; demolished in 1956
      Detroit International Fair and Exposition opened
1890 Jan. 15. Hazen S. Pingree took office as mayor; progressive movement in Detroit began

1891 Y.M.C.A. established vocational classes which grew
      into Detroit Institute of Technology
1892 Detroit College of Law established
1893 Nov. 23. Detroit joined Western Baseball League;
      league's first organizational meeting held at
      Grand Hotel in Detroit; name changed to Amer-
      ican League on Oct. 11, 1899; league play be-
      gan in 1901
      Ernst Kern opened his first store; company dis-
      banded in 1959
      Electricity first available for home lighting
      Electric streetcars began operating out Woodward
      avenue
1894 Detroit Yacht Club founded; moved to Belle Isle
      in 1923
1896 Mar. 6. Charles B. King operated first automobile
      on streets of Detroit
      June 4. Henry Ford drove his first motor vehicle
      Majestic Building opened; torn down in 1962
      Detroit Opera House showed several reels of film
      through an eidoloscope, forerunner of motion
      picture
1897 Sebastian S. Kresge opened his first notions store
1899 Ransom E. Olds established Detroit's first automo-
      bile factory; moved to Lansing in 1901
1902 Sept. 2. George W. Bissell became Detroit's first
      auto accident fatality
      Oct. 11. Wayne County Building opened
1903 June 16. Ford Motor Co. incorporated
      Cadillac Automobile Co. produced its first car
      Buick Motor Car Co. organized
      Packard Motor Co. moved to Detroit from Warren,
      Ohio
1904 Jonathan Dixon teamed with Benjamin Briscoe to
      organize Maxwell-Briscoe Co.
1907 Oct. 29. Pontchartrain Hotel opened; closed Jan.
      31, 1920

1908   Sept. 16. William C. Durant founded General Motors Co.; General Motors Corp. formed in 1919
Crowley, Milner & Co. founded, took over Partridge store at Gratiot and Farmer on May 13, 1909
Ford Motor Co. produced first Model T
1909   Feb. 20. Hudson Motor Car Co. incorporated
July 4. First mile of concrete road pavement in U.S. opened on Woodward avenue from Six Mile to Seven Mile roads
1910   Jan. 1. Ford Motor Co. Highland Park plant began operation
July 14. First airplane in Detroit flew at State Fair Grounds
1911   May 1. Herman Kiefer Hospital opened; originally opened as a pest house in 1893
1912   Cadillac adopted self-starter as standard equipment
1914   Jan. 12. Henry Ford announced $5 per day minimum-wage scale
Feb. 26. Detroit Symphony Orchestra gave first concert in Detroit Opera House
July 14. Dodge Brothers started production of Dodge automobile
Kiwanis Club No. 1 formed in Detroit
1915   Oct. 1. Henry Ford Hospital opened
Oct. 12. Municipal Receiving Hospital opened; name later changed to Detroit General Hospital
1916   Detroit Automobile Club founded, forerunner of Automobile Club of Michigan
1917   Apr. 6. United States entered World War I
Henry M. Leland organized Lincoln Motor Co.
1918   May 1. Prohibition went into effect in Michigan
June 25. New city charter adopted; nonpartisan government set up
Nov. 11. Armistice signed, ending World War I
Merrill-Palmer Institute established
Last electric arc street-light tower taken down

1919   Kern store at Woodward and Gratiot rebuilt; went out of business in 1959; razed in 1966
1920   Jan. 16. Prohibition Amendment to the United States Constitution went into effect
Aug. 17. First airmail in Detroit; seaplane flew to Cleveland and back
Ford Motor Co. moved to River Rouge plant and established offices in Dearborn
Double-deck buses appeared on Detroit streets
1921   June 3. Detroit Public Library main building at Woodward and Kirby opened
Oct. 13. WWJ licensed, first radio station in U.S. to broadcast regularly sponsored commercial programs; first broadcast on Aug. 20, 1920
General Motors Building at Second and Grand Boulevard completed
1922   Apr. 17. Department of Street Railways took over last of Detroit United Railway lines
Detroit Historical Society founded
Police Headquarters on Beaubien erected
1923   Sept. 10. College of the City of Detroit founded; renamed Wayne University in Jan. 1934
1925   Henry Ford developed his tri-motor airplane
Maxwell-Chalmers reorganized as Chrysler Corp.
1926   Sept. 26. Detroit Cougars entered National Hockey League; renamed Falcons in 1930, then Red Wings in 1933
1927   May 20. Charles A. Lindbergh, Detroit born, flew Atlantic
May 26. Last of more than 15,000,000 Ford Model Ts produced
Oct. 6. Detroit Institute of Arts building on Woodward opened
Oct. 14. Detroit City Airport opened
Oct. 15. Olympia Stadium opened
1928   Fisher Building at Second and Grand Boulevard built

New Wayne County Jail erected

1929 Oct. 14-Nov. 13. Stock market fell; great depression began

Nov. 15. Ambassador Bridge opened

Detroit Aircraft Corp. organized; height of Detroit aircraft industry

1930 July 22. Mayor Charles Bowles recalled by Detroit voters

Sept. 9. Frank Murphy elected mayor, assumed office Sept. 23

Nov. 3. Detroit-Windsor Vehicular Tunnel opened

1931 192,000 Detroiters received welfare aid

Collingwood Massacre, Purple Gang at its height

New Detroit House of Correction opened in Plymouth

Lawrence Institute of Technology opened

1932 Mar. 7. Ford Hunger March: 3,000 march on Dearborn

1933 Feb. 14. Governor William A. Comstock closed all Michigan banks

Apr. 27. City treasury empty; city employees paid in scrip

June 1. Sales tax passed by Michigan legislature

Dec. 5. 21st Amendment to the United States Constitution repealing Prohibition ratified

Various city colleges combined as a university; named Wayne University, 1934; renamed Wayne State University, 1956

1934 Apr. 23. Federal Building and Post Office on Lafayette opened

Detroit Lions football team moved to Detroit from Portsmouth, Ohio

1935 Aug. 26. United Automobile Workers organized

1936 Dec. Chevrolet and Fisher Body employees in Flint staged automobile industry's first major sit-down strike, which lasted until Feb. 1937

1937 Jan. 13. Lone Ranger program began over radio station WXYZ

Feb. 11. U.A.W. became sole bargaining agent at General Motors

Apr. 6. U.A.W. became sole bargaining agent at Chrysler

May 26. Battle of the Overpass, clash between Ford Motor Co. guards and U.A.W. leaders

June. Detroiter Joe Louis became heavyweight champion of the world

1941 Apr. U.A.W. became sole bargaining agent at Ford Motor Co. after 10-day strike

Aug. Auto production curtailed; halted after Pearl Harbor (Dec. 7)

Dec. 8. United States declared war on Japan; Detroit became "Arsenal of Democracy"

1943 June 20-21. Riot: 34 killed, 2,500 federal troops called in

1945 Aug. 14. Japan surrendered, ending World War II

Sept. 21. Ford Motor Co. reorganized, Henry Ford II president

1947 Mar. 4. WWJ-TV began television broadcasting

May 29. Willow Run Airport became center for commercial airlines in Detroit area

Walter Reuther elected president of U.A.W.

1948 June 15. First night baseball game at Briggs Stadium

Oct. 6. Parking meters installed on Detroit streets

1949 United Foundation held its first drive

1950 June 11. Veterans' Memorial Building opened

Construction of John C. Lodge expressway began

1951 July 24. Detroit Historical Museum at Woodward and Kirby opened

U.A.W. moved into Solidarity House on Jefferson avenue

1954 Hudson Motor Car Co. absorbed by new American Motors Corp.

Packard Motor Car Co. taken over by Studebaker

1955 Apr. 12. Mariners' Church moved to site of Old Council House in Civic Center; moving began Dec. 17, 1954

Sept. 23. City-County Building opened

1956 Apr. 7. Last streetcar operated in Detroit

Oct. 18. Henry and Edsel Ford Auditorium opened in Civic Center

Detroit Packard plant closed

Medical Center proposed on 250-acre site bounded by Mack, Woodward, Warren, and Chrysler freeway

Wayne University taken over by State of Michigan, renamed Wayne State University

1957 Detroit Pistons basketball team moved to Detroit from Fort Wayne, Indiana

Last two Detroit & Cleveland Navigation Co. vessels scrapped; last run was during 1950 shipping season

1958 Last Packard automobile produced

1959 National Bank of Detroit Building at Woodward and Fort erected

St. Lawrence Seaway completed

1960 Aug. 15. Cobo Hall opened; Convention Arena opened June 16, 1961

July 24. Dossin Great Lakes Museum on Belle Isle opened

Nov. 6. *Detroit Times* ceased publication

1961 Aug. City Hall torn down; site is now Kennedy Square

New Post Office at Fort and Eighth opened

1962 July 1. City income tax instituted

1963 May. Michigan Consolidated Gas Co. Building at Woodward and Jefferson opened

June 23. New wings of Detroit Public Library main building opened

June 23. Walk to Freedom: 125,000 Detroiters

marched to Cobo Hall, addressed by Rev. Martin Luther King Jr.

1964 Dec. 7. Detroit Bank & Trust Co. Building on Fort street opened

1965 Aug. 2. First Federal Savings & Loan Association Building at Woodward and Michigan opened

Giant model of Garland Stove moved to State Fair Grounds on Woodward from East Jefferson avenue

1966 June 20. South wing of Detroit Institute of Arts opened

Last commercial airlines left Willow Run Airport; all airlines now centered at Metropolitan Airport

1967 July 23-30. Riot: 44 killed, 7,331 arrested, 4,700 federal troops called in, 1,600 fires

1968 Apr. 30. Aaron DeRoy wing to Dossin Great Lakes Museum opened

July 24. Kresge wing to Detroit Historical Museum opened

Oct. 10. Detroit Tigers defeated St. Louis Cardinals 4-1 to win seventh game of World Series

Notes on Illustrations and Maps

Frontispiece. Fireworks Display, Detroit-Windsor International Freedom Festival. This annual event, June 25—July 4, celebrates the independence of both Canada and the United States. (Courtesy, Detroit Department Report and Information)

Pages 75–98

1. Detroit City Limits Today. Map. Detroit reached its present extent of almost 140 square miles about forty years ago. It completely surrounds Hamtramck and Highland Park. Adjacent cities and towns are, starting clockwise downriver, (south) River Rouge, Ecorse, Lincoln Park, (west) Melvindale, Dearborn, Dearborn Heights, Redford Heights, (north) Southfield, Oak Park, Ferndale, Hazel Park, Warren, East Detroit, (east) Harper Woods, Grosse Pointe Woods, Grosse Pointe Farms, Grosse Pointe, Grosse Pointe Park. Grosse Pointe Shores, east of Grosse Pointe Woods and north of Grosse Pointe Farms, does not touch Detroit. (Courtesy, Detroit Department Report and Information)

2. Detroit in 1796. "Map of the Old Town of Detroit, projected on the present [c. 1880] map of the city," based on Thomas Smith's map of 1816. Smith's original drawing has not been located, but there are various other copies, and a quite similar one is in Silas Farmer's *History of Detroit and Wayne County,* 1884, vol. 1, p. 33. To judge from the latter and John Jacob U. Rivardi's map of 1799 (original in Clements Library, Ann Arbor), the plan of Fort Shelby (Fort Lernoult or Fort Detroit in 1796) on the present map is perhaps somewhat too large. According to Bellin and Farmer, at the time of the American occupation in 1796 the four principal east-west streets in Detroit were, from south to north, Sts. Louis, Ann ("Main Street"), James (Jacques on

Bellin's map; see Fig. 4), and Joseph. (On this map—others differ —the north-south streets, going west from the church, are Campau alley, St. Honore st., McDougall alley, L'Erneau st.) Present-day widened Jefferson avenue apparently covers most of what used to be Sts. Louis, Ann, and James streets. The exact location, size, and shape of Fort Pontchartrain are unknown; however, the stippled area around "A" on this map would be a good educated guess even today. (From Robert E. Roberts' *Sketches and Reminiscences of the City of the Straits*, 1884, p. 41)

3. Statue of Antoine de la Mothe Cadillac, Founder of Detroit. One of four sculptures of early Michigan French heroes (the others were La Salle and Fathers Marquette and Richard) commissioned by Bela Hubbard, who presented them to the city. They were made by Detroit sculptor Julius Theodore Melchers and were placed in niches on the late City Hall in 1884. Some time after it was demolished in 1961, they were acquired by the University of Detroit. For a group photograph, see George S. May's *Pictorial History of Michigan, the Early Years*, 1967, p. 31. (Burton Historical Collection)

4. Fort Detroit, about 1750. Drawn by Charles V. Kerns for the late Clarence M. Burton to represent "Cadillac's Village," but actually based, as the late Milo M. Quaife pointed out (*This is Detroit*, 1951, p. 13), on Joseph G. Chaussegros de Lery's MS. map dated 1749, which was engraved for Jacques N. Bellin's *Petit Atlas Maritime*, the first known printed plan naming the streets of the town. By the time Bellin's atlas was published in Paris in 1764, two later maps of Detroit had been made, another by De Lery, dated 1754, and one by John Montresor dated 1763 (there are versions of the latter in the Detroit Institute of Arts and the William L. Clements Library, Ann Arbor, Mich.). Englished tracings of both De Lery maps are reproduced in Clarence M. Burton's *When Detroit was Young*, 1951, pp. 21, 25; the later one shows that by 1754 the picketed cemetery (just east of the church and not indicated on Bellin's engraving), approximately located in an area later covered by the intersection of Griswold street and Jefferson avenue, had been removed and the town stockade extended that much farther upriver. Cadillac's village (Fort Pontchartrain) was probably only about one-fourth the size of the town shown in this drawing (compare our Fig. 2, and also the so-called "Cadillac Plan of 1702" and the model based on it—both illustrated in Quaife's *This is Detroit*, p. 9). (Burton Historical Collection)

Notes

5. Henry Gladwin. From a life portrait by British artist John Hall, in the collection of the Detroit Institute of Arts. A professional soldier to the core, Major Gladwin was British commandant at Detroit during Pontiac's Conspiracy of 1763. (Courtesy, Detroit Institute of Arts)

6. "Mad Anthony" Wayne. From a life portrait by the famous American artist Charles Willson Peale, in a private collection. General Wayne's headquarters were at Detroit when the county of which it is the county seat was named for him in 1796, the year of his death. (Burton Historical Collection)

7. Ribbon Farms in 1810. Map. Detail of "Plan of Private Claims in Michigan Territory, as Surveyed by Aaron Greeley." The "10,000 Acre Tract" branches out into a rectangle north of the fort and the farms on either side of it. The base line north of the tract is now Base Line (Eight Mile) road, and Hog Island has since been renamed Belle Isle. (Burton Historical Collection)

8. Pontiac's Siege. An imaginative painting of the Indian attack on Fort Detroit in 1763, by Frederic Remington, the famous illustrator of the American West. Location unknown. (Burton Historical Collection)

9. Detroit in 1794. The earliest known authentic dated view of Detroit, this watercolor was discovered in England by Lady Nancy Astor, who presented it to the city. It is initialed E. H. and has been tentatively attributed to Lieut. Edward Henn. In the Burton Historical Collection, Detroit Public Library. (Burton Historical Collection)

10. Hull's Surrender. General William Hull, the American commander, capitulated to British General Sir Isaac Brock on August 16, 1812, and Detroit thereby won the dubious distinction of being the only major American city ever occupied by a foreign foe. Engraving by Augustus Robin after H. L. Stephens' imaginative drawing. (Burton Historical Collection)

11. Father Gabriel Richard. A Roman Catholic priest, Father Richard was also an educator, publisher, politician, and champion of liberty and democracy. From a posthumous portrait by James Otto Lewis, in the collection of Ste. Anne's R.C. Church, Detroit. (Burton Historical Collection)

12. The Woodward Plan. Redrawn detail of "A Plan of the City of Detroit, Drawn by Abijah Hull, Surveyor of Michigan, January 1807," in the Detroit Historical Museum. The small area, darkened in the redrawing, bisected by Woodward and crossed by Jefferson— hardly more than a third of one hexagon—represents the extent the plan was actually followed before it was abandoned in 1818. For the design of this part today, virtually unchanged for 150 years, see Fig. 51. (Adapted from W. Hawkins Ferry's *Buildings of Detroit*, 1968, Fig. 17)

13. *S.S. Walk-in-the-Water.* This ship, the first steamboat on the upper Great Lakes, first docked at Detroit on August 27, 1818, and foundered near Buffalo in 1821. For a copy of her manifest, "Job Fish . . . Master," see May's *Pictorial History of Michigan*, 1967, p. 92. From a drawing by Samuel W. Stanton. (Courtesy, Dossin Great Lakes Museum)

14. General Lewis Cass. Territorial governor, secretary of war, ambassador, U.S. senator, secretary of state, nominee for the presidency, Lewis Cass was one of Michigan's leading citizens. Engraving by W. J. Edwards after a daguerreotype by M. B. Brady. (Burton Historical Collection)

15. Detroit in 1838. A print after a drawing by William A. Raymond, in the Detroit Historical Museum. From Robert E. Roberts' *Sketches and Reminiscences*, 1884, p. 161. (Burton Historical Collection)

16. Citizens' Meeting in 1861. This mass meeting was held at the outbreak of the Civil War in front of the new Post Office, April 18, 1861. The old State Capitol is in the distance at the head of Griswold street. The new First Baptist Church, in the middle distance at Fort street, had not been finished yet. None of these buildings exists today. (Burton Historical Collection)

17. Election Scene in 1837. This famous satire, now in the Detroit Institute of Arts, is described by Robert E. Roberts, who may well have witnessed the event, under the heading "The Boy Governor of Michigan," in his *Sketches and Reminiscences of the City of the Straits*, 1884, p. 106: "It was painted in 1837 by Thomas Burnham, an amateur artist, and is a faithful representation of the election scene in the Campus Martius, in front of the old [then new] City Hall, where the whole vote of the city was polled. The candidates for Governor were Gov. [Stevens T.]

Notes

Mason, Democrat, and Charles C. Trowbridge, Whig. Gov. Mason is the central figure [in a high hat], represented as placing in the hand of John Weiss, the butcher, a dollar, given him, as was charged, for his vote. Frank Sawyer, editor of the *Advertiser* (Whig), and Kinsburry, editor of the *Detroit Post* (Democrat), with a copy of their respective papers in their hands, engaged in earnest dispute . . ." Silas Farmer also cites the painting (*History*, pp. 112–13). The artist, whose full name was Thomas Mickell Burnham, is usually incorrectly called T. H. O. P. ("Alphabet") Burnham. (Courtesy, Detroit Institute of Arts)

18. Second Michigan Infantry Troops in 1861. Formation photographed by Jex Bardwell at Fort Wayne, Detroit. (Burton Historical Collection)

19. *S.S. Philo Parsons.* This ship was captured by Confederate agents in a plot to free 3,000 Confederate prisoners held on Johnson's Island in Sandusky harbor, September 19, 1864, which failed. After a watercolor by the Reverend Edward J. Dowling S.J. (Courtesy, Dossin Great Lakes Museum)

20. Recruiting Poster. To increase enlistments, bounties were offered to recruits as herein indicated. (W.S.U. Archives)

21. Michigan Central R.R. Depot. Built in 1848 near the foot of Third street, it was destroyed by arsonists in 1854. (Burton Historical Collection)

22. *S.S. Frank E. Kirby.* (Courtesy, Dossin Great Lakes Museum)

23. Excursion Announcement. (Courtesy, Dossin Great Lakes Museum)

24. *S.S. Put-in-Bay.* The *Frank E. Kirby* and *Put-in-Bay* represent the fast, luxurious, passenger steamships that operated on the Great Lakes during the late 19th and early 20th centuries. (Courtesy, Dossin Great Lakes Museum)

25. Detroit in 1887. Supplement to the *Detroit Evening Journal*, May 7, 1887, after a drawing by John R. Chapin. (Burton Historical Collection)

26. Woodward Avenue in the Eighties. Photograph of shoppers and strollers by Jex Bardwell. (Burton Historical Collection)

All Our Yesterdays

27. Fire Engine Co. No. 3 in 1871. The firemen were photographed with their equipment in front of their Clifford street engine house after their return from the great Chicago fire. Stalwart firefighters such as these used the tower of the new City Hall, completed the same year, as a fire watch station. For a photograph of the same company in 1865, see Quaife's *This is Detroit*, p. 47. (Burton Historical Collection)

28. Woodward Avenue in the Eighties. View of the east side of the avenue just north of the Campus Martius. (Burton Historical Collection)

29. Ford Motor Company in 1903. The company's first factory building, it was on Mack avenue at the Belt Line R.R. (Courtesy, Automotive History Collection, Detroit Public Library)

30. Early Horseless Carriage. A Michigan law of 1905 required motorists to pull over and stop if approaching horses appeared to be frightened. (W.S.U. Archives)

31. Baseball Game in 1886. The score for the game at Recreation Park, Detroit, on June 19, was Detroit 1, Chicago 0, in 13 innings. (Burton Historical Collection)

32. King's and Detroit's First Auto. Charles B. King at the tiller of his car in 1896. (Burton Historical Collection)

33. Campus Martius in 1912. View looking south along Woodward from in front of the City Hall. The old Hotel Pontchartrain (1907) and the Soldiers and Sailors Monument (1872) are to the left (east). By now motorcars were common in downtown Detroit. (Burton Historical Collection)

34. Seven Mile Road in 1914, Near Gratiot Road. Because of roads such as this, the Wayne County Road Commission laid the world's first mile of concrete highway on Woodward avenue in 1909. (W.S.U. Archives)

35. Henry Ford in 1924. He poses with his first and 10,000,000th Fords. (Burton Historical Collection)

36. Liberty Bond Drive Parade in 1918, in the Campus Martius. Note the Soldiers and Sailors Monument, still in place, the Detroit Opera House, since razed, and in front of it, the Merrill Memorial

Fountain, since moved to Palmer Park and replaced by the Bagley Memorial Fountain. (Burton Historical Collection)

37. "Bread Line." Scene at the Salvation Army during the great depression. (Burton Historical Collection)

38. "Bootlegging." This photograph was published in the *Detroit News* of February 20, 1934, with the following caption: "Time was when the laws of the United States prohibited the bringing of liquor into this country. That didn't bother some folks. For instance, here is a picture taken by two *Detroit News* cameramen in 1928 showing rum-runners from Canada unloading the forbidden beverages at the foot of Riopelle street, within one mile of the City Hall. Were the photographers detected and chased? They were, and how!" (Courtesy, *Detroit News*)

39. "Stout Air Pullman." William B. Stout's Air Pullman "Maiden Detroit," built in 1922, was a forerunner of the famous "Ford Tri-Motor." (Burton Historical Collection)

40. "Ford Hunger March" Aftermath. Scene of a crowd at Central Methodist Church during the funeral of a victim of the March 1932 incident. (W.S.U. Labor History Archives)

41. Before the "Battle of the Overpass." Walter Reuther, Richard Frankensteen, and other union organizers posed for news photographers before the incident at the Ford Rouge Plant in 1937. (W.S.U. Labor History Archives)

42. "The Battle of the Overpass," May 26, 1937. (W.S.U. Labor History Archives)

43. "Blind Pig" Origin of 1967 Riot. The police raid of a speak-easy on Twelfth street near Clairmount occasioned the explosion which resulted in the July 1967 Detroit riots. The after-hours drinking spot was on the second floor of the Economy Printing Co. building. This photograph was taken on July 25 before the riots were over. (Burton Historical Collection)

44. Aftermath of July 1967 Riot. One of many blocks that were almost entirely destroyed. (Burton Historical Collection)

45. Detroit in 1968. Aerial view looking north from Windsor, Canada. In the park-like Civic Center along the waterfront, from west to

All Our Yesterdays

east, are Cobo Hall and Convention Arena, Veterans Memorial, Bob-Lo excursion steamers' dock, and the Henry and Edsel Ford Auditorium. North of the auditorium is the City-County building, and across Woodward avenue to the west, north of the Bob-Lo dock, is the Michigan Consolidated Gas Company tower by Minoru Yamasaki. Northwest of this is Detroit's tallest skyscraper, the Penobscot building, and in the distance about three miles north of it, the tower of the Fisher building is discernible. (Courtesy, Detroit Department Report and Information)

46. River Rouge Plant of the Ford Motor Company, Dearborn, Mich. This automotive giant, perhaps the world's largest industrial complex, maintains its own Great Lakes fleet. (Courtesy, Ford Motor Co.)

47. Ford-Lodge Freeway Interchange. Completed in the 1950s, this was the first of Detroit's major freeway interchanges. Aerial view looking south along the John C. Lodge freeway. Downtown Detroit, about three miles away, the river, and Windsor, Ontario, Canada, are in the distance. (Courtesy, Detroit Department Report and Information)

48. Cultural Center. Aerial view, looking east, made in 1966. In the foreground, from north (left) to south, are the W.S.U. General Library, moated Helen L. DeRoy Auditorium, and State Hall. Beyond the auditorium to the east are the Meyer and Anna Prentis building on Cass avenue, and the Detroit Public Library, facing the Detroit Institute of Arts along Woodward avenue. Northwest of the latter and north of the library is the Detroit Historical Museum. The tall structures are apartment or hotel buildings. Practically all the former residences in the foreground are utilized by Wayne State University. (Courtesy, Detroit Department Report and Information)

49. Thanksgiving Day Parade. A view at Woodward and Grand River of part of the J. L. Hudson Company's annual presentation. (Courtesy, J. L. Hudson Co.)

50. McGregor Memorial Conference Center. Minoru Yamasaki's architectural gem on the W.S.U. campus, 1958. (W.S.U.P.)

384

Notes

Pages 293-300

51. Downtown Detroit Today. Map. In the Civic Center along the Detroit River are the City-County building in the block bounded by Jefferson, Woodward, Larned and Randolph; the Henry and Edsel Ford Auditorium, directly south of it; and the Veterans Memorial, between the auditorium and Cobo Hall and Convention Arena. Two new commercial buildings on the north side of Jefferson avenue, the Michigan Consolidated Gas Company, between Woodward and Griswold, and the Hotel Pontchartrain, between Shelby and Washington boulevard, are on sites originally designated for the Civic Center. The Campus Martius, with the Soldiers and Sailors Monument and the Bagley Memorial Fountain, and Kennedy Square (southwest corner), the site of the late City Hall, are at the intersection of Woodward and Michigan-Cadillac Square; Grand Circus Park is on either side of Woodward south of Adams. Judge Woodward had planned a full circle at Grand Circus Park crossed by six throughways (see Fig. 12): Madison (boulevard) to continue due west, Broadway and Woodward (avenues) to diverge west and north of northwest, Washington (boulevard) due north, and Bagley and Adams (avenues) to diverge northeast. (Courtesy, Detroit Department Report and Information)

52. Downtown Detroit. Cobo Hall, with the John C. Lodge freeway approaching Jefferson avenue under it, and the Convention Arena are in the foreground. Belle Isle appears in the distance to the right (east). (Courtesy, Detroit Department Report and Information)

53. Washington Boulevard, "Detroit's Fifth Avenue." View looking true north from Michigan avenue. The Sheraton-Cadillac Hotel is to the right and the Book building and tower are in the middle distance on the left. Grand Circus Park is at the head of the boulevard. (Courtesy, Detroit Department Report and Information)

54. Detroit Harbor Terminals. Aerial view along the Detroit River near the foot of West Grand boulevard. Downtown Detroit lies to the east (right) beyond the Ambassador Bridge to Windsor, Canada. (Courtesy, Detroit Department Report and Information)

55. *S.S. Ste. Claire.* This Bob-Lo Company steamer has been in service since 1911 and has a capacity of 2,414 passengers. The *Ste. Claire* and the *Columbia* make excursion runs to Bob-Lo (Bois Blanc) Island daily during the Memorial Day to Labor Day season from the dock at the foot of Woodward avenue. (Courtesy, Detroit Department Report and Information)

56. Detroit Harbor Terminals. View on the dock during the unloading of a foreign freighter. (Courtesy, *Detroit Free Press*)

57. Ford River Rouge Plant, Dearborn, Mich. View on an assembly line. (Courtesy, Ford Motor Co.)

58. General Motors Technical Center, Warren, Mich. View looking north. The research laboratories building is at the far end and headquarters for the styling, engineering, and manufacturing staffs are to the right. (Courtesy, General Motors Corp.)

59. Chrysler Corporation General Offices, Highland Park, Mich. (Courtesy, Chrysler Corp.)

60. Football. Detroit Lions star Lem Barney (left), National Football League defensive rookie of the year 1967. (Courtesy, Detroit Lions)

61. Boat Race. Ecorse Marathon on the Detroit River in 1963. (Courtesy, *Detroit Free Press*)

62. Hockey. Detroit Red Wings star Gordie Howe in action. (Courtesy, *Detroit Free Press*)

63. Basketball. Detroit Pistons star scorer Dave Bing dribbles the ball. (Courtesy, Detroit Pistons)

64. Baseball. Pitcher Mickey Lolich, hero of the Detroit Tigers when the team won the 1968 World Series. (Courtesy, *Detroit Free Press*)

65. Baseball. Pitcher Denny McLain, winner of 31 games for the Detroit Tigers during the 1968 season. (Courtesy, *Detroit Free Press*)

66. Baseball. The Detroit Tigers won the World Championship on October 10, 1968, and the city went wild. (Courtesy, *Detroit Free Press*)

67. In Greenfield Village, Dearborn, Mich. View of the Village Green. Greenfield Village, a pioneer "outdoor museum" founded by Henry Ford in 1929, contains more than one hundred historic buildings moved from various sections of the United States and even abroad. (Courtesy, Henry Ford Museum)

68. Menlo Park Laboratory, Greenfield Village, Dearborn. Thomas A. Edison, the "Wizard of Menlo Park," accomplished most of his greatest achievements, including the invention of the first practical incadescent lamp, in this gray clapboard building, the world's first industrial research center, 1876–1886. Henry Ford had it moved to Greenfield Village from Menlo Park, New Jersey. James E. Fraser's statue of Edison is in the left foreground. (Courtesy, Henry Ford Museum)

69. United Automobile Workers of America International Union Solidarity House Headquarters, East Jefferson Avenue, Detroit. The General Douglas MacArthur Bridge to Belle Isle Park is in the right background. (Courtesy, U.A.W.)

Selected Bibliography

Automobiles of America; Detroit, 1968

F. Clever Bald: *Detroit's First American Decade;* Ann Arbor, 1948

F. Clever Bald: *Michigan in Four Centuries;* New York, 1961

Norman Beasley and George W. Stark: *Made in Detroit;* New York, 1957

Clarence M. Burton: *The City of Detroit Michigan;* Detroit-Chicago, 1922

George B. Catlin: *The Story of Detroit;* Detroit, 1923

Detroit Public Library: *Detroit in its World Setting, a 250-Year Chronology, 1701-1951;* R. E. Ripps, ed.; Detroit, 1953

Silas Farmer: *The History of Detroit and Michigan;* Detroit, 1884

W. Hawkins Ferry: *The Buildings of Detroit;* Detroit, 1968

Irving Howe and B. J. Widick: *The UAW and Walter Reuther;* New York, 1949

Bela Hubbard: *Memorials of a Half-Century;* New York, 1887

Alman Parkins: *The Historical Geography of Detroit;* Lansing, 1918

John B. Rae: *The American Automobile;* Chicago, 1965

George W. Stark: *City of Destiny, the Story of Detroit;* Detroit, 1943

Frank B. Woodford: *Lewis Cass, the Last Jeffersonian;* New Brunswick, 1950

Frank B. Woodford: *Mr. Jefferson's Disciple, a Life of Justice Woodward;* East Lansing, 1953

Frank B. Woodford and Albert Hyma: *Gabriel Richard, Frontier Ambassador;* Detroit, 1958

Index

All Our Yesterdays

Avenue Theater, 236

Baby, François, 117
Baby family, 60; house, 117
Bagley, John J., 210, 224; Memorial Fountain, 224
Baldwin, Henry P., 128, 211
Bank of Michigan, 199-200
Banks and banking, 198-200, 316-18
Baptists, 154, 156
Bar Harbor, Maine, 34
Barbour, George H., 208
Barnum, Phineas T., 236
Barstow School, 148
Bas Blanc (horse), 239
Base Hospitals #17 and #36, 271
Baseball, 240-44, 369, 370, 374
Basketball, 244, 375
Bateaux, 61
Bates, Frederick, 104, 107, 364
Battle Creek, Mich., 272
Battle of Antietam, 184
Battle of Bloody Run, 16, 61-63, 363
Battle of Bull Run, 184
Battle of Fallen Timbers, 73-74, 364
Battle of Gettysburg, 184, 187
Battle of Lake Erie, 122, 124-25, 365
Battle of the Overpass, 328, 374
Battle of the Thames, 122, 365
Battle of Tippecanoe, 115
Beaubien, Antoine, 59; Mrs., 167
Beaubien family, 41, 58
Beaver, 18, 27
Belèstre, François de, 51-54, 363
Belgians in Detroit, 250
Belle Isle, 14, 25, 38, 42, 197, 309, 346, 354; bridge, 197
Beller, Jacob, 237
Bennett, Charley, 243; Harry, 307, 315, 328, 329, 357

Bennett Field, 243
Berry Brothers, 204
Bessemer process, 203, 367
Bicycles, 230
Biddle House, 139
Big Three auto makers, 262, 264, 286, 328, 329, 357
Billy Boushaw's Saloon, 174
Bird, Capt. Henry, 66, 69-70
Bird's store, 227
Birmingham, Mich., 134, 287
Bison, 18
Bissell, George W., 268, 370
Black Hawk War, 140
Black Horse Tavern, 163
Black Legion, 341-42
Black Rock, N.Y., 130
Black Swamp, 129
Blackburn, Thornton *and* wife, 180
Blacksmiths union, 323
Blackstone Ballroom, 237
Blessed Sacrament R.C. Cathedral, 153
Blindpigs, 302, 305-6, 350
Bloomfield Hills, Mich., 161, 287
Blossom Heath, 305
Boating and sailing, 239-40
Bob-Lo Island, 198
Bonstelle Playhouse, 157-58
Book-Cadillac Hotel, 210
Boone, Daniel, 66
Booth, Ellen S. *and* George G., 161
Bootlegging, 301-4
Bouquet, Henry, 53
Bourgmont, Lt. Etienne de, 39
Boushaw, Billy, 174
Bowles, Charles, 308-9, 312, 373
Boxing, 244
Boy Scouts of America, 241
Boydell Brothers, 205
Braddock, Gen. Edward, 50
Bradish, Alvah, 172
Brady, Gen. Hugh, 144, 172
Bridges, Tommy, 243

390

Index

Briggs, Walter O., 243
Briggs Manufacturing Co., 265
Briggs Stadium, 243, 374
Briscoe, Benjamin, 264, 287, 370
Briscoe Manufacturing Co., 257
Broadway-Capitol Theater, 331
Brock, Billy, 290; Gen. Isaac, 117-20, 364
Broderick Tower, 227
Brodhead, Daniel, 69
Brodhead Naval Armory, 346
Broommakers union, 325
Brown, John, 181; Noah, 130
Brulé, Etienne, 22-23
Brush, Elijah, 101; farm, 101, 108; Capt. Henry, 117-18
Brush automobile, 264
Brush Street R.R. Station, 194
Buckley, Jerry, 308-9
Buffalo, N.Y., 25, 133, 196, 289, 323
Buhl Aircraft Co., 290
Buhl building, 228
Buick, David D., 262
Buick Motors Co., 262-63, 370
Buildings, 222-30, 359-61
Bulgarians in Detroit, 251
Burlesque, 236
Burroughs Adding Machine Co., 268
Burroughs Corp., 268
Bush, Donie, 243
Butler, Walter, 66
Byrd, Adm. Richard E., 289

Cabacier's Creek, 16
Cadillac, Antoine, 30-41, 363; birth and early life, 32; commandant at Ft. de Buade, 30, 34; death, 41; description of Detroit, 38-39; governor of Louisiana Terr., 41; home, 113; landowner in Maine, 34; lands at Detroit, 36; marries, 33; plans Ft. Pontchar-

train, 36; plans forts in New France, 30-32; removed from Detroit, 41
Cadillac, Antoine (son), 35; Marie-Therese, 33, 38
Cadillac Hotel, 210
Cadillac Motor Car Co., 262, 276, 370
Cadillac Theater, 236
Cahokia, 68
Caille, Arthur, 238
Caldwell, Billy, 66
Camp Backus, 186
Camp Beauregard, 332
Camp Custer, 272
Campau, Jacques, 62; Joseph, 137, 159; house, 113-14
Campau building, 228
Campau family, 41, 60, 102
Campbell, Capt. Donald, 53-55, 57, 59
Campus Martius, 186
Canada, 14, 27, 28, 47-48, 143-44, 185, 270, 273, 303-4, 335, 357
Canadian Indian Department, 114
Canadian National Pacific R.R., 194, 196
Canadians in Detroit, 245
Canals and locks, 132-33, 135, 189-90, 203, 366-67
Canard River, 117
Cape Kennedy, 358
Capitol (Mich.), 137-39, 141, 230, 363
Capitol Park, 137, 143
Capone, Al, 303, 306, 307
Carmel Hall, 308
Carpenters union, 323
Cartier, Jacques, 28
Casino Theater, 238
Cass, Lewis, 115, 118, 119, 123-24, 134, 136, 139, 140, 147, 148, 170, 171, 192, 365; appointed territorial governor, 126; as sol-

Index

Detroit Historical Society, 171, 187, 372
Detroit Hockey Club, 244
Detroit House of Correction, 178-79, 367, 373
Detroit Institute of Arts, 44, 172, 369, 372, 376
Detroit Institute of Technology, 284, 370
Detroit International Fair and Exposition, 231-32, 369
Detroit Journal, 161
Detroit Junior College, 282
Detroit Light Guard, 183-84
Detroit Lions football team, 243-44, 320-21, 373
Detroit Mechanics Society, 170, 332; building, 229
Detroit Medical College, 167, 282
Detroit Memorial Hospital, 167
Detroit Motorbus Co., 280
Detroit Museum of Art, 172, 369
Detroit News, 160, 161, 369
Detroit Normal School, 283
Detroit Opera House, 173, 221, 234-35, 237, 270, 368, 370
Detroit Pistons basketball team, 244, 375
Detroit Public Library, 139, 171-72, 174, 310, 348, 368, 369, 372, 375
Detroit Red Wings hockey team, 244, 321, 372
Detroit River, 13-14, 16-17, 24, 25, 36, 45, 196, 239, 303, 363
Detroit River Navy, 240
Detroit Savings Bank, 200
Detroit Savings Fund Institute, 200, 367
Detroit Scientific Society, 172
Detroit Stove Works, 208
Detroit Symphony Orchestra, 172-73, 359, 371
Detroit Tigers baseball team, 243, 320, 376
Detroit Times, 161, 375
Detroit Trades Assembly, 324, 368
Detroit Traffic Court, 178
Detroit Typographical Union, 322-23, 367
Detroit United Railways, 280
Detroit White Lead Works, 205
Detroit Yacht Club, 240, 370
Detroits baseball team, 242-43
Detroit-Windsor Tunnel, 198, 303, 304, 333, 373
Deutsches Haus, 246
Diggs, Charles, 352
Dilhet, Father John, 106
Dime building, 229
Dioceses, P.E., of Mich. and Western New York, 156
Dioceses, R.C., of Baltimore, Bardstown, Cincinnati, Mich. and Quebec, 152
Diphtheria, 166
Dixie highway, 276
Dixon, Jonathan, 370
Doc Brady's, 305
Dodemead, John, 105
Dodemead's Tavern, 105, 106
Dodge, Horace and John, 257, 258, 264-65, 371
Dodge Brothers Co., 264-65; automobile, 371
Dollier, Father François, 24-25, 363
Donaque River, 34
Doolittle, James, 336, 337
Dossin Great Lakes Museum, 125, 144, 171, 375, 376
Douglass, Frederick, 181
Draft, military, 184, 272, 333
Drugs, see Pharmaceuticals
Drydocks, 198
Dubisson, Charles R., 40
Ducharme, Charles A., 208
Duffield, Rev. George and Dr.

Index

Index

Index

White Star Line, 197
Whitefish, 190
White's Grand Theater, 235
Whitney, Clark J., 235; David Jr.,
   201
Wickersham Report, 310
Wilcox street, 226
William Penn (steamboat), 131
Williams, John R., 137, 159, 365
Williams street, 137
Williamsburg, Va., 68
Willow Run Airport, 291-92, 337,
   338, 374, 376
Willys Motors Corp., 338, 357
Wilson, Charles E., 287; John M.,
   180
Wilson Theater, 173
Winchester, Gen. James, 121
Windsor, Ontario, 143-44, 195,
   197, 257, 270, 303-4
Wisconsin, 271
Witherell, James, 147
Wolfe, Gen. James, 52
Wolverine Tube Co., 339
Woman's Hospital, 169
Wonderland, 236, 238
Wood, Gar, 240
Woodbridge, William, 127, 136
Woodbridge farm *and* Grove, 242
Woodmere Cemetery, 71
Woodward, Augustus B., 104, 108-
   10, 112-13, 119, 120-23, 127,

131, 146, 148-51, 364; *A System
   of Universal Science*, 144; ap-
   pointed territorial judge, 104;
   criticizes Proctor, 122; plans for
   rebuilding Detroit, 108; plans
   for university, 148
Woodward avenue, 20, 109, 192,
   193, 268, 371
Woodward Plan, 108-10, 137, 364
Woodworth, Ben, 113, 125, 177,
   178, 223, 233; Samuel, 113
Works Progress Administration,
   319
World War I, 270-77, 288, 332, 371
World War II, 331-40, 374
Wright Brothers, 288
Wright, Kay Co., 224
Wyandotte, Mich., 203-4, 303

Yax, Michael, 43
York, Rudy, 243
Yosemite (U.S.S.), 231
Young Men's Christian Associa-
   tion, 171, 273, 284, 367
Young Men's Society, 170
Ypsilanti, Mich., 141, 184, 195,
   214

Zeder, Fred, 287; James, 264, 287
Zion Lodge, 64-65, 111
Zoos and circuses, 242-43, 288

Frank B. Woodford, a native of Detroit, was born in 1903 and died in 1967. He graduated from Hillsdale College in 1923 and earned a B.S. degree from the University of Pennsylvania in 1925. In 1931 Frank B. Woodford joined the staff of the *Detroit Free Press*, which he served in various capacities for over thirty years. He was the author or co-author of numerous books, including *Lewis Cass, the Last Jeffersonian* (1950), *Mr. Jefferson's Disciple, a Life of Justice Woodward* (1953), *Parnassus on Main Street, a History of the Detroit Public Library* (1965), *Gabriel Richard, Frontier Ambassador* (1958), and *Harper of Detroit, the Origin and Growth of a Great Metropolitan Hospital* (1964). *All Our Yesterdays*, his final work, a fitting tribute to Mr. Woodford's appointment as City Historiographer of the City of Detroit, was virtually ready for the press at the time of his death.

Arthur M. Woodford, also a native of Detroit, was born in 1940. He was educated at the University of Wisconsin, Wayne State University, and the University of Michigan, from which he received his master of library science degree. Mr. Woodford is Assistant to the Personnel Director of the Detroit Public Library.

The manuscript was edited by Charles H. Elam. The book was designed by Don Ross. The type face for the text is Times Roman designed by Stanley Morison in 1931; and the display faces are Goudy Heavy designed by Frederic Goudy, 1926, and Cooper Black designed by Oswald Cooper, 1921.

The text is printed on Hammermill's Lock Haven Antique Offset. The hardcover book is bound in Columbia Mills' Fictionette Natural Finish cloth over binders board. The paperback is bound in Riegal's Foldcote Cover. Manufactured in the United States of America.